# PAPER
# GIRL

## ALSO BY BETH MACY

*Raising Lazarus*

*Dopesick*

*Truevine*

*Factory Man*

# PAPER
# GIRL

◈

## A MEMOIR OF HOME AND FAMILY
## IN A FRACTURED AMERICA

## BETH MACY

PENGUIN PRESS
NEW YORK
2025

PENGUIN PRESS
An imprint of Penguin Random House LLC
1745 Broadway, New York, NY 10019
penguinrandomhouse.com

Excerpt from *Where You Come From Is Gone* by Annie Woodford,
copyright © 2022. Used by permission of Mercer University Press.

Page 331 is an extension of this copyright page.

*Designed by Nerylsa Dijol*

ISBN 9780593656730 (hardcover)
ISBN 9780593656747 (ebook)

Printed in the United States of America
1st Printing

The authorized representative in the EU for product safety and compliance is
Penguin Random House Ireland, Morrison Chambers, 32 Nassau Street,
Dublin D02 YH68, Ireland, https://eu-contact.penguin.ie.

*For Liza*

## Those Factories Had Heart-Pine Floors

When I think of all the wood and people we've wasted,
the piles of fire-bent metal stacked almost as high as the
buildings that burned,
I want to make these words into a handmade knife,
tapped together in a backyard shed in Bassett or Fieldale.

Or a skirt sewn without a store-bought pattern,
lined with a scrap of golden polyester my grandmother would
have prized.

Or a bird dog with a mouth so soft no training quail ever died.

The loom and the finishing room held us in their spell.
The lathe turned and turned but we didn't listen.
We took all the overtime we could get.

*—Annie Woodford*[1]

Where you come from is gone, where you thought you were going to never was there, and where you are is no good unless you can get away from it.

—*Flannery O'Connor*[2]

❖

It is easier to build strong children than to repair broken men.

—*Frederick Douglass*[3]

# CONTENTS

**Part I.**
## SCHISM

**Part II.**
## SILOS

**Part III.**
## SHOWING UP

# *PAPER GIRL*

# SCHISM

*Hunter Woodruff, a tenth grader in 2024, had fallen
behind in credits at Urbana High School, struggled
with truancy, and eventually dropped out of school.*

*One*

# PRECIPICE

*Silas James was lucky to get a scholarship to attend
community college, but unreliable transportation
turned getting to campus into a regular struggle.*

It was June 2023, and Silas James had just graduated from Urbana High School, forty-one years after I wore that same insignia. It was a moment that was supposed to be the launching pad for his new identity and new life, as my graduation had been. It was meant to signify a break from the family chaos that had permeated most of his eighteen years.

Two full scholarships were all teed up and waiting for him at a community college in a nearby city. He planned to become a welder. Companies need welders, he knew. The nation needs welders. The pay was more than anything anyone in his family, save a few drug dealers, had ever made. And this was legit.

For Silas, manipulating metal and gas wasn't just a way to get the hell out of Urbana, Ohio; it made him feel like an artist.

He'd been so nervous about starting college that when I asked if he took a test-drive to Clark State in Springfield, Ohio, the week before, he shot back: "One hundred percent, I drove an hour away just to practice."

After his first class, he called me from the cafeteria: He'd just ordered a chicken quesadilla and a strawberry smoothie, and he was thrilled. He loved that he'd flashed his student ID to the cafeteria workers, he loved the sliding-scale health center, and he adored Toni, the mentor they'd assigned to him as a first-generation college student. "Everything you can think of, they have it here," he marveled. He'd even made a potential new friend in a classmate who wore ear gauges the same size as his.

And the fact that the college webmaster had posted *his photo* on the home page during the first week of school? Silas had never imagined that when he was homeless, during long stretches of his junior and senior years of high school, nearly dropping out several times.

But on the third day of class, the head gasket blew on his Saturn Ion, a beater that was older than Silas by three years. The car was a goner. The next day, a relative he was staying with was injured in a car accident and left the hospital with a concussion so severe she required around-the-clock supervision. Which is how he ended up a college dropout before the end of his first semester's first week. The family organizing and caretaking had fallen to Silas, as it often did.

Even his graduation had been a bust. He found himself ruminating on his grandparents, who'd spent four days driving from Texas on the back of a single motorcycle for his commencement, only to skip the ceremony because their vision prevents them from driving at night. He hadn't seen them since the eighth grade, and at the restaurant they took him out to for lunch, they barely managed three sentences. "They seemed burdened to be here," Silas told me.

He thought about his favorite high school counselor, Mrs. Flowers, who came to his graduation party at the city park and handed him a card with $100 cash as the skunk of his relatives' weed enveloped her. His older sister had gone camping and skipped the festivities altogether. He thought about his truancy officer, Brooke Perry, who'd pulled strings to get the school district to send a van to pick him up from one of his several temporary homes outside the county.

For years, teachers and counselors had been praying and pulling strings for Silas to graduate, extending shoulders and untold hours of support and sometimes even their spare bedrooms. For his own safety and mental health, they wanted him to get the hell out of Urbana.

As drum major, Silas wasn't just the leader of the Urbana High School Marching Band; he was also the student who spent every lunch period in the band director's office, sometimes crying, sometimes joshing with Mr. Sapp, but always plotting ahead with his favorite teacher about the next band routine, the next test, the next step of his life.

He'd pursued the drum major position his sophomore year with a single-mindedness that impressed Mr. Sapp. To become the one who led the marching band onto the field and directed songs and twirling routines, there were two requirements: You had to be able to fully execute a back bend, with the feathers of your hat plume kissing the ground; and you had to fit into one of the two drum major uniforms that Mr. Sapp, with his dwindling band budget, could afford to buy.

"He took it very seriously," Mr. Sapp told me. "He went to all the clinics, and he practiced and practiced and practiced."

*Former UHS drum major Silas James, between work
shifts and his community college classes, participated
as an alumnus in the 2023 homecoming game.*

The small uniform fit Silas's 120-pound, five-two frame as if it were
tailor-made. Though his legal name was still Elizabeth James, he'd
become trans and changed his name during junior year. When we
met in early 2023, he was eighteen and just beginning to give himself
testosterone injections. He picked the name Silas because it sounded
like "silos"; he'd always been surrounded by farmland, always reveled
in the way the grain storage towers punctuated the rolling midwestern landscape. His mom chose Cole, his new middle name, from a list
of names he'd sent to her in jail. In his heart, he would always be a
proudly rural kid.

Mr. Sapp often still slipped and called Silas "she" or "Elizabeth"
or even "Shug," the name he went by for a brief period before he
landed on Silas. The students all call Mr. Sapp "David M. Sapp, director of bands," which is a mouthful. It's one of the many band-kid
jokes they make about him, along with ribbing him about his goofy
ties and ever-present Crocs.

# PRECIPICE

---

I COULD IDENTIFY with Silas. I too had been a student bandleader at this same high school and came from a childhood with its share of chaos, addiction, and utility cutoff notices. In a region where most of the industry is based on transportation—not far from where Orville and Wilbur Wright first invented flight—I could pinpoint exactly how much a crap car limited a rural kid's ability to improve their lot. It didn't just keep you from getting back and forth to your shift job; it had the potential to keep you from arriving at a new and better life.

It's not just having a car that actually starts every time that people on the other side of poverty take for granted. My mom struggled to buy me a used trumpet in the fifth grade, paying another family in town for it in monthly installments. While I have never been homeless—mainly because my grandmother next door owned the house we lived in rent-free—I'm not exaggerating when I say it was a miracle that I left Urbana for Bowling Green State University in my mom's rusted Mustang, praying the whole way that its slippy clutch would not give out. I had the good fortune to leave town before falling into premature parenthood or addiction, both of which have saddled many of my family members for four generations that I know of, maybe more.

As I got to know Silas, I was struck by how much harder the situation was for him than it was for me. The more time I spent back in my hometown, the more I recognized the unprecedented forces that were actively turning the community I loved into a poorer, sicker, angrier, and less educated place.

IT'S NOT AS IF Urbana had ever been utopia for me; I was among the poorest kids in my class, and I felt it. Not just as I delivered newspapers from the back of my ten-speed, befriending people up and down the class ladder, but also on my block of South Walnut Street, where slurry voices from inside our house sometimes pierced the joyful noise of our kickball games and hide-and-seek.

I found refuge in my friends' homes and on the pleather ottoman inside the living room of my grandma Macy, who taught me to read and write and how to play checkers. I took solace in the public library down the street, the public school I could also walk to, and the women in charge of these sacred places who were my demigods.

Decades later, around 2015, as my mom began her descent into dementia, I began noticing something different during trips home to see her. Something was rotting beneath the surface of my postcard-cute hometown. It wasn't just that kids like me weren't going away to college anymore; many weren't even finishing high school.

The newspaper I used to deliver and later wrote for had become a ghost of its former self, no longer employing paper girls like me or much of anyone. Where it used to cover everything from DUIs to city council meetings to fire station fundraisers, readers were now left to rely on press releases and Facebook posts, creating a gaping information void in my community's understanding of itself. People now knew every detail of what their national political candidates were saying and doing, but almost nothing about the lives of their neighbors.

A few years ago, an old friend and I were driving around Urbana when we passed a middle-aged man riding a bicycle in the afternoon. When I admired the new-to-me bike path stretching from Cincinnati to Toledo that bisected the heart of our hometown, my friend set me straight: Unless they're donning spandex, middle-aged dudes riding bikes without helmets signifies they're on probation for DUI and can't drive. If I saw those same men sitting on a front porch in the middle of the day, it was safe to assume they were on disability and/or out of work.

Something was happening to our beloved hometown that didn't quite fit the pat explanations offered by economists and sociologists, important as they were.

IT'S NOT THAT THE USUAL WAY of understanding what happened to a town like Urbana isn't fundamentally true. It's just so much more complicated, as invisible and ingrained as the air we breathe and the way we talk to each other—and don't talk. But yes, absolutely, in my once prosperous hometown, the middle class had imploded by way of technology, offshoring, and the decline of unions, beginning in earnest not long after I left Ohio in the mid-1980s.

Back then, many homegrown companies were already morphing into international conglomerates. As production moved to countries with cheaper wages, our nation's leaders talked a good game about training young people for new jobs. But American students fell behind other nations in science, technology, and math, and the free market, freed to send the jobs away, did just that. Politicians from both parties saw globalization as inexorable, just a natural part of American capitalism's aging process. As long as our 401(k)s were still growing, it was easier to look away.

France, Germany, and other countries that also participated in globalization haven't suffered the same levels of child poverty, wage stagnation, or income inequality that the United States has. But that truth is not very palatable. Many Americans, especially those who have the good fortune to be wealthy, argue that low-wage suffering is the cost of national greatness or what economists call creative destruction; that Europe doesn't have a company like Apple; that it's one thing or the other. There's a magnificent cruelty embedded in those sentiments.

I'll never forget that moment in the 1970s when my dad landed a coveted union job painting the brand-new Upper Valley Mall in Springfield. For years after, we marveled every time we drove past the shiny white automotive bay doors he'd painted, recalling that rare window when we got to eat T-bone steak. One in three full-time workers carried union cards when I was coming of age, but now that number is one in ten.

But any real reckoning with all the changes to the American heartland must extend beyond economics. If I lay out life in Urbana today and measure it against life there when I was growing up, the biggest shocker to me is the staggering decline of education, in both the formal and the informal senses of the word. Not just how we acquire skills, but also how we learn to be human beings with each other. How we learn structure and responsibility and ambition, formally but more important through role models, including bosses at after-school jobs, other people's parents, and, most of all, life-changing teachers—all the bulwarks of a thriving middle class. However desperate my circumstances, it was unthinkable to me not to go to school. School was my sanctuary, the place where I felt most appreciated and most myself.

How does a community lose contact with its faith in schools? And what happens when it does?

PART OF THIS STORY is what happens when the middle class vanishes. But another crucial element is something Americans have paid far too little attention to—the fact that government stopped thinking of higher education as a public good and basically privatized it to the tune of $1.75 trillion in individual student debt. At the precise moment we were supposed to be preparing young people for the so-called knowledge economy, tuition skyrocketed. The same countries that held on to their unions have also heavily subsidized, if not outright paid for, higher education and advanced vocational training, including apprenticeships.[1] The United States now falls thirteenth in the world for college completion, behind Russia, South Korea, Canada, and other countries.[2] In the mid-1980s, when I became a journalist, the United States ranked first.[3] From first to thirteenth. Without debate or even much in the way of discussion.

College has become so out of reach that many Americans have bought the story that they wouldn't want to go anyway. That flywheel of economic fatalism and resentment has been spinning now for two generations, becoming one of the primary drivers of partisan hatred and inequality, of people feeling resentful and betrayed.

And of being unevenly informed, judging from the fact that I can no longer talk about the news (even the weather!) with my relatives or many of my high school friends because we don't agree on the simplest of facts. The more we try, the more we find ourselves flung into opposing corners.

Our impasse reminds me of that old carnival ride at our county fair, the Gravitron: The cylinder spins so fast that the floor drops, and before you know it, you're just stuck there pinned to the wall, immovable.

IN MY HOMETOWN, the number of children living in poverty has more than tripled since I left.[4] The number orphaned by the opioid crisis has tripled just since 2015.[5] After the jobs went away, heroin helped itself to my hometown, followed by fentanyl and meth. The result of that one-two punch has been a preponderance of trauma that is overtaxing every system meant to address it. "Backward mobility," economists call this devastating trend, exacerbated by the Great Recession.

As corporate profits soared, the median wage for workers, adjusted for inflation, stagnated, and the cost of housing, education, and health care far outpaced inflation. In the four decades between my graduation and Silas's, inequality grew so dramatically in the United States that the richest 0.01 percent of Americans have accumulated the same amount of wealth as the poorest *50 percent*.[6]

Presidents, governors, and state legislatures defunded higher education under Republican and Democratic leaders alike. The purchasing power of the federal need-based financial aid program that I credit with effectively saving my life—the Pell Grant—is so meager that very few bright poor kids like Silas can afford to pursue four-year degrees.[7] Now the average Pell Grant pays just 30 percent of a poor kid's public school tuition,[8] far less than what it covered for me.[9]

As a society, do we care half as much about poor kids getting a leg up as we used to? I'm not sure, honestly. But the defunding of higher ed rarely comes up among the pundit class, which tends to parse economics from their big-city bubbles and fancy colleges, rarely venturing to places like Urbana.

When I left for college in 1982, the Pell Grant paid the entirety of my tuition, my room and board, and even my textbooks—an investment in my future that I have paid back through taxes many times over. When you consider that the government recoups the money spent on a typical Pell grantee, through taxes on their increased earnings, in just ten years,[10] the gutting of Pell's purchasing power is extremely shortsighted. But the plundering of this federal program, birthed in the last gasp of America's War on Poverty, is also rarely discussed.

AMERICA'S STUDENT-LOAN DEBT MACHINE is now larger than Americans' combined credit-card debt.[11] Think about how many college graduates have amassed five- and six-figure student-loan debts, and yet a third still earn less than half the nation's median wage.[12] While economists argue that a four-year degree is still the best long-term path forward,[13] only half of Americans participate in any form of higher ed at all.

When they pulled the ladder of upward mobility away from low-wage families, they took away the thing that soothes misery and distress; they took away their hope. What the free-market boosters failed to account for is that, without the potential for advancement and the general sense that fairness and justice will prevail, our social compact is screwed.

The more divided our education levels, the more divided our nation.

SOMETHING DRASTICALLY FLIPPED during the course of my lifetime: Some of the fundamental things Americans once took for granted are no longer true. How has this epic shift played out on the ground in places like Urbana? It is no longer unusual to drive through my hometown—once a Union stronghold and a proud stop on the Underground Railroad—and see Confederate flags. I first noticed this in 2020 during trips home to see my mom, whose health had turned for the worse.

For a decade, I'd also clocked growing tension over politics among my family members and some of my oldest, dearest friends, most of whom now hated "the media," even though they still loved me and, as I tried to remind them, I'm the media too.

I had a hard time understanding how we'd even arrived at this moment. These were my people. I didn't want to write them off, and I didn't want them to write me off. With my family, the desire to hold even vaguely similar views feels baked into our DNA, not unlike our propensity for sweets (and type 2 diabetes), our terrible nearsightedness, and our premature gray.

What was my own role in these breaches, and were they beyond repair? What happened to Urbana? And what did that have to do with the fact that a kid like Silas, with his above-average IQ and the hustle to match, was struggling so desperately to catch a break?

In 2023, I was invited to join a media roundtable in the elite enclave of Cambridge, Massachusetts, featuring two dozen journalists who write about the economy, with rural America top of mind. The hand-wringing was intense. A prominent National Public Radio host shocked us all when he said he gave democracy "another two or three years at most." I was the only journalist in the room who both hailed from and reported on rural America. But it was clear that almost every one of us now lived in bright-blue urban bubbles. (Where I live—Roanoke, Virginia—is now an urban blue dot in a sea of rural and suburban red.) Few in the group had connections to towns like Urbana, where the 2020 stolen-election narrative is so embedded that the town's community center held showings of the "documentary" *2000 Mules*, alleging a vast conspiracy among left-wing nonprofit groups and paid ballot "mules" to steal the 2020 election.

Having written three rural-centered books about the aftermath of globalization followed by the parallel whammy of the opioid crisis, I wasn't sure to what degree our national estrangement was Trump's fault and to what degree the so-called elite—including newsmakers, the media, and a thoroughly deregulated business class—had brought it on ourselves. I left the roundtable with more questions than answers. And I worried, a lot, about potential violence.

All that weighed on me in the aftermath of my mother's death, when I could not get over the feeling of being an outsider in my hometown, a place where I had once known people on just about every block of every street. I decided to return in earnest to Urbana, to re-engage in its culture and its quirks. I wanted to figure out what the hurdles were today for promising poor kids like Silas James, who was as desperate as I had been to thread the needle of upward mobility. How did my high school go from graduating 186 seniors in 1982, my class, to just 91 students four decades later?

I WANTED TO SEE from the inside how politics factored into the lives of the small-town neighbors I grew up knowing, including the people on my old newspaper route and the friends whose parents often helped me—folks who went out of their way to give me rides home from sports and band practices, like the mom who could just tell when I needed a hug because her dad, too, had been an alcoholic. That same mom also made me lunch nearly every day of high school—something I tried to pay forward when my own kids brought home friends who didn't have rides home or field-trip money or the benefit of a free tuna-salad sandwich.

I wanted to understand how our sweet class reunion organizer had turned to organizing our former classmates around conspiracy theories like Pizzagate and adrenochrome. ("You didn't get the vaccine, did you? . . . *Bad move!*") What happened to my old boyfriend, a former reporter and Bernie Sanders supporter who was now spending hours every day watching Russian propaganda on YouTube and prepping for the end-time?

I want to be clear about something: I don't think every young person needs to go to college to "save their lives." This isn't the damned and the saved. I do think that the more messed up a given family and community are, the more kids benefit from having a chance to step away, to experience a nontraumatic—even peaceful—environment.

But, of course, by definition, that requires outside help. Like reliably having a roof over your head. Like Pell Grants. Like public school teachers and librarians who stand up for marginalized kids in the face of racism, homophobia, and anti-intellectualism. (In Ohio, the Southern Poverty Law Center now counts fifty hate and antigovernment groups, several of which are devoted to the decimation of public schools.)[14]

Four years before her death, my mom, a bookish woman who was also my first proofreader, told me I should stop writing about sad things. "You should write a love story," she said.

And though my fellow Urbanans might not view it this way, I have tried here to honor my fierce mom's wishes, with love, by figuring out what happened to my country, my hometown—and my family.

EVERYONE I SPOKE TO at my Urbana High School alma mater brought up the tiny drum major. "There's something about him, I don't know. Even when everything's in chaos, he somehow manages to do whatever he needs to do," said Chris Flowers, a school liaison who helps students transition to college, the military, or the trades.[15] She, too, had grown up poor and surrounded by family dysfunction, and she, too, believed that going to college transformed her life.

When Silas was homeless for most of his junior and senior years, he couch surfed with friends or stayed at his girlfriend's house even after they broke up, which was crazy in retrospect: One argument ended with the destruction of his cell phone, another with his ex parading a date in front of him at senior prom. His mom was in jail on another round of drug charges, and his dad died of a methadone overdose, combined with COVID and a heart blockage, his junior year. A distant relative had taken in Silas and his siblings for a while, but he ended up in jail on charges related to molesting minors. (Silas was also considering pressing related charges against the man.)

This was a reality I could not have conceived of in Urbana forty

*Silas and his siblings released lanterns on
the anniversary of their father's death.*

years before, when I knew of no homeless people and certainly no one
who'd lost a parent to overdose. But, as I would soon learn, Silas's
level of trauma is not an outlier among Urbana students today. What
was different was his ability to make do by turning friends, teachers,
and counselors into substitutes for a functioning family, another trait
we shared.

It had troubled his band director that Silas regularly smoked marijuana, but about that they agreed to disagree. "He was self-medicating,
for sure," Mr. Sapp told me. "He started smoking at a young age. . . .
He wanted to forget about things."

When Mr. Sapp came to Urbana to teach in 1995, most band kids
came from middle- and upper-middle-class two-parent families. Because of school fees, the cost of instruments, and the need for transportation home from after-school practices, the band is now so small
that it can no longer spell out the word "Hillclimbers," the school's
team name, as we did when I marched in it. It's no longer big enough,
even, to spell "Urbana."

Now, at the annual homecoming game, the marching Hillclimbers are reduced to scripting out "Ohio." The best tuba player still dots the letter *i*, then solos, as the band and audience sing the "Buckeye Battle Cry."

Asked if he thought Silas would make it through college after his rocky first attempt, Mr. Sapp was realistic: "It could go either way."

Brooke Perry, the homeless liaison, thought Silas had college potential if his living situation could be stabilized, but the math wasn't in his favor. Even if he ever made it back to Clark State, Silas would be the first among her growing roster of homeless students to even go to college at all.

His English teacher Cassie Cress, the most prescient of the bunch, prayed that he'd leave the area, because otherwise "his family will just keep dragging him down."

Emotions are temporary, Silas kept reminding himself. But first, he had to get through the pain of right now. And right now, he could not muster the energy to put his McDonald's uniform back on and get back to his drive-through shift. He had a blazing headache and no motivation to talk to anyone or do anything.

He'd thought about suicide before, but this time was different. This time, with a pocketknife in one hand and a handful of tranquilizers in the other, he had a plan.

In his mind, he kept replaying the awkward meal with his grandparents. He didn't think their lack of connection stemmed from his being

*Cassie Cress, a UHS English teacher, became a lifeline for many struggling students.*

trans; surprisingly, they seemed okay with that. It was more that they wanted a relationship with him, but like many fractured families in America today, including my own, they had no idea how to pull it off.

Neither did Silas. The precipice was so wide he could no longer even picture the other side. He spread out the forty pills in front of him.

*Two*

# TRUST

*When I left home for college in 1982, Mom knew
I would likely not be moving home again. But
she tried to keep our drop-off moment light.*

My mother was used to hard work, and her dying was no exception. Felled by a stroke the week of the 2020 election, she was already in hospice by the time I made the seven-hour drive and landed at her bedside. Her kids and grandkids took turns rearranging her pillows, wetting her lips with a sponge, and watching for changes as her small chest heaved, her breath uneven and crackling. It was the height of COVID-19, and we could only visit in pairs, fully masked and gowned.

Mom had always been the glue of our family. She was stubborn, no-nonsense, and rock-solid, her footfall so pronounced that the floor vibrated when she moved from her kitchen sink to the stove. If you were a teenager with a hangover, she was not above vacuuming the carpet in front of your bedroom door, over and over, until you hauled your ass out of bed and commenced being a productive human being.

Now she was a wisp of a thing, unable to speak or even squeeze our hands. An institutional gown hung from her bony frame, and her shoulder-length hair was all wrong, nothing like the cropped cut she'd always worn. The philodendron on the windowsill of her memory-care unit was spindly and parched—the last remnant of an arrangement I sent when she moved into assisted living two years before. In her right body and mind, Mom would never let a houseplant go dry.

I watered the vine and hugged my torn-up siblings and my niece Liza, who lived closest and helped coordinate Mom's care, bringing her chocolates and other essentials every week. But for the life of me, as our matriarch lay dying, I could not produce a single tear. While my relatives wept for days, I couldn't help but see Mom's transition as a welcome relief from the indignities of her dementia. She was due her rest, and now here she was, powering through her death just as she powered through her life, getting the damn job done.

NOT LONG AFTER I CAME ALONG IN 1964—the midlife accident, the youngest by far of four kids—Mom became our family's primary breadwinner. When the bills got paid, it was on Mom to pay them, even if that meant showing up at the VFW hall on Friday nights to snag Dad's infrequent paychecks before he drank or gambled them away. Sometimes she took me along, the two of us intuiting that the sweet spot of catching Dad in a decent mood sat somewhere between the second beer and the fifth. If we timed it right, he might even invite us to join him at the dark, smoke-filled bar, setting me up with a cold Coke and a pack of cashews, and Mom with a Miller Lite. I loved going there because the entrance to the club had a secret passcode and a two-way mirror to keep nonmembers out. In the staid small town of Urbana, Ohio, it was a tiny whiff of *Mission: Impossible.*

The night I was born, Dad won a hundred bucks gambling at the VFW, but Mom never saw a dime of it. For generations, women in our family suffered from the burdens of addiction, poverty, and what I now see as the broken masculinity of their men, though we never had such an elevated term for it; it was just what we knew.

Mom was born to an alcoholic father and a mentally ill mother, then had the bad luck to marry another drunk—a junior-high dropout who served in World War II. They met at the Dayton filling station where he worked, in boom-time America. An early photo at a bar shows them dark, handsome, and lithe, Dad with a cigarette and drink in the same hand.

Dad was mainly an absent figure in my life. My oldest sister, Terry,

*Sarah and Ted Macy, not long after Dad*
*came home from World War II.*

fifteen years my senior, will tell you he was not a bad person, and that is her truth: When she was sixteen, he borrowed a truck to drive her to Columbus because she'd won tickets to a Dave Clark Five concert. It was winter, and he sat patiently outside the arena, a six-pack of beer on the floorboard of the truck, while she enjoyed the show.

By the time I was that age, he had emphysema and late-stage alcoholism, and sometimes he turned mean, once beating me with a bent coat hanger he'd been using to scratch the itch beneath his cast. He'd broken his leg in a bar fight at Spainie's, another of his regular watering holes. After Terry married and moved out, one night in an alcoholic rage Dad wanted me to know that Terry had always been his favorite child and I was a slut. Such eruptions were rare and impossible to predict, so I avoided him mostly and adopted a kind of vigilance in the form of a knife I sometimes tucked into my back pocket as I vowed to myself, after the hanger, that he would never touch me again.

I stayed out late partying with friends, and several times I "borrowed" my brother's car at the age of fifteen to buy beer at Dickie Pooh's Drive-Thru when the ABC agents from Columbus—"the staties," we called them—weren't in town. You could tell when they were by the unmarked white van they parked around the corner. Back home, I'd refill the fuel I used with gas from our lawn mower can, and I never got caught.

Trying to get a rise out of me, my dad had picked the wrong slur: I admit to sometimes being a wild child, but I didn't sleep around.

Dad did not bother attending my high school graduation, nor did I bother asking him to come. Terry remembers him as some benign cross between Fred MacMurray and Otis the town drunk, but she never had a school friend laugh at her as he described watching Mom prop up our fifty-year-old dad, walking him from the bar to the car.

She never made a joke about forgetting to buy Dad a Father's Day card, only for him to snap, "That's okay. You're probably not my kid anyway."

In my thirties it took a therapist to acknowledge my suffering but also to note, "It's better that you were more neglected than abused; it could have been worse." She added, "As a writer, being an outsider helped you notice things other people don't."

When I told her my parents' preferential treatment of Terry made me so resentful that I once peed in a bottle of Terry's favorite perfume, she howled laughing and said, "You were one angry little girl."[1]

It fell to the women to do the business of running the family, mowing lawns, paying bills, and shredding cabbage for slaw. It was Mom's idea, when Dad's truck was about to be repossessed, to keep it idling in the driveway overnight, temporarily stymieing the repo man who showed up to retrieve it, only to find the truck with its tank on *E*. Mom despised that truck, because Dad had traded in *her car* to buy it in one of his late-night bar deals. ("It doesn't even have bumpers!" she fumed.)

Occasionally Dad would bring home a mess of bluegill he'd caught when he should have been working, though he left it to Mom to scale, gut, and fry up the fish. After the truck was repossessed, Dad's boss gave him a beat-up sedan, which he hand painted using leftovers from his scant few house-painting jobs. (His friends called him Shaky because it was said that he could paint a perfectly straight line even with the DTs.) He made the top half tan, the bottom Day Glo orange. If there was a worse-looking car in Urbana, Ohio, in 1977, I challenge you to find it.

As a teenager, I refused to ride in it, except for one fishing trip to

Muzzy Lake. On the way home, Dad's fishing poles rattled against the metal minnow bucket in the back of the two-toned car as he, my mom, and I sang along to "Ya picked a fine time to leave me, Lucille" on the AM radio. The requisite bottle of Wiedemann's was lodged between Dad's knees, which were bony and frail, like the rest of him—his emphysema morphing into lung cancer.

As far as fond memories with Dad go, that's my one and done. Thanks, Kenny Rogers.

WHEN THE ECONOMY WAS GOOD, Mom soldered airplane lights at Grimes Manufacturing, the company that dominated our town for most of the twentieth century. It was founded in 1933 by Warren G. Grimes, a ninth-grade dropout and consummate tinkerer who'd talked his way into a job at Ford Motors by lying about his age. Grimes ended up inventing the red, green, and white navigational airplane-light system still in use to this day. By the time I was growing up, everyone called him Old Man Grimes because he basically ran the town, serving not only as its largest employer by a long shot but also, for a time, as mayor. He gave away much-coveted Ohio State University scholarships to employees' kids, bought radio equipment for the Urbana Police Department, offered free haircuts to employees, and opened a downtown movie theater, the Gloria, naming it for his daughter. To help school nurses examine students for ringworm, he donated a cockpit light.

But he also maneuvered to keep Interstate 75 from being built too close to Urbana—to block the arrival of competing factories that could force him to raise wages.[2] When the Japanese automotive maker Honda was casting about in western Ohio for a spot to open its first American factory in 1979, it chose nearby Union County, even though its county seat of Marysville was much smaller than Urbana at the time. But Union had a nearby interstate, U.S. 33, connecting it to

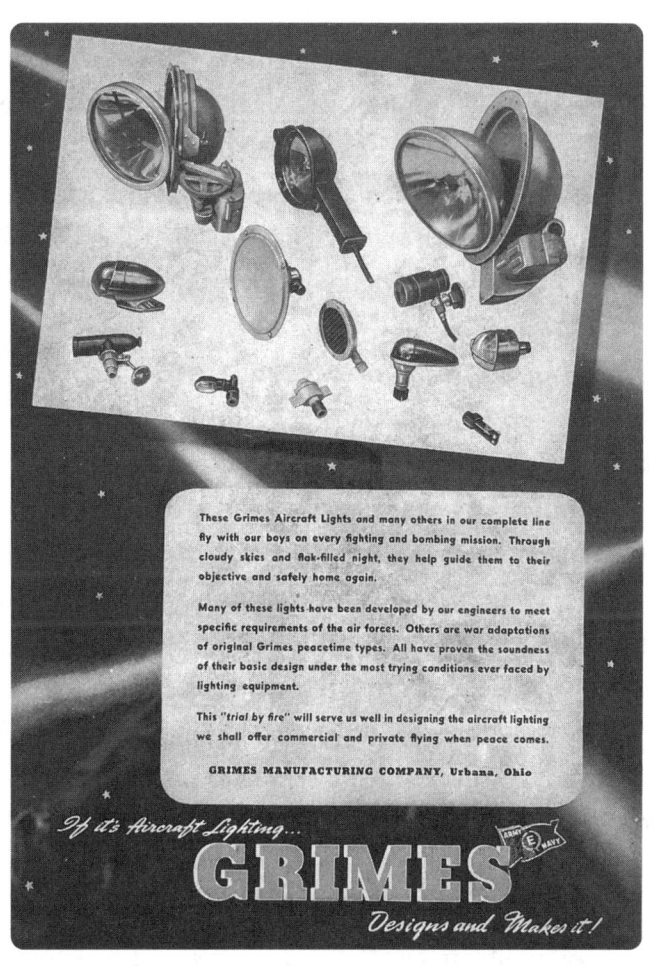

Warren Grimes made his mark on Urbana
and on worldwide aviation practices.

Columbus as well as to multiple other highways. Marysville's growth nearly quadrupled, making it one of the fastest-growing communities in Ohio, while Urbana's remained flat.

FROM THE BEGINNING, farming was baked into our region's landscape. It's for good reason that we produced the likes of A. B. Graham, a nationally known educator and agriculture luminary who created the youth program 4-H, which stands for head, heart, hands, and health. If the word "wholesome" started with an *h*, Mr. Graham would have surely included that too.

With fertile soil and plentiful rivers and creeks, Champaign County was from the beginning an alluring place to raise livestock and to grow wheat, grain, and corn. ("Champaign" is a derivative from the French word meaning open, flat country.) A pioneer town, founded by land speculators eager to exploit the new Northwest Territory and chartered as the county seat in 1805 on former Shawnee land—near the longtime home of Chief Tecumseh—Urbana was for a time the nation's largest settlement between Cincinnati and Detroit, with aspirations to become the next Pittsburgh. Initial plots sold for $1.25 an acre,[3] drawing New Englanders seeking relief from rocky soil and Virginians who were tired of banging their hoes against the tobacco-depleted earth.

Once Tecumseh's people were killed or pushed farther west, the land-hungry migrants, many of them Germans, English, and Scots-Irish, were deeded land; some as payment for their Revolutionary War service. Leaders at the time liked the idea of dividing Americans into two classes—*plebs rustica* and *plebs urbana*. The former lived in rural districts and were farmers, while the *plebs urbana* lived in villages and tended to be artisans. The name Urbana, then, was intended to give the town a leg up and a sophisticated air. In its first decades, Urbana

*Early-morning fog lifts as the sun rises over
a Champaign County soybean field.*

was the nation's No. 1 producer of brooms and was also known for its carriage and cigar making.[4]

In its initial growth spurt, it was also an important staging head-quarters for the U.S. Army during the War of 1812, with Ohio's governor setting up shop at Doolittle's Tavern on the public square. From that spot, a seventy-year-old freed slave named Richard Stanhope was dispatched to deliver war provisions to army troops in Detroit. Stanhope had been George Washington's valet, fighting alongside him and standing at his bedside as he drew his last breath. Rewarded with a four-hundred-acre land grant, Stanhope was among the rush of people, Black and white, making their way to Champaign County's prairie-like landscape,[5] a "promised land" for the oppressed, the downtrodden, and the poor, its lush soil seen as the ticket to independence and wealth.

A PROMINENT STOP on the Underground Railroad before the Civil War, the county also attracted the state's most famous runaway. Addison

White had fled slavery in Kentucky and never quite made it to Canada's promised land, settling just east of Urbana in Mechanicsburg, a village full of New England Quakers and known abolitionists. The town's residents liked White so much that in 1857 they ended up buying his freedom for $950 from his former enslaver, after months of legal and physical battles with the posse charged with capturing him. At the time, White lived and worked for the region's busiest Underground Railroad conductor, Udney Hyde, a Vermont native who sheltered 517 runaways in his time.

Once White's freedom was secured, he stayed on to help Hyde with farm chores as well as to serve as his "night conductor." The pair hid runaways in cellars, attics, and stables and inside hay-covered wagons. They coordinated their secret passage to Canada with other like-minded Ohioans. Building a trapdoor to the cellar in the bedroom of his log cabin and a platform inside his well where they could hide, the irascible Udney Hyde told people he was "breaking the laws of man but keeping the laws of God."[6]

Animosity over slavery divided the county from its earliest days. The western half—now home to the far-right congressman Jim Jordan as well as one of the lead January 6 insurrectionists—was then home to pro-slavery so-called copperheads who favored "states' rights" in the lead-up to the Civil War. In the eastern half, a person like Addison White could walk free even after his enslaver traveled from Kentucky to Mechanicsburg to reclaim him, in clear violation of the Fugitive Slave Act of 1850. One runaway recalled being told that "I could travel in broad daylight if I'd hold up my head and act free." White railroad conductors liked to taunt slave hunters by yelling, "Run, boys, run," when no runaways were there, and area farmwives gathered in sewing circles to make new clothing for runaways who arrived with their garments in tatters after weeks of walking through brush, hiding in thickets, and swimming across streams.[7]

During one antislavery meeting in nearby North Lewisburg, "rowdies from the town would come with drums and literally drown us out so that we couldn't hear." At other times, the dueling Virginia and New England camps threw eggs at each other and got into fistfights over slavery at local pubs.[8] Churches splintered over the issue, too, as pro-slavery residents dismissed Urbana as a "black abolition hole." But the work in Ohio, home to the busiest Underground Railroad terminals in the nation, became vital to ending slavery. It inspired Harriet Beecher Stowe's *Uncle Tom's Cabin*, which built antislavery support that became part of the groundwork for the Civil War.

When it came time to tally votes in the 1860 presidential election, Lincoln won Champaign County with 2,325 votes, edging out Stephen A. Douglas (1,810).[9] By that time, Addison White's story was so well known that it caught the attention of Frederick Douglass, who befriended him, invited him to his home in Rochester, New York, and later recruited him to serve with the Fifty-Fourth Massachusetts Infantry, the Union's first Black regiment. Their bravery was heralded in the film *Glory*. Of the 3,235 Champaign County men who served the Union—an above-average proportion, roughly half of them volunteers—578 didn't return.

In 1870, a statue of a cavalryman was cast from a bronze Civil War cannon and erected in Urbana's picturesque public square. With his head bowed in sad meditation, the figure has one hand resting on his hip and the other on his saber hilt. The Man on the Monument, as he is known, faces north on U.S. Route 68 to symbolize the Union's victory and the hope that all the suffering would one day mend our nation's tattered fabric.

When I began my home-going project in early 2023, I did not yet see how brittle that fabric had become.

IN THE CHAMPAIGN COUNTY where I grew up, no one mentioned Addison White. Few paid much mind, either, to the downcast Man on the Monument erected to honor the local men, Black and white, who'd helped to save the nation and abolish a disgraceful institution.

In 2013, a biracial classmate of mine, Mark Evans, finally got a historical marker for the Underground Railroad placed in Urbana in honor of his Black, Native American, and white ancestors who helped run it. But no one spoke about Charles "Click" Mitchell, a Black man who was accused of raping a prominent newspaper publisher's widow and lynched for it. In a photo taken of the 1897 lynching, Mitchell's battered body hung from a maple tree, above a crowd of smiling and jeering young men who displayed the twenty-three-year-old's corpse in the courthouse yard later that day.

When Evans tried to present Mitchell's story at a local Juneteenth festival in 2022, "they flat out told me NO WAY!" he said.[10] In 1963, no minister in Urbana would marry Evans's parents in a church, so they coaxed a retired Black pastor to perform the service in a relative's living room. Mark's mom's family, who is white, wanted nothing to do with her after that, or her kids. Mark's maternal grandmother "has never even hugged me," Mark said.

Mark's dad, Johnny Evans, a retired Urbana police officer now in his eighties, told me his family was discriminated against regularly for decades—denied apartments and home loans, fired from jobs without cause, treated poorly by co-workers and neighbors alike. Shortly after his retirement, Johnny and his wife, Peggy, moved to the capital of Columbus, an hour away, searching for more open-minded neighbors.

"I got so many pains about this town," Mark said. He reminded me that he'd dated a white girl through most of our high school years, but they'd had to sneak around because her parents forbade her to see someone of mixed race. Mark lives in a Columbus suburb now too, happily married to a biracial woman whose Champaign County roots also include Underground Railroad conductors. He spent the entirety of the January 6 insurrection glued to the TV, clutching his gun for protection and worrying about his police officer neighbors who still had Trump signs planted in their yards. "They think we're taking something from them when we talk about it."

The tensions among members of Mark's and my old graduating class had grown so heated during Trump's presidency that one reunion organizer dropped out after receiving a death threat and friendships built over sixty years dissolved. Some of my oldest friendships seemed on the brink of dissolving too.

MARK'S FAMILY'S EXPERIENCE hadn't been visible to me. It's fair to say that I, along with most of my classmates, grew up seeing Urbana through a rose-colored lens. Urbana had long touted its status as a patriotic World War II factory town. As much of the nation morphed from farm to workshop, Grimes Manufacturing heralded itself as a company that helped "our boys on every flying and bombing mission" win World War II. There was a time when every airplane in the nation used lights manufactured in my hometown. Grimes lights even made their way into space on Project Mercury, Apollo, and Gemini missions.

Mom didn't mind soldering airplane lights, even tolerating the smarmy boss who liked to pinch her butt when she walked past. As a little girl, I was proud of her work, too, and used to point it out to friends when a plane, any plane, passed overhead.

According to Betty, my first friend, when we were four, I told her I could whisper to the wind and make it stop, and she believed me, "because you rode a big-girl bike when I was still on training wheels."

Betty said recently that her parents considered me "feral" as a child, a word that stung.

When we were in high school, her mom, Kim, a frugal immigrant from Korea who was a driving force behind the transformation of the family's small truck-driving business into a developer of corporate warehouses and industrial parks, resented the fact that Betty routinely gave me rides home from band and sports practices. To be fair, gas prices were steep at the time, and my house wasn't on her way home. Also, when we were five, apparently, I talked Betty into exchanging her family's empty soda bottles (pop bottles, Ohioans call them) for money to buy candy at Carmazzi's, a newsstand and candy store on the town square. Kim considered that stealing—a fair point, I now realize, but come on.

A longtime neighbor, asked what he remembered of our family, recalled only that I was the town's "paper girl" and my dad was "the town drunk." When I told my sister Terry this, she reared up and said, "He wasn't the only town drunk!" She worried that I was unfairly picking on Dad and pointed out that he did try to get sober a few times. "It's a disease, Beth; you know that," she said, reminding me that I have publicly talked and written about the disease model of addiction many times.

*Ted "Shaky" Macy found solace in cheap beer and cigarettes at the Urbana VFW, where he won $100 on the night of my birth.*

When I was in the fifth grade, Dad's boss sent him to an Indiana rehab to dry out for a month. Not long ago, I found a letter he wrote to Mom from his 1974 stay, time-stamped 3:30 a.m.: *Sweetheart, I love you. Please rite me. Tell kids to rite to Dad. Tell Mom am OK.*[11]

Afterward, Gideon-sized Alcoholics Anonymous devotionals would appear next to the toilet. I used to sit there scanning them, praying they wouldn't disappear. "The drinking career of almost every alcoholic has been marked by escapades, funny, humiliating, shameful or tragic. The first impulse will be to bury these skeletons in a dark closet and padlock the door," an Al-Anon book I later found read.

When you're a sensitive kid, though, it's damn near possible to hide an alcoholic dad when everyone in town seems to comment on him. Once, when Dad caught Mom having an affair with a family friend and carpet installer named Bernard—we got a really nice living room wall-to-wall out of the deal—Dad tracked him down at a bar on Monument Square and punched him off his barstool, a story Terry told me, laughing as she recounted it.

I didn't find the anecdote funny, but, unlike Terry, I had few positive memories to counterbalance the drunken forays. As the poet Anne Sexton wrote, "Pain engraves a deeper memory."

MY MOM TRIED to make up for him by working her tail off and loving us roughly but well. When I complained of boredom, she told me to "go play in the traffic." (There was very little traffic on our street.) I learned to cuss by watching her struggle to light the natural-gas pilot on our rickety clothes dryer with a match rubber-banded to the end of a yardstick. Later, during my first reporting job for a weekly newspaper in Columbus, I made $235 a week (before taxes), and it was Mom who schooled me on the poor people's art of check kiting.

At my first daily paper in Savannah, Georgia, I earned so little that I couldn't afford to use my crap health-insurance benefits. For my confidence-killing case of adult acne, a dermatologist prescribed medicine that cost more than $100 a pop—until Mom, then in her sixties, managed an end run. With the help of her niece, a medical receptionist, wily Mom figured out how to get an Accutane prescription of her own; then she mailed it to me in Georgia.

When I mentioned being homesick for Ohio's glorious autumns, living in the coastal South, where the trees didn't even change colors—they just turned brown one November day and fell—Mom mailed me a box of fallen leaves from the sprawling buckeye tree in Grandma Macy's yard, with instructions to burn them, something she did every year. I did; the smell was intoxicating.

My friends *adored* my mom, swooning over her fried chicken and marveling at her can-do attitude. My friend Betty still lays her sweaters out to dry flat on newspapers because Mom showed her how. She still remembers the smell of our house: cut grass in the summer, kerosene in the winter, and bacon year-round. "It was comforting," she wrote to me a few years ago. "As was your mom. The lighting was low, and it always seemed cool and comfortable and was always tidy. Your mom accepted me even tho I looked different. She taught me that little house dogs were awesome."[12] (Betty has six tiny shih tzus.)

My dad rarely spoke to any of us, a by-product of being hungover whenever he wasn't at the bars. "I could just tell he didn't like people like me," my friend Joy recalled. Black people, she meant.

Throughout the 1970s of my youth, when the economy tanked and layoffs descended, Mom picked up under-the-table work waitressing and babysitting. A sucker for babies, dogs, and chocolate, she made noodles by hand and whipped up fudge and cakes without a recipe, not because cooking from scratch was healthy or cool, but because it was cheaper than the popular prepackaged items most of my friends' moms made. We never went on vacations, but once we rented inner tubes and floated down the Mad River, after Mom carefully tucked her cigarettes inside a plastic baggy. When a current tipped her over, she lost her bifocals, while her cigarettes stayed safe and dry—something we laughed about long after she quit smoking and became a hardcore antismoker.

When my second-oldest sister, Cookie, became a single mother of three after her second divorce in the mid-1970s, Mom somehow found room in our cramped cottage for four more souls. There was never a morning when Mom didn't play short-order cook, making French toast for my nieces and a bacon sandwich (on toast, a schmear of mayo) for me, wrapping it in a paper towel so I could eat it on the way to school. I was perennially late and also, then as now, not much of a morning person.

*Mom, with me in her lap and flanked by Terry (left) and Tim. She was frugal through her final days but always made sure we had a decent Christmas.*

Mom would deadpan, "Good morning, glory," handing me the sandwich. Bacon with a side of sarcasm—that was our love language.

A CHILD OF THE DEPRESSION, Mom wasn't above spending five minutes scraping the last teaspoon of mayonnaise from the jar, and you were a fool if you didn't do the same. She rarely bought bait for her fishing excursions, preferring to wait for a nighttime rain and dig up the night crawlers herself, a flashlight in one hand and an empty Folgers can in the other.

Giant blocks of yellow government cheese sometimes appeared in our Frigidaire, but the few times she applied for food stamps, she returned deflated. The social workers seemed to delight in the fact that Mom made a couple dollars more than the eligibility cutoff. At the height of her earnings when I was in college, she was a widow who test-drove cars for a Honda subcontractor, making $8,000 a year. But she could stretch a dime further than anyone I knew.

She even put my birth on layaway, paying $110 over several months, money she scrimped and handed over in installments of five and ten bucks a month. Decades later, she handed me the small, yellowed folder she'd tucked away for posterity—the doctor's office payment record from her prenatal visits and my birth.

I was twenty-six and soon to wed, and as we hugged goodbye in the doorway of her house, her throat caught as she bestowed on me the kind of respect I had never before received from her. "You have practically raised yourself," she said.

No matter how far from home I went, no matter how much our paths diverged, she wanted me to never forget: *We* are your people; *this* is your stock.

THE WOMEN HELD OUR FAMILY TOGETHER. My sister Terry helped pay our bills with her receptionist's salary, splurging for Michael's Pizza on Thursdays—the night *The Waltons* aired—made by an Italian grandma, Mrs. Michael, who used a blackened cleaver hauled over from the old country to chop her pies into tiny squares. (The crunchy corner pieces were best.) When Mom became a widow, a family friend helped pay for Dad's funeral, and Terry helped her buy a decent car.[13]

My family read widely, books (always from the library) and newspapers, and watched Walter Cronkite every night. Before I was out of diapers, President Lyndon B. Johnson told the nation, "At the desk where I sit, I have learned one great truth. The answer to our national problems—the answer for all the problems of the world—comes down to a single word. That word is 'education.'"[14]

It was the dawn of his Great Society, a time when most Americans believed both the president and Cronkite, when every house in my neighborhood read *The Urbana Daily Citizen* and many also took the bigger *Springfield News-Sun* or the much-bigger *Columbus Dispatch* on Sundays. I know because I delivered the *UDC* door-to-door six afternoons a week on my Huffy ten-speed.

My route customers called me "Paper Girl" with a wry smirk. I'd pursued the job so I could buy my own clothes, and I desperately wanted to go on the seventh-grade field trip to Washington, D.C., so I could experience, for the first time, what it felt like to cross the Ohio state line.

Also, I did not wish to be left behind. If you couldn't come up with $225 for the weeklong trip, you could stay home and go to school instead, and it wouldn't count against your grades. But then everyone would know you were poor.

Not that they didn't already know. The one time I invited our future homecoming queen to our house to work on a school project with me, her eyes widened and her jaw dropped. It was nothing like her expansive house on a horse farm. "It's so *fifties* in here!" she cackled. "You don't even have a shower!" A gleam shone from her gorgeous smile, from the braces we couldn't afford, as if what she'd just said was really a joke instead of an insult I'd still be recounting, word for word, some fifty years hence.

My grandma Macy pitched in for the D.C. trip. When both Mom and Dad were out of work, Grandma shared her wages from the uptown clothing store where she worked into her mid-eighties and nailed a homemade sign on her front-yard buckeye tree that said FLOOR SANDER FOR RENT. Dad hit her up constantly for bar money, and

Mom swore he was the way he was because she'd spoiled him his entire life.

As our chartered Greyhound rolled into West Virginia, I closed my eyes and held my breath, hoping that something cellular inside me would be changed.

LITTLE DID I UNDERSTAND that politicians on both sides were actively promoting programs to ensure it would not be my last trip across state lines. An outgrowth of LBJ's War on Poverty, access to higher education for poor kids was spurred by America's need to remain competitive in a rapidly globalizing world. Back then the government took a more active role in training its workforce; it did not just leave things to the market's invisible hand.

A few years before my Washington field trip, a quirky, blue-blooded Rhode Island senator named Claiborne Pell designed what he called the "G.I. Bill for everybody" so that promising poor kids would have the same right to a higher education as those whose families, like Pell's, went to the Ivy League.

While my mom soldered airplane lights at night in dimly lit Quonset huts, working what she called "second trick," the millionaire senator sketched out my escape hatch on a ski lodge place mat. The formula for administering the new federal financial aid program had come to him as he was skiing down a mountain in the Swiss Alps.[15] While Pell and I didn't seem to inhabit the same universe, his ability to see outside the comforts of his waterfront mansion would transform this layaway baby's life.

UNLIKE PELL'S FAMILY, I didn't lay eyes on an ocean until my twentieth year, and only then because the parents of one of my dorm buddies owned a beachside condo. Mom didn't see the beach until her early sixties—and only then because, a few years after Dad's death at fifty-seven, she married a middle-class widower with a federal pension and a paid-off suburban ranch house. Ten years her senior, Gene had a sweet disposition and a weak spot for her lean dancer's legs. (In Dayton, where they'd both grown up, people still recalled her teenage nickname: Jitterbug.)

Not long after her 1989 wedding to Gene, Mom beamed as she described owning real jewelry for the first time, driving a car manufactured in the present decade, and buying the kind of long-term care insurance that would one day allow her to leave the four of us real money when she died. Which is not to say she ever stopped scraping the hell out of the mayonnaise jar.

"They say money isn't everything, but you know what?" she asked me, pausing for dramatic effect.

"It's *pretty nice.*"

*Three*

# BUBBLES

*I graduated from Bowling Green State University in 1986, the tail end of a time when Pell Grants covered a poor kid's tuition, housing, and books.*

I f Mom's golden ticket into the middle class was marriage, then going away to Bowling Green State University, courtesy of Senator Pell's grants, was my portal to stability. It led me to things like affordable health insurance (eventually) and meaningful work and a husband who was not only pretty nice; he treated me as his equal and never had trouble stopping after a second beer. His parents, who'd met at Cornell, taught all six of their kids how to ski. (The one time I tried skiing in my early twenties I couldn't make it past the bunny hill.) They learned to swim early, too, in their backyard pool. There are still times when being with his family feels as if I've immigrated to another country—one where degrees far outnumber divorces—but as I type, we have been married thirty-four years.

Without a four-year degree, I could have easily ended up underemployed or unemployed, ruled under the thumb of some "man of the house." The ability to earn a bachelor's degree is one of the single most important factors protecting Americans against deaths from addiction, poverty, and hopelessness, what the economists Angus Deaton and Anne Case call deaths of despair. Higher education is a stronger link to a longer life than even household income, according to Deaton and Case.[1] A college diploma, in fact, is correlated to an extension of the average American's lifespan by eight and a half years.[2]

Just 37 percent of Americans have a bachelor's degree. In Urbana, that number is only 16 percent, five points lower than the national average for rural adults.[3] That means that most Urbanans end up with far less earning potential; over a lifetime, they make 80 percent less than those with bachelor's degrees.[4] They also endure higher levels of family instability and mental distress.

In Urbana, the number of police calls for mental health incidents has increased ninefold in the decades since I left.[5] In the past twenty years, general EMS calls have increased by 3 to 5 percent every year.[6]

I saw the ripple effects of these heightened emergencies during every visit home, one way or another.

FOR YEARS, I thought the Pell Grant had the ability to lift the weight of poverty because it had lifted mine. I couldn't understand why the government didn't erect billboards about it so that poor kids from kindergarten onward would know that if they did well in school, there was a brighter and much easier world awaiting them beyond shift work and clunker cars.

But maybe I was too busy being "elite" to understand how disconnected I'd become from the landscape of my roots. In a 2022 poll, 37 percent of voters agreed with the statement that "college makes you lose common sense," and four out of five Republicans reported believing that high school and college teachers alike are simply "trying to teach liberal propaganda."[7] But was it the MAGA people who'd turned brittle with antipathy, or was it me and my ilk who'd turned fancy and aloof?

While rural people still rally around their flagship universities' sports teams—my siblings and former classmates all proudly wear Ohio State University apparel—the level of contempt rural people have for universities has soared. The University of Wisconsin political scientist Kathy Cramer, author of *The Politics of Resentment*, offered that she, too, had wildly underestimated the "reservoir of hate" that rural people felt.

Even though he's an Ivy Leaguer himself, Trump tapped into that reservoir, not just giving it a voice, but lighting it on fire with such rhetoric as "I love the poorly educated." And: "Too many Universities

*Sports are still a popular topic, as crowds cheered the announcement of the 2023 UHS Homecoming Court.*

and School Systems are about Radical Left Indoctrination, not Education."[8]

"It's no longer just whether you can afford college. It's the whole 'If you go to college, you'll leave home, move to a city, and you'll turn into a liberal,'" said Sarah Flanagan, a former aide to Senator Pell who's now a higher-ed lobbyist.

BY THE LATE 1990s, average tuition in the United States had more than doubled from when I went to school, while the value of the top Pell award dropped 25 percent. When President Bill Clinton touted his Hope Scholarship and related tuition tax credits as a doubling of federal funding for financial aid, it was a sleight of hand, catering solely to middle-class students who were already going to college. That same decade, Clinton oversaw the country's catastrophic entry into NAFTA in 1994 and paved the way for China's admission into the World Trade Organization in 2001. He predicted that offshoring would eventually prove to be a "win-win" for American workers.

Our country still suffers the fallout of those disastrous decisions, which were cheered by business schools and Nobel Prize–winning economists, including several who have since recanted their pro-offshoring views.[9] "I . . . no longer defend the idea that the harm done to working Americans by globalization was a reasonable price to pay for global poverty reduction," Angus Deaton wrote in 2024. "We have largely stopped thinking about ethics and about what constitutes human well-being."[10]

NAFTA took nearly a million jobs away, and the trade agreements that followed it were responsible for the loss of a staggering four million more jobs, most of them in manufacturing. The Great Recession slashed another two million jobs and twenty-five thousand businesses.[11] The average laid-off factory worker suffered a 19.2 percent fall in their standard of living, with Chinese imports reducing roughly a third of all Americans' incomes, delivering a disproportionate blow to rural areas and small towns.[12]

The international conglomerate Honeywell Aerospace would end up owning Grimes Manufacturing. "I don't even know where it's based," said Rich Ebert, the county's director of economic development.[13] (Honeywell's corporate headquarters are in Charlotte, North Carolina.) There is no Old Man Honeywell who has at least some of Urbana's interests at heart.

Cheaper furniture and blue jeans notwithstanding, displaced American workers are still waiting on Clinton's win-win to land. In the transition to a "twenty-first-century economy," hollowed-out communities and even whole regions were largely treated as collateral damage.

For blue-collar workers left to fend for themselves, many of them now working service jobs for half their previous pay and no benefits, the shift to unfettered free trade was like opening a velvet box and finding a turd inside. The Democratic strategist David Axelrod had a better (or at least more polite) metaphor: "I'm so proud of my association with Barack Obama, but the Democratic Party was the party that brought and heralded free trade. We lied to people and said all boats would be lifted somehow. Well, it was a tide that lifted a lot of yachts. A lot of the smaller boats got shipwrecked. A lot of people's lives were changed for the worse."[14]

The displaced were told to get an education and move to where the jobs were. And among those who didn't or couldn't, "their apparent resistance to doing so is taken as further evidence of their self-destructive nostalgia for the good old days and, later, as proof of their white male privilege instead of understanding how strongly rooted rural and small-town people tend to be," said Anthony Flaccavento, a Virginia farmer and onetime congressional candidate who now heads the Rural Urban Bridge Initiative.[15]

The Trade Adjustment Assistance program designed to retrain dislocated workers was so minimal and poorly executed that only a third of the displaced even participated, and most who did ended up making far less than they had in the factories. According to the Economic Policy Institute, international trade costs American workers without a college degree $2,300 a year in lost wages, even after factoring in the lower cost of consumer goods.[16]

I saw this firsthand as I traveled the heartland promoting my first book, *Factory Man*, in 2014, about the implosion of small American factory towns and a lone Virginia factory owner who fought back. By the time the paperback published the following year, I learned to keep a box of gratis copies in the trunk of my car for the dislocated workers who came to my events but couldn't afford to buy a copy.[17]

But most politicians and pundits still fail to acknowledge that the majority of American people fared worse under free trade, even as the nation's combined income rose.[18] In 2016, exit polls confirmed that anger over free trade was the prime reason Donald Trump flipped Wisconsin, Pennsylvania, and Michigan from blue to red.[19]

*Senator Claiborne Pell saw his namesake grant as a kind of "G.I. Bill for everybody." Illustration by Tim Foley.*

Average tuition has more than *tripled* since I went to college, and the neediest students now have only roughly a third of their costs covered by Pell Grants,[20] thanks to paltry budget allotments advanced by Congress and state legislatures headed by both parties. Had I been born just a decade later, I would not have been able to go to college.

When I interviewed the retired senator Pell a decade before his death in 2009, his biggest regret was that his namesake program had not achieved entitlement status, leaving its fate in the hands of politicians who were more interested in garnering reelection campaign funds from their corporate donors than governing for the greater good.

It is true that leaving home and going to college ended up separating me from my family—physically, culturally, and politically. That separation was never clearer to me than the Saturday after the 2020 presidential election. As the suburban Georgia votes were being tallied, my sister Cookie and I were sitting in Mom's memory-care unit with a hospice nurse. The lights were dimmed, and we tried to make small talk as Mom gasped for breath. About the only thing we agreed on was not to discuss the orange elephant in the room.

Cookie and I had never been especially close. She's thirteen years older than me, and our lives diverged early. I was five when she got pregnant during her senior year of high school, then married, then divorced. Three daughters later, after her second marriage failed, she was a single mom working for Old Man Grimes, checking her mailbox for child-support checks that rarely showed. In the mid-1970s, she made $1.67 an hour putting together helicopter instrument panels.[21]

Around the time Grimes Manufacturing was sold and resold before being gobbled up by Honeywell, replacing workers like Cookie with machines or sending their jobs overseas,[22] she found solace and community in a Pentecostal church, led by a charismatic preacher who chaired the local "decency league" and introduced her to her third husband. This one, finally, was a teetotaler who wanted her to stay home and be a housewife, which sounded good to Cookie after so many years of scraping by. "We were so excited for her, remember?" our oldest sister, Terry, recalled.

By 1988, Mom and the rest of our family stopped speaking to husband number three or including him in gatherings because of his abusive treatment of Cookie's kids. The youngest two ended up moving in with their dad, who, when they became justifiably angry teenagers, sent them to a veteran-run orphanage. Which may explain why Cookie skipped my 1990 wedding and instead attended a revival at her rural, fundamentalist church.

Over the decades, we exchanged Christmas cards and played fiercely competitive games of Boggle when we got together, and online Scrabble between visits. She usually won. At family potlucks, she was known for her "chocolate dessert," a crunchy-gooey marvel that's a medley of prepackaged items (heavy on the Cool Whip) and might be the tastiest thing I've ever put in my mouth.

I'd never known Cookie to express political opinions or follow the news, but a few years back, like many people in my hometown, she started posting pro-Trump memes on Facebook. An animated cartoon of Trump doing the twist as victory dance the morning after he beat Hillary Clinton springs to mind. She knew not to talk about Trump in front of Mom, though; even in her mental decline, Mom saw right through Trump's bluster, harrumphing, "I cannot stand the way he talks!"

I was closer to my brother, Tim, who used to visit us in Virginia every spring and fall to see our youngest in high school plays. But we, too, had grown apart since Trump's election in 2016. Tim had missed the invitation to Sasha's senior play, which he would have loved—our kid hamming it up as Nathan Detroit in *Guys and Dolls*—after unfriending me on Facebook.

"Because of all the liberal shit you post," he explained.

I wasn't sure what he meant—the fact-checked articles from papers I occasionally write for, including *The New York Times* and *The Washington Post*? But his absence bewildered me.

My FAMILY HAD ONCE been proud of me. In March 2011, my sister Terry went to the trouble of stuffing Post-it notes into every issue of *O, the Oprah Magazine* in the checkout line of her grocery store, noting, "My sister wrote this article!" After Mom's death, I inherited a cataloged box of every newspaper and magazine article I'd written, including a scrapbook Grandma Macy made of my honor roll mentions, a newspaper photo of me *missing a first-base catch*, and some awful stories I'd written for *The Urbana Daily Citizen* as a college intern. Apparently, during the week of the Champaign County Fair—which is still the biggest happening in Urbana—I was so low on the reporter totem pole that my beat assignment was sheep. (A headline on one of my stories: MICHELE MEYERS REINS [*sic*] AS LAMB AND WOOL QUEEN.)

In 2021, Cookie reminded her church friends to watch the Hulu

*A sibling snapshot in the mid-1980s perm years.*
*From left: Cookie, Tim, Terry, and me.*

show based on my book *Dopesick*, only to cringe at the gay storyline and multiple f-bombs in the first episode. I know this because she accidentally included my husband in a damage-control message she sent to her friends: "No nudity so far. But if Beth wasn't my sister, I would not be watching. I probably won't finish."

I had settled in a medium-sized Virginia city, lived for a time in Boston and New York. My siblings all lived in rural places within half an hour's drive of our hometown. I worked for newspapers and then wrote books, and they no longer believed "the media" unless it came from Fox News or, in Cookie's case, Newsmax. The newspapers they'd once read had become skeletons of their former selves, their content reduced to crime, high school sports, and ads for gun shows and shooting ranges.

When our eldest son announced he was getting married to the young man he'd been living with for two years, Tim and Cookie ignored it at first. My sister Terry offered a single like on Facebook. She had married John, an early computer tech and champion Hillary-hater. Whenever I asked John how he was doing, he replied, "deplorable," and the peacemaker Terry would scold, "We already discussed this, John; no politics!"

When a fellow patron at their small-town library overdosed in the bathroom in 2017, John was stunned. He'd been watching Fox News obsessively for a decade and no longer took the local paper, so he had little inkling that heroin had arrived in their small Ohio town, until he heard the thump in the bathroom stall.

AN ARMY VETERAN WHO worked as a technician on the manned Apollo 7 mission in Spain, John retired in the early 1990s and spent hours listening to Rush Limbaugh every day. The internet and twenty-four-hour cable news were exploding at the time, and measured political debate and news you can use were soon replaced by stories that favored shock value and partisan rancor. Political fevers heightened with the near-constant barrage of national cable news, usually spun by left- or right-leaning media and amplified by taunting tweets.[23] As Craigslist, Google, and Facebook usurped most of what newspapers counted on for ad revenue, my beloved industry cratered in all but the urban power centers. Non-city people like John began identifying more with national politics and less with their geographic communities and the kinds of shared narratives that once dominated newspapers, including feature stories that explained who your neighbors were—and sometimes who you were—warts and all.

Those feature articles were the bread and butter of my twenty-five-year newspaper career in Roanoke, Virginia, where I still live. I wrote about everything from artists to caregivers for the elderly to a Congolese immigrant who drove the city's immigrant kids to school.

For eight years I witnessed the travails of a young Black woman born into poverty. Salena Sullivan wasn't just the first in her family to go to college; she was the first in her neighborhood to go. I was with her at the library counter where she worked after school when she learned she'd been accepted, with a full ride, to Harvard. I got to witness the scene as her longtime library patrons, many of them elderly and former civil rights leaders, put down the newspapers they were reading and wept. And I followed Salena to Harvard the following year, after winning a Nieman Fellowship for Journalism for my work on outsiders and underdogs—one of only two from our class of war correspondents and urban-based national reporters who hailed from smaller news outlets.

My newspaper pay was lousy. When I quit *The Roanoke Times* to write books in 2013, none of us had received a raise in eight years. But traveling outside my zip code to witness the breadth of my community and explain it to readers was a joy most days, and it felt like public service. As James Baldwin put it, "The world changes according to the way people see it, and if you can alter, even by a millimeter, the way a person looks at reality, then you can change it."

When my first story ran, titled "The Library's Child," as Salena's patrons called her, a local hairdresser who was white and gay created a college spending-money fund in her name. He didn't want her to feel like a food-stamp recipient in line at a Whole Foods. This, too, is why local newspapers were once society's glue.

At *The Roanoke Times*, the newsroom had 125 employees when I joined in 1989. Now it has six reporters and an editor, Brian Kelley, who routinely works seventy hours a week; his bosses at Lee Enterprises have him regularly laying off reporters and editing three smaller papers in the chain as well. He could retire if he wanted to, but the responsible Eagle Scout in him will not abandon the ship, even though his corporate overlords long ago abandoned him. Before Brian, my favorite editor, Carole Tarrant, was escorted out of the building by a security guard when Berkshire Hathaway bought the paper in 2013. Warren Buffett's people thought she made too much money, not understanding that she loved journalism so much, as her successor does, that she would have worked for less pay. She was tough as hell, a Philly-bred redhead who thought nothing of drawing a line of ZZZZZZs on my story drafts to indicate boredom.

But when a Virginia Tech shooter killed thirty-two students and himself in 2007, Carole worked two months straight, brought in counselors and massage therapists, and created a pay-it-forward care system for journalists in other markets who were increasingly covering mass shootings and experiencing secondary trauma.

On the way home from her dismissal, with her work belongings stowed in her trunk, she stopped to cry in my backyard. Ten years later, she still mourns what's happened to journalism, and her displacement from it, every day. When I told Carole that Brian had canceled an interview with me at the last minute—he said he was just too depressed—she said, "Every day I read the paper and wonder how he's keeping it together by threads." At 125,000 subscribers in 1989, *The Roanoke Times* often had among the highest penetration rates in the nation. In its last publicized circulation count, it sold fewer than 11,000 copies a day (20,429, counting online subscriptions).[24] For decades we were known as a scrappy paper that punched above its weight, with three Pulitzer finalists and scores of national awards. But the capacity that made that possible had all been slashed.

Investigative series and empathy-building stories like the one about Salena, reported over months and years, rarely appear in local newspapers anymore, which are now largely filled with easier-to-land stories about cops and courts, giving the false impression that crime is so rampant that surely everyone ought to run out and buy a gun. In 2022, when the scandal of the Long Island congressman George Santos's made-up résumé came to light, press experts gnashed their teeth about *The New York Times* having missed the story. Turns out the tiny *North Shore Leader* had broken the news months earlier, but the bigger outlets were either too complacent or too strained to pick it up. And so a wealthy New York suburb, home to Sean Hannity and Billy Joel, elected a con man.

In Carroll, Iowa, a fourth-generation newspaper publisher named Doug Burns joined forces with the Democratic California congressman Ro Khanna to ask Khanna's Silicon Valley donors to help Iowa's newspapers by putting $4 million toward a project to combat misinformation. The goal was for social media companies to atone for the damage they had done to democracy by backing a proposal to push accurate reporting and buoy struggling newspapers. When he was turned down, Burns told a Facebook executive, "When the revolution starts, and we have a civil war in this country, and someone's dragging you and your family out of your Silicon Valley homes, before the knife goes into you, you're going to think, maybe I could have stopped this."[25]

Facebook ultimately gave his newspaper a $150,000 grant, and Burns's nonagenarian mother re-mortgaged her house, but it wasn't enough to fight off the onslaught of digital advertising and the demonization of the press. In 2022, the newspaper group that had been operated by Burns's family for ninety-three years, Herald Publishing Company, folded as the family was forced to sell *The Jefferson Herald* and the *Carroll Times Herald* at a devastating loss.[26]

Khanna told me there should have been a federal policy to tax digital corporations; he'd proposed such a thing under Biden's "Build Back Better" economic plan, but it didn't go anywhere. "They were thriving because of content generated by newspapers while at the same time they were displacing them," turning local news consumers into national news consumers and internet outrage into the reigning version of America's religion, he said.[27]

"Facebook needs to be made accountable for its harms," said Nancy Gibbs, director of Harvard's Shorenstein Center on Media, Politics, and Public Policy. "The minute one of its algorithms magnifies defamatory or harmful content and it's monetized, it should not be shielded from liability."

But a direct line can be drawn from Section 230 of the 1996 Communications Decency Act to online organizers of the January 6 riots, the sexual exploitation of children on sites like Backpage and Pornhub, and illegal online sales of fentanyl and assault weapons. Thus the law, typed out during a naive era of technological optimism, paved the way for social media companies to police their sites for harmful content generated by third parties—but, unlike newspapers and other legacy media operating under good-faith duty-of-care standards, online platforms aren't required to remove objectionable material and can't be held liable for socially harmful content on their sites.

"People engage around negative emotions," Gibbs added.[28] As long as there are incentives for politicians and platforms to keep feeding the outrage industry, gone is the coverage that once held neighborhoods together—not just local investigations, but also editorials and news of local businesses, schools, and neighbors in need and community-celebrating stories about people like Salena Sullivan (who, by the way, now *runs* a library and owns a house around the corner from me).

Halfway home to Urbana on one of my visits, I stumbled on something outside a Subway restaurant that reminded me just how low my industry—and the health of our people—had sunk. In Charleston, West Virginia, where the *Gazette-Mail* won a 2017 Pulitzer for Eric Eyre's investigation into the corrupt distribution of opioid pills, many of that city's newspaper boxes had been turned into free "little libraries" offering naloxone and fentanyl test strips.[29] In Sharpie marker, the scrappy harm-reduction volunteers who man it had written: KEEP CALM & CARRY NALOXONE.

Local news once served as democracy's immune system. As Thomas Jefferson put it, "Were it left to me to decide whether we should have a government without newspapers or newspapers without a government, I should not hesitate a moment to prefer the latter."

THE ARC OF MY LIFE parallels an era during which our institutions, including the daily newspaper, have become despised, a time when more than half of Republicans have come to consider reporters "the enemy of the people."[30]

More than a third of Americans don't even read the news,[31] and an astonishing number of people from both parties report actual hatred for one another—including 23 percent in 2023 who favored violence should the opposing party win the next election.[32] Unlike newspapers, the digital platforms where many now get their news aren't held to fact-based reporting standards.

This erosion of trust hasn't just kneecapped the newspaper industry; it's hit every source of authority that existed when I was born in 1964—in a hospital whose creation was spearheaded by Old Man Grimes.[33]

*Four*

# DESCENT

*It was always best to arrive with chocolate in hand:*
*Mom clutches a giant brownie I brought to*
*her assisted-living apartment.*

s Mom struggled for her final breaths, the woman who was
her last new friend on the planet paced up and down the
hallway outside her room, singing "Georgia on My Mind"
in a deep tenor. An insular person her entire life, Mom was never big
on making friends outside the family, but one good thing about her
dementia was that she forgot that too.

The nursing staff called them Thelma and Louise. When I asked
one what Mom and her new friend, Yvonne, talked about, she said,

"Escaping." A relative found actual escape bags in Mom's closet: Yvonne's had a tracksuit and pictures of her kids and grandkids; Mom's contained Hershey's Kisses and a threadbare bra.

Mom had moved into the facility in 2018 against her will after a brief hospitalization. She lost the right to drive her car after repeatedly becoming confused by the sameness of the surrounding cornfields. When I mentioned that she wasn't supposed to be driving anyway, she snapped, "Oh, the doctor didn't mean the store." A library regular, she borrowed novels from the library long after losing her ability to keep the characters straight.

Her primary diagnosis was vascular dementia. She'd fought it for five years before being forced out of her condo, clinging to independence through sheer force of will. The weekend we moved her into assisted living (not just kicking and screaming, but also crying and telling Terry, "But I took care of you!"), my youngest, Sasha, was the only one able to distract her by singing, dancing, and playing the Ink Spots song "I Don't Want to Set the World on Fire."

I keep a video of them dancing to it on my phone. Each time they danced, she marveled anew at how her youngest grandkid could possibly know all the words to a song from the 1940s, and each time Sasha patiently explained it was from the soundtrack to *Fallout 4*, a favorite video game.

WHILE SOME PEOPLE CHANGE personalities with dementia, my mom's feistiness and frugality only got stronger. Her hearing was terrible, but she refused to get hearing aids. In her late eighties at the time, she said they were too expensive and, besides, "They're for old people."

For her ninetieth birthday party, my sister Terry arranged to have a Frank Sinatra impersonator perform. The gathering was scheduled for three hours, and for the life of me I couldn't imagine Mom being serenaded to for that long—I thought she'd find it awkward and off-putting. But when we danced in a kick line to "New York, New York," to the crooning of a guy who billed himself as Cincinnati's Sinatra, old Jitterbug kicked her legs higher than anyone else.

Nine months before her stroke, I called to see if she had gotten the Valentine's Day gift I'd mailed earlier that week, and she drew a blank.

"It was a card?" I said, trying to help. "In a big manila envelope?"

Silence.

"With a bar of chocolate inside?"

"Well," she shot back. "If you'd sent me *two chocolates*, I would have remembered!"

In 2014, I dedicated my first book, *Factory Man*, to my "long-ago factory mom, Sarah Macy Slack, whose airplane lights I still imagine I can glimpse, up among the stars." When she saw the dedication in an early copy, she wanted to know if it appeared in everyone's copy or just hers, a question she'd never ask in her right mind.

That's when I knew she couldn't live at home alone much longer. A home-care aide was out of the question—an invasion of privacy, she said; it would "get on my nerves." And what would they talk about? What if someone stole her stuff?

After COVID restrictions forbade in-room contact at her memory-care facility in early 2020, we were only permitted to visit through an open screened window. For the first time, I couldn't tell whether she recognized me. Mostly she complained about the cold air coming in through the window and obsessed over the other visitors milling on the porch behind us; in her confusion, she couldn't figure out why they were there.

At the end of the visit, I said goodbye and told her I missed her.

"I miss me, too," she said.

It was her final side dish—the last snappy retort.

FOUR DAYS AFTER MOM'S STROKE, my sister Cookie and I sat watch next to her hospice bed and tried to avoid news of the Georgia recount in favor of safer topics. I pointed to the small pillow I'd had made for Mom two Christmases ago, its edges now worn from use. I'd had a friend cross-stitch a riposte that our late stepdad, Gene, made to Mom on their first date, five years after Dad's death. Early in their courtship, Gene was broiling Mom a steak—the first time a man had ever made her a meal—when, alarmed by a little broiler smoke, she kept trying to intervene. He gently admonished her to relax.

In cross-stitch cursive, the pillow quoted what Gene told her that night: "Just sit there & look cute."

When Mom could remember little else, that moment of sweetness still resonated. Some time after COVID hit but before the stroke, she had taken a purple ink pen to the pillow and printed her response beneath his words, as if communing with her late husband: "OK."

Cookie and I were marveling over the pillow, now propped under one of Mom's limp hands, when the hospice nurse's phone pinged.

"News alert," the nurse said, her tone incredulous. "They're calling it. For *Bid-den!*"

As I sat in a rural red county in a red state, it was unclear whether she'd intentionally mispronounced the president-elect's name.

"No!" Cookie fumed. "You wait, it's fraudulent! He won't win."

I said nothing as Mom's jagged breath filled the silence.

IN MY HOMETOWN, I'd heard, some of my old friends were finding community not in religion but in QAnon, spending hours every day sharing links about crazy things, like Tom Hanks's alleged pedophilia and the equally bonkers belief that Michelle Obama is a trans woman. Politics had intruded on our class Facebook page so much that several of my buddies sat the fortieth reunion out.

An old boyfriend and liberal Deadhead I hadn't seen in thirty-eight years had turned his entire backyard into raised vegetable beds and was now an ardent fan of Vladimir Putin—though he still hung beaded hippie curtains between his couch and his dining room deep freeze, now stuffed with his homegrown produce and half a cow. His oldest friend told me they'd had a heated argument over Trump. The friend thought maybe my ex had been swept into QAnon, but he wasn't sure because, after a friendship of fifty years, they no longer spoke.

*The Urbana Daily Citizen* was now a misnomer, printing only twice a week. With a staff of two—down from seven full-timers in the mid-1980s, when I worked there—it no longer covers city council, and its twice-weekly pages are largely relegated to press releases and high school sports. Owned for decades by a local publishing family that included the long-standing Republican congressman Clarence J. Brown and his son, Bud—who inherited both the paper and his dad's seat in Congress—it's now owned by out-of-state hedge funders.

"Today's news and yesterday's corrections," the townsfolk have long joked of the UDC. But people in Urbana knew Bud Brown, as they'd known his dad. They knew exactly where his family lived—in that big, shade-dappled mansion on Scioto Street. "They had to work to be reelected," the longtime reporter Steve Stout, a former classmate, told me. (It was Steve's dad, a manager at Grimes, who pinched my mom's butt.) "If a stray dog showed up in the Browns' yard, they actually had to keep it."[1]

In a county where Trump took 73 percent of the 2020 vote,[2] readers regularly phoned the paper's editor, Brenda Burns, to castigate her for running Associated Press wire copy, which they deemed fake news. "The AP is a bunch of liberal wokesters not reporting the truth," one woman shouted on the phone, begging Burns to run copy from *The Epoch Times*, a far-right religious newspaper, instead.[3] An old schoolmate of mine from a prominent Republican family, the caller had taken her children out of school to attend the January 6 riot at the Capitol— a completely different kind of field trip to Washington, D.C.

One of the insurrection's chief planners, in fact, turned out to be a bartender from my home county, a veteran who'd spent weeks training her militia friends for the protest and was sentenced to eight and a half years in federal prison.[4] A few towns over, in St. Paris, the congressman and House Judiciary chairman, Jim Jordan, also led efforts to undermine faith in the 2020 election results.

AFTER A LONG DAY at Mom's bedside, I found myself wondering if we could ever be a real family again after her death, or were we now among the one-fifth of Americans who've lost connections to close friends and family members over politics.[5] More than half of Americans, 54 percent, believe another civil war is looming.[6] Could we patch things up? What would that even mean?

I struggled to understand this moment. How had these radical ideologies seeped so deeply into America's water table? People are so distrustful of government that my own diabetic nephew refused a lifesaving transplant not once but twice after learning the donors had received a COVID vaccine.

The tension came from all directions. A sister-in-law on my husband's side of the family tried to debate me after the election of 2016, when I mentioned in a mutual grumbling session that my siblings had all voted for Trump. She and I had gotten along fine before, and I'd loved participating in her family's seder.

But the conversation turned sharp when she said angrily, referring to my Ohio family, "Your people don't want my people to exist." We were just starting Christmas dinner at another relative's house, and her comment jarred me, not unlike Cookie's "It's fraudulent!" It felt as if I were being held responsible for something painful that I hadn't done and was struggling myself to comprehend.

How could I not love the relatives who took care of my demented mother when I live seven hours away, including my brother-in-law John, who flings around the word "deplorable" at me but also resets Mom's TV every other day, or the sister who takes her to every doctor's appointment? As untenable as their political positions may seem, I tried to explain, they are solid, decent people. "My people don't hate your people; they don't even know your people," I said.

"Exactly," she said.

My sister-in-law is a poet who graduated from Yale and now works for another Ivy League school. If our interests were plotted on a Venn diagram, our main areas of intersection would be politics, our love of literary fiction, and the jugs of maple syrup she brings us every year from the sugar shack down the road from their Vermont home. I cheer every poem she publishes, read every novel she recommends.

But I resented having to explain my relatives and my love for them when I found myself just as aggrieved by their beliefs as my sister-in-law was.

WHEN I WAS GROWING UP, we lived on South Walnut Street, in the crappiest-looking house on a block mostly peopled by factory workers. Before my parents moved to Urbana from Dayton in the 1950s, our home sheltered the likes of welders, grocers, and machine operators.[7] But walk down the street and around the corner, and the neighborhood became a holy jumble of architecture and ancestry. Like small towns across America in those days, Urbana was a place where a poor kid could benefit from living right around the corner from somebody rich.

When our dentist fashioned an ersatz retainer for me, he'd known that Mom couldn't afford the braces I really needed because he lived in a big Victorian right around the corner from our run-down house. There were bona fide mansions up the street from him, including stately nineteenth-century homes built by factory owners and other prominent people who'd migrated to west-central Ohio to start Urbana College in 1850. The founder's wife, from high-society Philadelphia, apparently didn't think much of Urbana, describing it as "the fag end of the world."[8] A cigarette butt, she meant.

Established by members of the Swedenborgian Church, the college was the second-oldest coed institution in the nation, part of a movement inspired by the British philosopher and theologian Emanuel Swedenborg "to encourage and promote the diffusion of knowledge, in the branches of academic, scientific and exegetic instruction."[9] The English poet William Blake was an adherent of this tradition, which blended religion and art with scientific facts in service of the greater good, as was John Chapman, a.k.a. Johnny Appleseed.[10]

Elsewhere in town, the Curry Institute opened in 1889 with aspirations to become "the northern Tuskegee," an industrial training ground for Blacks. Urbana artists with national reputations during that period included the early movie stars Lillian and Dorothy Gish, the Broadway composer Raymond Hubbell, and the sculptor John Quincy Adams Ward, whose best-known work, *Indian Hunter*, resides in Central Park. As a child, Ward learned to make figures out of mud from a Champaign County creek.

Strong schools that proudly promoted science, literacy, and art were touted in the region's newspapers, of which I counted more than twenty titles during the town's first century. As a county historian boasted in 1917, "The magic touch of education is the 'open sesame' to the fabulously rich accumulation of cultural and social efficiency. . . . If one has no children, the expenditure he makes for the education of his neighbor's children adds to the sum total of social welfare, and in the long run he is also benefited."[11] That historian was also an elected county judge. He would surely have been shocked at Urbanans' embrace of book banning, homeschooling, and other anti–public school sentiments a century later. He'd be unelectable at best.

THE JUDGES I HAVE GOTTEN to know in Urbana were stymied by the town's decline. Lori Reisinger, a family court judge since 2009, told me that by 2012—the year heroin blasted into Champaign County—students stopped being afraid of school administrators, police officers, and even her.

"They're not being taught respect for authority or for the rule of law. They're not being taught the value of education," Reisinger said. Her colleague Nick Selvaggio, a common pleas court judge, pointed out that fleeing and eluding cases had quadrupled between 2022 and 2024; when an officer flashes his lights atop a cruiser, many refuse to pull over. Among those who do, when an officer asks to see the person's license, many rear up with "Why?" Two-thirds of his cases are drug related, most involving meth, and 70 percent stem from addiction or untreated mental health problems.[12]

One of Reisinger's revolving concerns is a meth-addicted mother with four children who'd lost custody of all four kids and was pregnant with a fifth. "She even got clean during COVID, but then she got hooked up with somebody bad, started using again, and had another baby. At first, she was desperate to get the little girl back," Reisinger said, her voice trailing off. "So . . . we're bringing kids into this world with issues at birth."

A young man had recently attempted to hang himself from his parents' rooftop, and with no psychiatric beds available anywhere nearby the only safe place Reisinger could place him was in juvenile detention, where he stayed for two weeks with no psych meds or counseling. "I spent two hours yesterday deciding whether to let him out."

When I asked if she slept well at night, the judge wrung her hands and lowered her head. "No," she said. "I don't."

In her early days on the bench, Reisinger used to tell her teenage offenders, "I raised three kids, and I was known as the strictest mom in Champaign County. And now I'm yours."

But that line no longer landed.

"There's no value of education anymore. None. Truancy is rampant," she said. "And when you really call certain parents out on it, they take their kids out of school and do online school, or they say they're 'homeschooling' them."[13]

*Friends Hunter Woodruff, eighteen and a tenth grader,*
*with Dalton Dorsey and another friend from a neighboring*
*school district on a hot August afternoon a few blocks*
*from Urbana's Monument Square.*

According to a recent survey of UHS students, the No. 1 goal of Urbana's teens was to become a social media influencer.

"For the first time in history, the individual is the basic unit of society," the journalist Bill Bishop, the author of *The Big Sort: Why the Clustering of Like-Minded America Is Tearing Us Apart*, from 2008, told me. "People don't want community; they want a platform."[14]

The scramble for burnished egos and platforms had been orchestrated by far-off tech bros, billionaires who addicted us to amped-up outrage that pitted us against one another and made it downright impossible for us to collaborate on our shared economic concerns.

No wonder the block I grew up on looked more like a bunker now than a diverse but tight-knit neighborhood.

I STRUGGLED TO RECOGNIZE my hometown. In Silas's class, only two students were admitted to OSU; in my class more than a dozen were. In the 1970s and 1980s, my neighborhood felt bathed in the idea that learning mattered, and I helped myself to every inch of it, disappearing for hours in a stand of lilacs down the street, reading books like *Harriet the Spy*. I didn't know what a reporter was back then, but I loved hiding out in those lilacs and taking notes on passersby à la Harriet. A paper girl by the age of ten, I felt my world broaden when I came to know people like our mailman (our routes were nearly identical, and we sometimes walked together), as well as the bankers, teachers, and paper-mill workers I talked to along the way. Negotiating with skinflint customers who tried to dodge me on Saturdays when it was time to collect was good reporting practice, too.

My favorite customer was a retired paper-mill worker and widow named Lillian Huggins who lived on Eichelberger Drive. The street had the newest housing stock on my route, in a postwar suburban enclave, a semicircle that connected to my street at both ends, and I liked how the word "Eichelberger" rolled off the tongue. Also, most of that street's customers paid on time.

Mrs. Huggins gave me lemonade when it was hot and let me warm my hands and feet when it was cold, but mostly she just wanted to talk. In 1990, I was bereft to learn that she'd died from a horrible accident in the dead of winter.[15] She'd fallen on a hallway heating grate and, unable to get up, slowly burned to death. No one had stopped to check in on her until smoke came pouring from her house, and by then it was too late. She was eighty-seven. That's when I first clocked something shifting in the neighborhood.

BACK THEN, MY NEWLYWED MOM mailed letters to me in Virginia from her paid-off home in Kettering, a solid Dayton suburb. In one, her friend Jean had called to say that the Drackett Company—which employed 450 Urbanans who made Windex and other cleaning supplies—had just closed. She also noted that Grimes, where she and Jean had met on the job, was laying people off again. Chi-Vit, a union shop that made porcelain enamel for appliances,[16] would announce layoffs later that year, and Nabisco, which had recently bought Urbana's Corn Nuts facility, would soon close that long-standing factory, in a double whammy that also hurt local corn growers.[17] "Urbana is turning into a ghost town," Mom reported.[18]

On a typewriter she'd picked up at a yard sale—the letter *i* always made a little hole instead of a dot—Mom described force blooming forsythia and crab apple and putting out February feeders for the birds. She mailed me handwritten recipes ("First, wash your hands," she often began), gardening-tip clippings, and coupons for Maxithins. She was learning to sew and made tiny outfits for the ceramic goose she kept in front of her house, a trend that took midwestern retirees by storm in the late 1980s and early 1990s.

When I playfully asked if she ventured into the rain to put her homemade raincoat on the goose, she shot back, "No. I do it when it's clouding up." Of course she did.

Early in their courtship, her new husband, Gene, had wooed her by mail with an entry he'd written for a regional poetry contest, titled "Lady in the Morning":

*Her breath is the soft murmur*
*Of flowers in a summer wind*
*The fragrance of her hair comes*
*Soaring from a golden mass of gossamer*
*A tiny smile on her lips*
*Small pearls of sweat on her brow*
*Soon she will arise*
*And love me anew.*[19]

Not bad for a retired Wright-Patterson Air Force Base engineering technician. Mom retyped his poem and mailed it to me with a letter. It was 1989. "Sounds like a romantic old dude, huh? I just composed the following and am sending it off forthwith, if not sooner."

*What lovely lines*
*Of verse you wrote*
*I am impressed!*
*You get MY vote.*

For Christmas that year, Gene gave us sculpted birds and fish. He'd whittled them in his garage, Mom painted them, and together they mounted them on rocks or turned them into mobiles. Safely away from the weight of living in poverty for six decades, Mom had never had the bandwidth for such domesticity—or such unfettered happiness—before marrying Gene and leaving Urbana.

WHEN I WAS SLINGING NEWSPAPERS IN URBANA, not one person on our block locked their doors. Our across-the-street neighbors, the Williamses—Kentucky coal miners who'd migrated to Ohio for factory work—insisted that I didn't even have to knock on their front door when I visited their daughter Dixie Irene. It was less bother to them if I just walked in.

This range of humanity meant I was exposed to all kinds of people, from the down-home Kentuckians whose dad worked for a Grimes subsidiary and their McNeely cousins next door, whose dad worked for another, to friends from better-off households who were without question going to college, like my Black friend Joy, whose parents were teachers and later became principals. A few blocks away, Betty, too, was going places, if her hard-driving Korean mom had anything to do with it, which of course she would.

Those connections exposed me to solidly middle-class social circles, but it was Urbana's high-performing school system that became my real open sesame to opportunity, combined with a grandma next door who taught me to read before kindergarten using the same McGuffey Readers she'd used as a Champaign County farm kid—my own private Head Start. (She also gave me my first job, paying me to mow her lawn.) I absorbed intuitively that the kids with ski-lift tags and spring-break tans had opportunities I didn't, but they weren't necessarily any smarter than me. And maybe on some level they absorbed that lesson too.

As the work of the Harvard sociologist Raj Chetty has shown, poor kids from mixed-income neighborhoods have more interactions across class lines. When good schools are added to an economically diverse mix, not only do those kids do better educationally and financially as adults than their peers residing in concentrated poverty, but they live longer too.[20]

My hometown made me a striver. I might have seemed feral to Betty's mom, but I was also precocious and unapologetically ambitious—a word I didn't realize had negative connotations until an editor interviewing me for my first newspaper job asked me to describe myself in a single word, then acted startled when I said it. Naive enough to say the quiet part out loud, I didn't get the job.

Before I left Urbana for college, I knew Linn Wilson, who manned the desk of the local library down the street from our house. I knew her husband, the local judge Roger Wilson, because he swam laps at the city pool where I lifeguarded summers during high school and college. I'd never learned to swim properly because lessons cost money Mom couldn't spare. But when I manned the concession stand that first summer, my lifeguard pals coached me on my front crawl after hours until it became plodding but passable, and the following year I was promoted to lifeguard, which paid better and was easier than slinging ice cream and hot dogs, which was easier than slinging newspapers.

The soundtrack of those summers was the droning of the pool's *Donkey Kong* machine mixed with Billy Idol's "Eyes Without a Face," which a gaggle of preteens kept on permanent repeat. My tan was so deep that our pale Appalachian neighbors called me "Mr. Mosley's daughter" after our mailman, who was Black, mocking the both of us.

A kid I used to routinely blow my pool whistle at for breaking the rules astonished me when he grew up and into a cop and then a police captain, eventually becoming a source for two of my books. In one episode of Hulu's *Dopesick*, a carload of teens scramble to bring an overdosed friend back to life by stuffing a frozen fish down his pants.

I learned about that trick from the pool menace turned police captain Chad Seeberg, who'd witnessed it during OxyContin's early days. (In another two degrees of separation not uncommon in Urbana, Seeberg has arrested members of Silas's family.)

Although Seeberg's dad was a union factory worker who commuted to Dayton to build car parts, Chad went to Ohio State. He went on to become the local library board chair of a nearby town that's home to Honda and has seen its share of book-banning scuffles and church splits over female pastors and same-sex marriage. He can quote everything from Brookings Institution surveys to Stoic philosophers and George Washington's Farewell Address.

He'd been thinking about upward mobility in Urbana since I first brought the topic up in 2023. "It occurred to me after seeing my old friends in Urbana who've done very well: If you had a big family business or a farm, you either stayed, or you went away for college and came back."

If you didn't have inherited land or wealth in the form of an established family business and you went away to college, you didn't return.[21]

It didn't take a Harvard study to confirm what Chad and I have long known since our well-tanned days by the pool: When you're working class, good schools and social connections are sustenance. I'd never given it much thought before, but now that I was back in Urbana for long stretches and looking beyond its Mayberry facade, I realized I was seeing what happens to a town that loses many of its crucial lifelines. Its descent had begun long before my mother's.

"It's that loss of grit," Seeberg said. "It's mental health, parents' inability to parent, general population decline." He cited the new Intel microchip plant that was being developed in nearby New Albany, Ohio, boosted by $8.5 billion from President Joe Biden's CHIPS and Science Act. Seeberg wasn't sure the if-you-build-it-they-will-come strategy still worked in an era of sky-high childhood trauma and a severe shortage of tradespeople.

Dubbed Silicon Heartland, the plant promised to be the "largest silicon manufacturing location on the planet," part of Biden's efforts to re-shore manufacturing and make America less dependent on overseas supply chains. But builders were having trouble finding the seven thousand workers needed just to construct the plant, let alone staff it.[22] Competition for construction workers was also slowing the pace of home building for the growing workforce needed at Intel. Two years after the project was announced, only 11 percent of the construction crews had even been hired.[23]

In Urbana, a baking-pan factory looking to expand operations had to look elsewhere because the local workforce wasn't reliable enough, one civic leader told me. An assistant supervisor at the plant had recently quit after eleven years because of long hours, including mandatory overtime created by the employee shortage, and rampant sexism. "It takes a toll on one's body and mind," she said.

She was now working at a vape shop, earning half her factory salary. Her daughter Maddie Allen, a UHS senior with the same Clark State scholarship that Silas had, was planning to ride her brother's bicycle from her trailer park in Urbana to Springfield for her Clark State classes—some twenty miles away. The ride would take her an hour and a half, one way.

"Even in winter?" I asked.

Even in winter, she said.[24] The bike was rusty and presently lying on its side behind their trailer, with two flat tires. I thought of how hard it was proving for Silas to get to college, even with a car. I remembered my own tenuous first ride to college, in Mom's Mustang with the slippy clutch, and I never had a daily commute.

"Oh, honey," I told her, gently. "I don't think that's going to work." But Maddie remained upbeat, reminding me that she'd once ridden her little sister's pink scooter—with a bell and streamers—to her after-school job at Burger King.

*Five*

# MIGRATIONS

*Christina Flowers, one of Silas's UHS mentors,*
*encouraged him to go to community college.*

Christina Flowers remembers where she was the moment everything changed. She was lying on the carpet, coloring at her friend's house across the street. They were on their bellies, their socked feet wiper-blading happily in the air, when her friend casually asked her, "Why were the police at your house last night?"

"Oh, my dad beat up my mom again," Chris answered.

When the friend looked at her, mortified, Chris asked her, "You mean your dad doesn't beat your mom, too?"

She was a second grader when she learned that alcoholism and domestic violence weren't the rules of the day in everyone's home. Once, when her mom was pregnant, Chris's stepfather forced her to choose his method for battering her mom: Should he strike her with a cast-iron skillet this time? Should he hit her instead with a kitchen chair, or would it be best to throw her down the stairs?

"If I didn't pick one, he would do all of the above," she told me.[1]

She was seven when her friend's question stopped her in her tracks and made her think: Maybe one day, I won't have to live like this. Maybe I, too, can have a different life.


CHRIS GOES BY MRS. FLOWERS NOW. She was fifty-one when we met in 2023 as I began trying to unpack the transformation of the hometown and family that raised me. How had my bucolic home county turned into a place of homeless encampments, a tripling of youth suicides, and a school shooting?

Flowers, whose background was similar to mine (though I didn't experience daily abuse), is the one who introduced me to Silas James as an example of a promising poor kid and a modern-day me. Flowers, too, had barely eked her way through college. But unlike me, she graduated with significant debt.

Her first year at Muskingum College was mostly paid for by scholarships from businesses and civic clubs in her northeast Ohio hometown. But most of the aid didn't extend beyond her first year, and at the start of her sophomore year Flowers feared she would have to drop out for a year to work. Her family income was $11,000 a year, the lowest of any student on campus at the time.

Just eight years after I graduated from college, the Pell Grant no longer covered even half of an impoverished kid's tuition and room and board.

A college counselor intervened to keep Flowers from dropping out, and she ended up receiving forgivable loans (as long as she became a special education teacher), $20,000 in additional loans, plus a merit scholarship she didn't quite have the grades for, but the financial aid officer decided that she was so close and trying so hard that the school could give it to her anyway.

Flowers vowed to become that same kind of educator, one who refused to place test scores above humanity. She understood that a solid social safety net had the ability to make up for the twin perils of family poverty and bad luck. One should not have to become a unicorn, as Flowers was at her college—the poorest kid on campus by a long shot—solely because of an accident of birth.

BY THE TIME I was ensconced in my newspaper career in the late 1980s, Pell Grants were no longer viewed as a means of helping Americans compete globally. In a decade, need-based financial aid went from being perceived as an investment in future productivity and tax revenue to being looked down upon, its recipients mocked as welfare handouts.

Ronald Reagan's secretary of education William J. Bennett scoffed at the notion that education helps people recover from poverty, calling it "sociological flimflammery." Reagan denounced professors as elites and compared Pell grantees to welfare moms as he quietly, methodically set about cutting federal aid to education in half.[2] Democrats were cast as people who weren't interested in the good of America but instead wanted to siphon off the wages of hardworking people.

When the GI Bill was enacted to reward returning World War II veterans and to help America compete in the cold war, the notion of making public education free through the fourteenth grade was floated by the high-minded Truman Commission Report in 1947.[3] Had follow-up legislation and federal dollars been attached to the report during that optimistic postwar era, college access, including for

Black people and women, might have become a game-changing aspect of the American social contract, along the lines of Social Security and, eventually, Medicare. But the legislation went nowhere, partly because southern schools would have had to embrace integration to be eligible for federal funds.[4]

"Since the 1960s, the dominant idea in politics has been that government is bad, which was first coined by George Wallace and others, who claimed it wasn't really about race," the Pulitzer-winning author and civil rights scholar Taylor Branch told me. "They transmitted their hostility from race to the federal government, to 'the tax-and-spend liberals and the pointy-headed bureaucrats' because in the '60s the federal government announced that it supported racial equity." This is how white voters from all classes ended up breaking the working-class coalition that once united around the New Deal.

By the 1970s, it was no longer respectable to be overtly racist, but you could still cuss the government. "And for fifty years that's what they've done," Branch said. "There's no longer a shared noble purpose behind 'We the people.' Instead, people convince themselves that their liberty depends on taking a gun into Starbucks."[5]

When Democrats capitulated to Reagan's trickle-down theory, the government surrendered its ability to respond to economic dislocation, including the decimation of Pell Grants. "We were never going to prevent deindustrialization or the rise of China, but for a generation we basically shut down the whole government apparatus that might have led to serious interventions to respond to those consequences," the Harvard political scientist Steven Levitsky told me.

During that same generation, the United States stopped being a country where white men alone ruled our TV screens and our elected bodies and ran the boards of virtually every Fortune 500 company. "When you and I were kids, 85 percent of the country was white; today it's 58 percent," said Levitsky, co-author of *How Democracies Die.* "The number of Latino, African American, and Asian American members of Congress has more than tripled since my bar mitzvah. This kind of demographic shift has never happened in any democracy in the history of the world."

The 2008 election of the first Black president, Barack Obama, turned up the flames of an already simmering political divide, even though he rarely talked about race. White-identity politics soared as rural white Americans, still suffering from the aftermath of offshoring and hammered by the opioid crisis, watched their majoritarian status diminish. Donald Trump, Steve Bannon, and Tucker Carlson became the new Republican standard-bearers of white-identity politics, with their insistence that it's okay to be "anti-woke" and to dislike people who are different from you because they're probably just stealing your tax dollars.

"Good jobs require college education, and they're mostly in the cities, where people tend to be more secular" and where immigrants have long clustered, Levitsky said.[6] In ruby-red rural areas like Urbana with low higher-education rates and an explosion in homeschooling, religion also plays a larger role in people's lives, another sea change from 1980, when more evangelicals voted for Jimmy Carter than for Ronald Reagan.

Christian nationalists cling to Trump's performative machismo because it rhymes with their style of Christianity, in which men being in charge is God's will. Or as my dear high school friend Amy Hunter, an Atlanta educator, put it, "These women we know from home who get with a man and defer to all his tendencies and beliefs, I want to say, 'You married him, but do you have to share a brain with him?!' If a population was a person, they'd be that abusive person who is like, 'If I can't have a nice life, nobody else will.'"[7]

---

By the time Flowers graduated in 1994, four-year colleges were telling poor and first-generation students: Either take out student loans you'll spend decades paying back, or go to a community college.[8] And so Pell's emphasis on sending poor kids away to college for free died at the hands of a false and racist notion that Pell grantees were akin to welfare recipients, even though the most common recipients of both programs were white women.

"Higher ed always gets squeezed first because the average taxpayer doesn't notice," said the sociologist Sara Goldrick-Rab, the author of *Paying the Price: College Costs, Financial Aid, and the Betrayal of the American Dream.* When I told her my story, she noted that I talk about college with the same enthusiasm and awe as her grandfather, who attended on the GI Bill. "Somebody invested in you, so you did not have to pay the cost up front, and that's what they took away," said Goldrick-Rab, who named her orange tabby cat Pell after the late senator.

Just as Nixon's War on Drugs was used to justify incarcerating a disproportionately large number of Black people to score political points, Reagan and Clinton strengthened the playbook by adding a layer of demonizing poor students, Black and white. "It was pulling the ladder up behind us and then saying, 'You didn't bootstrap well enough,'" Goldrick-Rab told me.[9]

Busy working and raising young kids when the largest of these cuts rolled out, like most Americans I had no idea the trend was even underway. Then, in 1998, I took a leave of absence from my newspaper and, to supplement my schoolteacher-husband's salary, I taught remedial English at our local community college two nights a week.

The array of experiences in my classroom was astonishing and challenging, and sometimes it made me cry. One student in her forties had never read a book and told us that her husband routinely called her "retarded." Two sisters who drove school buses were trying to earn associate's degrees in business; their goal was to help their truck-driver husbands start a family company. A younger student, fresh out of jail, was the smartest person in the class but resisted everything I said, asking me why a syllabus isn't simply called "a list of stuff we have to do."

All were first-generation students and Pell recipients, and many worked full-time while also taking care of kids and, in some cases, parents, too. One of my favorite students, Meribeth Ingram, was a single mom so academically gifted that I threatened, only half joking, to jump off a nearby bridge if she didn't transfer to a four-year college after finishing her associate's degree. She went on to get her bachelor's at nearby Hollins University and now works on the risk management team of a local nonprofit hospital system.

"An older student in the midst of having and raising kids, my self-esteem had been shot down long before and was still being hammered down," Ingram remembered. "My college experience showed me a version of myself outside of being a mother and a scared child, and I was surrounded with people who believed in me, and that helped me believe in myself."[10]

She went from earning $4.15 an hour when we first met to making $72,000 a year with benefits. She got Pell Grants, too, but their purchasing power by then was so kneecapped that she ended up graduating with $57,000 in student debt.

MOST OF MY STUDENTS enrolled to get either associate's degrees or trade certifications; a few, like Meribeth, used the community college system as a cost-savings option on their way toward a bachelor's. The older ones had lost jobs to globalization and automation and were thoroughly miffed by the computer revolution, which had passed them by. A librarian friend in a county that was midway through losing half its jobs to offshoring described how laid-off workers would bring her their printed-out résumés, asking her to physically feed them into her computer, as if on a roller.

A forty-something mechanic in my class wrote about the best job he'd ever had, in construction, but he didn't have a single comma or period on the page. "If I get me a computer," he wanted to know, "won't that put in all the periods for me?"[11]

When the college sent me to in-service teacher training, a speaker complained vehemently about Pell grantees, calling them lazy slackers who were simply taking advantage of government handouts. I sat there taking it in for a while until finally I stood and, with my voice shaking, told him how wrongheaded he was.

Judging from the reaction—crickets—I might have been the only one among the hundred teachers in the room who'd gotten a full Pell. In the workplace and elsewhere in my adult life, I usually am.

Afterward, when I couldn't stop ranting about the anti-Pell professor, my husband pointed toward our home office and nudged me, "Go. Write about this." The following month an essay I wrote titled "The Scarlet P" appeared in *The Chronicle of Higher Education*, followed by a phone call from Washington, D.C.

Days later, in a suit I'd borrowed from a friend, I found myself standing face-to-face with Claiborne Pell. I'd been invited to talk about the miracle of Pell Grants in front of members of Congress and college presidents, for an assembly honoring the retired Rhode Island senator. To deliver the speech without choking up, I practiced and practiced and practiced, my husband coaching me to slow down and breathe.

When I hugged Pell before the speech and warned him that I might tear up, he said, "It's okay if you do."

I wasn't rich, I told the crowd in the ballroom of a D.C. hotel. I taught college writing classes part-time between shuffling my kids to preschool activities in my Volvo station wagon (odometer reading: 122,000 miles). My husband drove a 1985 Mustang with a leaky convertible roof to the low-income public school where he taught.[12]

But here I was, the daughter of a housepainter who'd dropped out of school in the seventh grade, pushing back on the false narrative that poor people weren't worthy of investment. I thanked Senator Pell and told the Washington insiders that my vacations weren't fancy and my cars didn't always start. But I was happy most of the time and productive as hell, even if I did sometimes resort to grading papers in the play zone of Burger King while my kids crawled through the primary-colored tubes. *The Christian Science Monitor* called me "Pell's poster child."

Shockingly, I didn't cry, but a priest sitting in the front row sobbed through my entire speech. He'd grown up working with his parents on a potato farm in rural northern Maine. When an eighth-grade English teacher referred to him as "dumb French trash," he found the slur motivating. But it also took federal aid and Upward Bound, a support program for first-generation college students, to get him to Dartmouth, where he graduated near the top of his class.[13]

IN THE SPAN OF A DECADE, Reagan had systematically shifted our federal financial aid apparatus from being need based to greed based, and now Clinton was upping the game to prove his "new Democrat" bona fides.[14] And no one, save a few writers, educators, and nonprofit organizations, said a word.

"Who's going to push back?" asked the higher-ed scholar Don Heller. By the 1990s, state college presidents were obsessed with improving their *U.S. News & World Report* rankings in their quest for prestige and research dollars, and adding amenities like sushi bars, fountains, and wave pools to stay competitive. "Very few presidents are going to go in front of their state legislatures and talk about expanding college access to poor kids," Heller explained.

"They're all going, 'Let the community colleges take care of it.'"

When I told him my story, Heller, a retired provost at the University of San Francisco, said, "If you would have been forced to stay home and go to community college, you would have never made it out."[15]

Made my way out of poverty, he meant, not necessarily Urbana, which I very much loved. Still, it is true that among the 80 percent of Americans in rural America who lack college degrees, only a quarter end up migrating from their hometowns. The few poor rural people who do get a bachelor's typically move to cities for better jobs and rarely live near their families again.[16]

My mom had intuited that I would not return home and that it would be good for me but hard on our relationship. She knew it when she made the two-hour drive home alone in her rusty Mustang after dropping me off at college. I still have a photo of her waving goodbye from the driver's seat and pretending to cry—or pretending not to cry; it was hard to tell. She said she'd read in a magazine somewhere that while your high school friends are important, it's your college friends who end up being your best friends for life.

When I called her two weeks into the first semester, homesick and crying next to the hallway pay phone, it took everything she had not to tell me to come home. And when I left the state for my first daily newspaper job in Georgia in 1987, she knew I'd probably never move home again.

As we hugged goodbye in her driveway, my things stuffed into my upgraded-but-still-used Volkswagen Rabbit, she deadpanned, "I've thought about it. You can't go."

MY EARLY MIGRATIONS were emotionally fraught for both my mom and me, but they paid off eventually. Flowers, too, marveled at her good fortune, including a supportive husband with a good job. A religious person who spends her summer vacations doing mission work, she thanks God for her career, her happy marriage, and her paid-off student loans, "which seemed like a lot at the time, but I now realize were nothing." She has a swimming pool in the backyard of her home in an Urbana subdivision. "If we need to buy a couch, we can just go out and buy a couch," she said. For someone who grew up attending multiple schools because her family was always being evicted, a middle-class lifestyle is a luxury.

We swapped stories of parallel traumas. We pondered how we'd been able to develop coping skills while some of our relatives remained mired in dysfunction. She, too, struggles with the fact that some in her conservative family won't accept her grown gay son. And she also battled bouts of intense anxiety in her twenties. When you move up a social class—sociologists call us class migrants—you're never totally comfortable in your past world or your present.

"You get used to just waiting for the next crisis to occur because that's what you're used to, and early in my career I would manifest that things were worse than they really were. It took me a long time and a lot of therapy to stop doing that. The anxiety of waiting for the crisis was worse than the crisis itself," she said.

A champion catastrophizer, I once told my husband that if my next book failed, "I might become a bag lady again—" He interrupted me with "Beth! You were never a bag lady!" Despite my relative success, the feeling of being on the precipice of disaster never completely recedes.

Survivor's guilt is huge. "I have to remind myself that I shouldn't feel bad about making good choices," Flowers said.

OFFICIALLY, Flowers's role in Urbana City Schools is to serve as the liaison between area businesses—factories, mostly—and the 5,173 students in Champaign County, who are much needier today than when I was among them.

Urbana's mayor, Bill Bean, told me with a straight face that kids today don't need college. "I have a religion degree, but did I use it? I'm not a minister."[17]

No, he took over his dad's successful insurance company, which had been in business since 1866.

*Longtime Urbana mayor Bill Bean thinks college is*
*overrated and said Urbana's 16 percent college*
*graduation rate didn't bother him.*

*Urbana students play basketball after school*
*a few blocks from Monument Square.*

Urbana City Schools consistently rank last in the region for gradu-ation, with a four-year rate of 81.8 percent. Only half of third graders meet reading proficiency guidelines, though nearly all get passed on to the fourth grade.[18] Forty years ago, just 6 percent of Urbana's third graders were below level.[19] And absenteeism has skyrocketed, espe-cially in the wake of COVID.

When it comes to helping a kid aim for a life better than the one they were born into—whether that means pursuing college or work-ing in a trade at one of several factories in the region that are consis-tently hard up for employees who'll actually show up at work—Flowers echoed what nearly every Urbana teacher I spoke to said: In terms of mental well-being, the kids are not all right.

There are no full-time psychiatrists in the county, though there are two psychiatric nurse practitioners.[20] At the one sliding-scale clinic in town, the waiting list for counseling appointments is six months long; the clinic holds a few slots every week for suicidal calls.[21] Urbana's po-lice chief, Matt Lingrell, told me he'd lost the child of family friends to suicide, not long after she'd been swimming in his backyard pool. "I had to tell my sergeant, 'I can't come to this one.' It broke my heart," Lingrell said.[22] Her funeral was held in the high school gym. Teen suicide attempts in Urbana now outnumbered overdoses.[23]

So it has fallen to public school workers, who are already beyond stressed, to provide much of the social safety net.

That was clear not just in Urbana's graduation rates but also in student behavior, which is often so disruptive that the high school principal keeps an app for phases of the moon on the home screen of his Apple watch. During our first interview, a student in the next room began shrieking and crying and pounding the desk in the assistant principal's office, and the principal just shrugged, pointing to his watch.

"See there?" he said. "I could have told you—full moon."[24]

As I began spending longer stretches back home, I noticed a much greater sense of anomie than I'd felt before. I saw it not just in the truncated high school band but also in the mileage of a truancy officer who spends most mornings traversing the county and personally hauling a couple dozen kids out of bed and taking them to school. Many students don't have the social skills to ask for a pencil—or understand that they're better off asking to borrow one from a friend than grunting at their teacher, "I don't have a pencil."

An English teacher had to dumb down her reading list from twelve books a year to four. After buying copies for all her students, she was too afraid to teach *Dear Martin*, about a young Black teen grappling with racism, after getting complaints about teaching *The Crucible* the year before. When a mom accused her of being a witch, the teacher said, "They're not really witches; that's the whole point of the book!"[25] A middle school math teacher told me she was astonished by how many seventh graders can't do multiplication or long division. When she checked their files, it was clear they'd been failing math all along but had been passed anyway.[26]

Out of necessity, it has become Flowers's chief occupation to teach Urbana's kids what she calls "how to human." By which she means teaching them not to answer "two weeks" when a prospective employer asks how many days of work is acceptable to miss during your first six months on the job. The correct answer is zero. By which she means looking a potential boss in the eye and shaking his or her hand. When I asked a career-fair recruiter how many employees he typically retains out of every ten new hires, he didn't pause: "One would still be here in six months. And he probably has an attendance problem or doesn't like the night shift."[27] Laborers at his Wisconsin-based crate-manufacturing plant make $24 an hour and get free health care.

Six months before, the company was so hard up for labor that it had to stop doing background checks and drug tests. Another employer told me his company had resorted to flextime: Employees forgo benefits in exchange for the option of showing up part-time whenever they please.

"You come in every day, and you don't even know who's going to be here," he said.[28]

Truman Johnson, a classmate whose family founded the automotive air-tank manufacturer Johnson Welded Products and ran it for fifty-three years, described how his family used to worry about electrical outages, earthquakes, and fires—anything that might disrupt their output.

"We never once talked about not having enough employees," he said. At the moment, the family employed 375 workers over two shifts, including 27 Haitian migrants who commuted daily from Springfield.[29]

Two days after our interview, the Johnson family sold the factory to a Kansas-based company with other production facilities in Michigan,

Illinois, and Australia. It was the last substantial locally owned factory in town.

Flowers bonded immediately with Silas James. Her daughter, Mary, was in the band with Silas, and together they'd advanced a history project to the state competition. Before she moved to Urbana from nearby Marysville, Flowers had also taught a close friend of Silas's, his sister's fiancé, in a neighboring district. The young man died at twenty-three from an accidental gunshot wound.

In mental health circles, a measurement technique called adverse childhood experiences (ACEs) is often used to gauge childhood risk factors. Silas's ACE score was a 10, the maximum on the trauma scale. His father overdosed and died in 2021, and his mom was jailed repeatedly on drug-related charges. Homeless in the middle of his junior year, he'd been offered a spare bed for a time by a relative in another town. But it fell to Chris Flowers, a pair of guidance counselors, and the division's homeless liaison to arrange transportation via the McKinney-Vento Act, which provides federal funds for homeless students to help them stay in school. "Silas stood out because he was very smart and very respectful," Brooke Perry, the homeless and attendance liaison, told me. "Even through all his insecurities and barriers, he persevered through everything."

It wasn't just his intellect that made teachers and counselors want to help him; it was also his pluck. Flowers once offered him the guest bedroom of her house, even though she knew it was crossing a boundary.

A guidance counselor managed to get his mom's sign-off from within jail so they could fill out the FAFSA paperwork required for his community college scholarship. And "David M. Sapp, director of bands," kept his spirits up, offering his office as a de facto counseling center and lunchroom. In Silas's phone contacts, Sapp is entered as "David M. Dadd."

When Silas was cited by police for driving without a license—he didn't have the money to take driver's ed and only had a permit—Sapp knew the judge because her kid had also been in the band. "When you go into that courtroom and she asks what you're involved in, the first thing you must say is marching band, and you're the drum major," Sapp instructed him. The judge gave Silas a modest fine, which he paid off with his McDonald's wages.

David M. Sapp was also the first teacher Silas came out to as trans. Sapp didn't really get it, but he loved the kid enough to keep an open mind. They talked about hormone treatments and surgeries, and the importance of having steady health insurance. "Many times, he just cried the whole time about what was going on at home or the lack of home," Sapp said.

When Silas was late or absent and missed the first two games of his

*UHS Marching Band director David M. Sapp leads*
*the band during the 2023 homecoming parade.*

senior year, they argued. Then Sapp played go-between with counselors to ensure that Silas was technically enrolled in Urbana schools
while he was couch surfing in an adjacent school district and had
trouble making it to school. It took bureaucratic finagling because
technically Silas didn't have an address. "The school district was like,
'One place or the other.' I tried to explain: But that's what happens
with homeless," said Perry.

Urbana High School was Silas's seventh school since kindergarten.

WHEN WE FIRST MET IN 2023, Silas said he had maybe two memories
from his childhood when his parents weren't doing drugs. He'd
mostly lived with his grandmother in a trailer, but she died when he
was nine, and then he moved back in with his mom, who eventually
moved the family into a friend's house in Urbana. When Silas's older
sister fell into the same drug-using pattern as their parents and ended
up in a psych ward, it hit Silas that it was up to him, and only him, to
break the cycle. He was twelve. He'd just been diagnosed with cyclo-
thymia, a mood disorder that manifests as a mild version of bipolar
disorder.

Mr. Sapp's father had been a welder, so he pushed Silas into the
trades. "I told him, if you become a welder, you can pick your line of
work and pick your paycheck," Mr. Sapp said. "My wife and I both
have degrees, but anymore it's so expensive, and if you go a trade
route, you won't end up with a lot of debt."

The masculine elements of the work appealed to Silas, especially
the flames.

Back then, Silas thought college would be easy compared with the
chaos of his high school years. He didn't understand the money part,
really. His scholarships and grants were substantial—including one
from the heavy-metal band Metallica, whose foundation offered schol-

arships in trades for scores of community colleges across the country. ("Welding is METAL," one Clark State administrator enthused. "Head-bangers rejoice!")[30] But the money could be applied only to tuition and books and didn't cover necessities like housing, food, and transportation. In the semester leading up to his UHS graduation, Silas told me he imagined getting a factory job after graduation, then saving up for a car, a legal name change, and testosterone injections as soon as he turned eighteen. A few months later, in the summer of 2023, Ohio legislators began the process of banning gender-affirming care for trans minors.[31] (The ACLU is appealing the ban.)

That spring, he envisioned going to work as a welder after a ten-month certification course so he'd always have a fallback job that paid well. Then he'd pursue his bachelor's in business administration while working as a welder. His long-term goal was to run his own welding and photography businesses as well as his own clothing line "because I like sketching and embroidery." Ultimately, he wanted to get his own place so he could raise his two younger siblings, who were currently in foster care.

Silas knew he had the chops for community college; it was the daily getting there he couldn't count on—something four-year residential students typically don't have to contend with once they land in a dorm. He lived in Marysville, an hour away from Clark State in Springfield, with his stepdad and mom; she was now on Suboxone, the medication-assisted

*Silas distinguished himself as a top student welder at Clark State University in nearby Springfield, Ohio.*

treatment for opioid use disorder, and fulfilling the conditions of her probation. For a time, she worked at Dunkin' Donuts, then landed a better-paying job on the night shift of a local automotive-parts factory. For a time.

"I'm always praying for her not to relapse," Silas told me. He parroted his therapist's advice on setting boundaries: "I've told her, 'This is a trial run to see if we can be in each other's lives.' If she keeps messing up, she can't be a part of my life."

It sounded like a lot, financially and emotionally. It sounded like something that would have sent a young me back to bed, anxious and overwhelmed.


AFTER GRADUATION and the messy interaction with his grandparents, Silas could not shake feeling sad and listless. He was bone-tired, with a headache that wouldn't quit and no motivation to do anything. "I was just sad about everything. I kept thinking about offing myself."

By the time he lined up those forty pills, he was feeling so hopeless that he decided his life was too much to bear. In case the pills didn't do the trick, he would also slit his wrists.

By his own admission, it was "a messy, half-hearted attempt." His mother found him in his bedroom unconscious and woke him up. He begged her not to take him to the hospital, and, reluctantly, she agreed on the condition that he'd go to regular therapy appointments, something he'd never done before. He slept for twenty-four hours straight.

He was groggy for the next three days. But he put his McDonald's uniform on anyway and went to work. We were talking every couple of weeks at the time, but he didn't tell me about the suicide attempt until months later, when it seemed far away enough that he could be matter of fact about it, almost flippant.

## PART II

# SILOS

*Jordan Collins, Jay Collins, and Catherine Lovejoy*
*(left to right) listen as the national anthem plays at*
*an Ohio Hi-Point Career Center graduation.*

*Six*

# HOMECOMING

*UHS students turn out to cheer at
the 2023 UHS homecoming game.*

Re-enrolled at Clark State that fall, Silas drove there in his stepdad's PT Cruiser. For the first time, he was a fully licensed driver. "I'm completely legal now, and I'm still afraid I'm going to get pulled over," he said, proudly adding, "I even have insurance!"

He was smarting from a breakup; a girlfriend in Michigan he'd met on Tinder that summer and visited by bus had started dating someone else, and she was refusing to mail back Silas's favorite hoodie, a Vans sweatshirt adorned with a gay pride rainbow and flames. He was still working full-time at McDonald's and going to school full-time, and he was thrilled that his mother had just gotten permission from Child Protective Services for unsupervised visits with his youngest half-siblings, who were then three and four and living in foster care.

"Have you seen Batman?" his little brother asked, trying to find his toy.

"I haven't seen Batman, buddy," Silas said.

He was both nervous for and proud of his mother; it was her longest spate of sobriety in years. Over a phone call I could hear her fixing supper, asking the kids if they wanted their sloppy joes on bread or on a tortilla. But judging from the lackluster tone of Silas's voice, which was growing lower from the testosterone, I wondered if he was still feeling down.

"No, I'm fine. It's just a lot to remember," he said. "Most days I go to school, then come home and go to work, then come home again and do my schoolwork, then go to bed. In high school, the teachers are on you about work and deadlines, but in college they tell you once. If you miss it, you miss it."

In the school's photo of his first day as a Clark State Scholar, he's wearing a UHS Marching Band hoodie featuring a drawing of a high-stepping drum major, plume high and baton clenched, marching atop cartoon flames (Silas really loves flames) with the caption THE ROAD OF FIRE. He's standing tall in the photo with a tentative half smile, trying his best to straddle his diverging worlds, if only the PT Cruiser would make it to the semester's end.

SILAS FOUND HIS ENGINEERING courses dry and theoretical—he much preferred the hands-on welding—but he was getting straight A's. He was most looking forward to joining the UHS band at the homecoming football game, to which alumni are traditionally invited to march. He dyed his short, cropped brown hair a bright shade of maroon, a UHS school color, for the occasion. He also found a sliding-scale therapist in Marysville who is trans.

On the way home from Clark State most afternoons he stopped to see Mr. Sapp and to help coach the drum major who'd replaced him. Unlike Silas, Mikey Dale was linebacker-sized, and he needed help

*Silas watches intently as his drum major successor Mikey Dale attempts a backbend.*

figuring out how to execute the required backbend. When you're six feet one, the plume on the top of your hat is a long way from the ground.

"Bend your knees!" Silas urged him. "You'll fall if your knees aren't out ahead of your toes."

Sapp invited me to march with the other alums, too, lending me a spare trumpet. I could barely sputter out an entire song before my lip gave out, but listening to Sapp describe the Script Ohio routine at homecoming, I blurted out, "I have a rush of positive feeling just hearing you talk about it."[1]

We shared stories about my own band director, Robert K. Martin, whose steady presence in my school career had instilled discipline and kept me out of trouble. When people talked during class, he'd pound his conductor's stick on the sheet music. When his favorite majorette errantly flung her baton and hit him on the head, he screamed out her last name, "*Copeland!*" But he was more bluster than bite.

During lessons in the summer, the two of us played old-timey swing duets, and he'd look over his clarinet and down his bifocals at

*Mr. Sapp lent me a trumpet so I could rehearse
with a handful of other band alumni at homecoming.*

me, as if to say "I'm watching you" when no one else was. When my dad died my sophomore year of college, he came to the funeral.

For years after leaving Urbana, I made my family stop and visit Mr. Martin every time we were in town. Robert K. Martin was definitely my version of David M. Dadd.

ON THE THIRD WEEK of Silas's second attempt at college, a wire jiggled loose from the starter on his stepdad's PT Cruiser, stranding him in Springfield, an hour from home. And even though they were still sleeping that morning after working the night shift, his mom and stepdad got up without complaint and drove to Clark State to fix the starter. "My stepdad taught me how to hook it back up if it happens again," Silas said. "That car is more bipolar than I am."

His college mentor, Toni Overholser, knew about his family's troubles during his high school years and was encouraged by their newfound support of him. It worried her that transportation remained such a barrier for most rural students. What good was a double schol-

arship if a student had no way to
get to their free classes? It helped
explain why 40 percent of community college students drop out
before getting a certificate or degree.[2]

In giant leather gloves and a
Darth Vader–like safety helmet
plastered with Adult Swim stick-
ers, Silas was a natural at bending
metal, keeping the welding torch
steady and his movements on
pace. He was not only the youngest in the class; he was among
the best. As the testosterone shots
took effect, Silas worked out regularly in the college gym, another

*Silas learned several styles
of welding for his Clark
State Scholars program.*

perk he couldn't believe he had access to. He delighted in his newfound strength and energy.

Jobs for welders in the region started around $49,000 a year. If he
completed the certification, he'd also get $1,600, a bonus from a state
program meant to encourage participation in the trades. With his Mc-
Donald's money and some help from his grandpa in Texas, he might
be able to buy a decent used car.

Another Clark State Scholar I met, who was a year behind Silas,
had also lost a father to addiction—her dad was presently homeless,
whereabouts unknown, somewhere on the streets of Dayton—and
she, too, had been molested by a guardian.

Almost every kid I interviewed had. That such trauma was so profound among the kids who were recommended to me—hand selected
by teachers as being both poor and exemplary—was a shocker. When

I circled back to share my surprise, the AP English teacher Cassie Cress nodded her head. "That's today's version of a young Beth Macy," she said.[3] Four decades after my own graduation, I'm still wrapping my head around how much harder things are for striving poor kids today.

Some days, it felt as if I'd stepped into the reality version of Barbara Kingsolver's Pulitzer-winning novel *Demon Copperhead*. A.k.a. the opioid crisis 3.0. Even friends I'd known for decades volunteered over dinner tables and on living room couches that they, too, had suffered from childhood sexual abuse—one by an uncle, another by her dad. One told me she'd purposely let herself get fat as a kind of protective layer. The Centers for Disease Control and Prevention has documented that childhood trauma reduces Americans' life expectancy and is more costly, even, than cancer or heart disease.[4]

When I processed what I was seeing in Urbana with a nurse-friend who used to be Huntington, West Virginia's fire chief, she told me that she regularly gives Narcan to the children and grandchildren of

*Cassie Cress asked me to talk about writing and growing up in Urbana during her class discussion of Jeannette Walls's memoir,* The Glass Castle.

people she'd first revived during OxyContin's heyday. "It's no longer people who got initially hooked on legal prescriptions; now the addictions are third and fourth generation, and they're starting because of all the trauma at home," said Jan Rader, now the city's opioid response director.

"We've got to develop strategies to deal with these incredibly broken people."[5]

BEFORE THE HALFTIME SHOW at homecoming, Silas and Mikey high-fived and shook hands like brothers, and the Friday night stadium lights sparkled on their matching maroon plumes. The tuba soloist charged with dotting the *i* in "Ohio" said he was "very nervous. It's my first time."

Silas was now dating a boy named Arlo, an art student he'd met online who went to college in Columbus, and they stole a kiss near the grandstands at the end of the second quarter. Urbana footballers were slaughtering Kenton Ridge, whose band was three times the size of Urbana's.

It was heartening to see the town turn out in the hundreds to cheer on the football team and the band. At the homecoming parade the night before, a two-mile route that started and ended at the high school on the hill, my friend Betty and I played our horns on the alumni-band float, throwing candy and waving at her family and other people we recognized in the crowd. We were both about to turn sixty, and our enthusiasm for reuniting around this thing we hadn't done together in forty years was strong enough to outweigh the initial embarrassment of it.

During halftime, my pal Karla, a lawyer in Cincinnati who had been responsible for getting me through Algebra II, sat with her nonagenarian mother, a retired school nurse, and cheered me on. (A

*Homecoming Court members are driven through Urbana in antique convertibles for the 2023 homecoming parade.*

former Ohio Innocence Project attorney, Karla has long kept an eye out for underdogs.)

In the reserved section, our class reunion organizer—the QAnon devotee—took pictures of us marching to post on the class Facebook page. After the game, several friends gathered in a downtown bar and danced to a boisterous funk band from Dayton. In my almost sixty years, it was the most racially diverse gathering I'd seen anywhere. And yet it was also true that the brother of a Black friend, visiting from Florida, had been called the N-word by a man driving by in an oversized truck as he shoveled snow from his sister's sidewalk. "Urbana," my friend's brother said, shaking his head.

The adult Urbanans who participated in the town's homecoming were mostly in the thin strata that constituted its middle and upper-middle classes. Most had no idea what was happening in the community beyond their information silos or the conspiracy theories they read online. They had no inkling that more than 20 percent of kids

*My buddy Karla, class of 1983, let me crash her*
*class reunion at an uptown pub owned by*
*one of our schoolmates.*

weren't even showing up at school. No one I spoke with, save for law enforcement and social worker types, had any idea how bad the mental health crisis had turned; two suicides had taken place the week of homecoming alone.[6] The newspaper was growing thinner by the week, and Betty said she looked forward to my visits because that was the only way that she, a local business owner, knew what was going on.

This reflected the collapse of vigorous local journalism, but it was deeper than that. Karla had fallen out with four friends from childhood, including two cousins, after meeting them for dinner and mentioning her COVID vaccine. "We were hanging out, our drinks had come but we hadn't ordered yet, and they all got up and left," she recalled.

"I said, 'You guys are joking, right?' And they were like, 'No, we don't want to get COVID, and you're actively sloughing the virus at our table.'"[7]

"These are super nice people who, if a neighbor's sick, they'll go and mow their grass and do their farm chores," Karla said. "But they feel threatened because the world's changing in ways they can't understand. They worry they'll be left out and what limited success they do have is going to be cut off. They see things through a lens of fear and scarcity."

Which is understandable, given that rural places have lost 48 percent of their jobs in agriculture, forestry, mining, construction, transportation, and production since 1970, according to Nicholas Jacobs and Daniel Shea, authors of *The Rural Voter: The Politics of Place and the Disuniting of America*. In the first decade of the twenty-first century alone, industrial employment in rural spaces dropped by a third, leading to a feeling of economic precarity, even among small-business owners who weren't themselves experiencing financial stress. Unlike in urban areas, rural workforce participation and unemployment never recovered to pre–Great Recession levels, leading to what scholars call a "shared fate" mentality in small towns, where people live, work, and worship in greater proximity than do those in cities.[8]

"Fewer things matter more to the average rural voter than the pride and identity that stem from living in a rural place," Jacobs told me.[9] Because it's easier for people in small towns to notice disparities, with poor and wealthy people living closer to each other, often that pride of place manifests itself as resentment toward well-off urban elites—even among well-off rural elites.

When Hillary Clinton tried to explain her loss in 2016, she noted, "I won the places that own two-thirds of America's gross domestic product. . . . I won the places that are optimistic, diverse, dynamic, moving forward."

But as Jacobs countered, "More Trump voters live in those moving-forward places than all of rural America combined."[10] In terms of sheer numbers, millions more Trump voters live in cities and suburbs than in small towns and the countryside.

"The Trumpiest people I've ever met are in Long Island or in the suburbs of Phoenix," Jacobs told me. "I don't like punching down on people, but it's hard not to punch down on the hellscape of North Myrtle Beach and all its hedonistic consumption, and *goddamn* they love Trump. They've got new houses, golf courses that are maintained by immigrants, and they're doing just fine."[11]

My HOMETOWN VISITS were also turning up connections with the Johns Hopkins political scientist Lilliana Mason's research on the increase in political vitriol in this country, and I reached out to talk to her. For a 2017 project she co-authored, 30 to 40 percent of Americans reported that members of the opposing party "don't deserve to be treated like humans because they behave like animals." Eighty percent called members of the opposing party "a threat to the United

States and its people." (The numbers were high for both parties but higher among Republicans, Mason said.)

Such views, historically speaking, are a precursor to violence, Mason pointed out. "It's a form of moral disengagement, a way to allow yourself to harm members of the other group while still feeling virtuous about yourself." Moral disengagement doesn't always lead to violence, but it always precedes violence.

According to a 2021 study commissioned by the National League of Cities, 81 percent of local officials nationwide reported experiencing harassment, threats, and violence.[12] A school board member in the northern Virginia locality of Loudoun County quit after receiving threats, explaining that her salary wouldn't even cover her funeral expenses.[13] The Champaign County Democratic chairwoman told me she planned to take her last name off her mailbox in the run-up to the 2024 election. She was having a hard time renting space in Urbana for their campaign headquarters, and the only quote she could find to insure a potential space was seven times higher than the going rate.[14]

"I think what is often lost in the story about Trump supporters is that it's not the poorest people who support Trump. It's the richest people in the poorest places," Mason told me.[15] Trump not only cut their taxes but also made it okay for them to hate political correctness of all sorts, including people of different gender and racial identities.

Being anti-woke scratches a deep itch for them. Like my siblings and some of my Urbana friends, people who aren't exposed to LGBTQ people and other minorities can't figure out where they belong in relation to them, Mason said. Under a Trump presidency, they don't even have to try.

Asked for advice on talking to my sister Cookie about my gay son's upcoming wedding, Mason advised me to skip politics entirely. "Go do something together and figure out who you are as people before you go into your memorized talking points," she said. "If it were me, I might say, 'What do you think about the wedding colors?' It's a wedding! It should be a fun thing to talk about."

The colors Max and Zack chose for their wedding—royal blue and green—would not end up at the top of my list of go-to topics.

BEFORE I SAT DOWN WITH COOKIE, I turned to other experts for advice. The rural sociologist Kathy Cramer encouraged me not to bring up politics but rather to meet her with curiosity. "Repair can only happen at the very human level," she said. If the subject of Trump comes up anyway, she advised me to say, "Wait a minute. I'm not seeing what you're seeing in your media or social media feeds."

"You've got to remember that you're a human being and so is she, and I do think so much of the way we think about each other now is because of our bifurcated communications environment," Cramer said. "You'll have to work at it, though; you've got to use those hope muscles."

"I'm afraid they've atrophied," I told her.

"You can do it!" she said.[16]

The counseling professor Tania Israel reminded me that "the most important thing is to have a warm relationship where you are trying to understand the person you're interviewing and to be compassionate." She explained that people attempting to converse across a political divide usually do so for four reasons: They're having trouble maintaining their relationship, they're trying to persuade or convince someone they're wrong, they want to heal the divide or find common ground, or they simply cannot fathom why people think or vote the way they do.

When I offered that mostly I hoped to better understand Cookie, Israel threw out another reason: "Maybe you just want your son to be loved, ya know?"[17]

A public-health activist in Baltimore suggested I approach my interviews "with the most compassionate version you have for what's happened with your family." Calling on the principles of trauma-informed care, Andrew Bell suggested I focus not on my family's deficits but on our strengths, like our resilient, plucky mom or the ancestral trip to Ireland my niece Liza and I were planning. He encouraged me to acknowledge the nuance of Cookie's situation, like the fact that she skipped my wedding not only to attend a church revival but also because she didn't have a car that would make the seven-hour journey from her house to mine.

"When you're from the professional or managerial class that you and I are functionally a part of, it's hard for the story not to feel hierarchical, which triggers a sensitivity around being condescended to," Bell said.[18] He read me a quotation from the philosopher Richard Rorty, who predicted in 1998 that globalization and growing inequality would eventually lead to widespread class resentment and, eventually, to fascism:

> Members of labor unions and unorganized unskilled workers will sooner or later realize that their government is not even trying to prevent wages from sinking or to prevent jobs from being exported. Around the same time, they will realize that suburban white-collar workers—themselves desperately afraid of being downsized—are not going to let themselves be taxed to provide social benefits for anyone else.
>
> At that point, something will crack. The nonsuburban electorate will decide that the system has failed and start looking around for a strongman to vote for—someone willing to assure them that, once he is elected, the smug bureaucrats, tricky lawyers, overpaid bond salesmen, and postmodernist professors will no longer be calling the shots. . . .

One thing that is very likely to happen is that the gains made in the past forty years by black and brown Americans, and by homosexuals, will be wiped out. Jocular contempt for women will come back into fashion. . . . All the resentment which badly educated Americans feel about having their manners dictated to them by college graduates will find an outlet.[19]

This prediction was published nearly two decades before Trump's election, which might not have happened had the liberals listened to Rorty, who told them to embrace blue-collar workers by blunting the pain of globalization, re-embracing labor unions, and focusing on up-ward mobility—basically the ideals that would eventually become Bernie Sanders's platform.

It was as if, sometime around 1980, Rorty wrote, "the children of the people who had made it through the Great Depression and into the suburbs had decided to pull up the drawbridge behind them."[20] Back then, students from the top quartile of American incomes were four times more likely to get a college degree than those from the bottom quarter; by 2000, they were ten times more likely.

What would it take, Rorty wondered, for the left to channel the rage of the newly dispossessed?

AN ADDICTIONS WORKER I know and admire describes Rorty's call to reform-minded action by using the Latin phrase *acta non verba*, which she had tattooed on her forearm. She says it translates to *Do shit, don't just talk about it.*

The minority Democrats in Urbana were adopting this philosophy, paying off school lunch debt for kids in arrears, sponsoring community Christmas films at the Gloria even though the theater refused to list their sponsorship on the marquee, holding blood drives, and starting a fund to pay for equipment for students entering the trades. But they were having a hard time getting anyone to run for office.

"It's too dangerous in this county to be seen as a Democrat," the chairwoman Heather Tiefenthaler told me. As we talked in an Urbana coffee shop, a news alert blinged on our phones: A Trump juror in the Manhattan trial, the porn-star hush money case, had just backed out of serving, citing fear of violence.

"It almost feels like a dream," Tiefenthaler said.

IN MY THIRTY-FIVE YEARS as a journalist, I've interviewed drug kingpins in prison cells, combative CEOs in corporate suites, and pharma bros who threatened to sue me if I didn't fall into line. Reporting from Haiti, I found myself in the crosshairs of rioters who threw rocks at my vehicle and came at the group I was reporting on with machetes. (I remember wishing they had guns instead, all the quicker to get it over and done with.)

Preparing to interview Cookie was scarier.

I picked up cupcakes on the way, a shameless appeal to the Macy sweet tooth. And for the first couple of hours of this family homecoming, I was able to hear my sister with empathy and curiosity—until I wasn't.

COOKIE AND I HAD never been especially close. In 1969, the year I started kindergarten, she became a teen mom and left home. For most of her life, she has lived either in or very close to our west-central Ohio hometown. I left Ohio in 1987 to work for newspapers and bounced around a bit before settling in Virginia in 1989, visiting my Ohio family on long weekends or holidays once or twice a year.

Cookie visited our home in Virginia once, a trip she found harrowing after missing a turn for the West Virginia Turnpike. She was a part-time secretary at her church at the time, and her husband worked at a local Japanese-owned factory that makes car parts for Honda and is now Champaign County's largest employer. They were renting a modest house in the countryside not far from Urbana. When I took her out to lunch at a nice Roanoke restaurant, the kind with white table-cloths, it was very much a splurge on my reporter's salary. She thanked me but made a point of saying it was foolish to spend eighty bucks eating lunch out.

It was a fair point, though I wasn't in the habit of asking her for advice. We were strangers, honestly, with different pastimes, beliefs, and tastes. I had grown up mostly without her, save for the couple of years, between marriages, when she moved into our parents' house with her daughters. She was new to her church at that point, and when her pastor introduced her to her third husband, we were hopeful for her and the girls. When the two of them went knocking on doors to proselytize—witnessing, she called it—I felt embarrassed. I knew everyone in the neighborhood from my paper route and can remember thinking, *Please don't tell anyone we're related.*

Cookie and her new husband "went out calling on people Saturday morning for the church," Mom wrote in a letter to our oldest sister, Terry. It was the fall of 1983, my sophomore year of college, and Dad was then in home hospice care for lung cancer. His death was imminent, though he had recently, after Mom left for work, taken off for the library down the hill from us, pushing his wheelchair and periodically pausing to sit down and rest. The library trek had gone so well, Mom wrote, that afterward he decided to take on five more blocks and pushed his wheelchair to the VFW for a final round of beers.

"I really thought he was making it up, but [a friend] called yesterday and said he was there with your Dad. Said he was supposed to come by the next day and take him for a ride," Mom wrote. "I told him I was going to lock up his wheelchair!"

During one of Cookie's outings to witness in the neighborhood, "they hadn't been gone too long when the pastor, his wife and another woman came in and he started preaching at your Dad. He got pretty upset, and I was about to tell [the pastor] to leave when [Dad] kinda calmed down," Mom wrote. "After they left, he said that Cookie had set him up! Was kinda funny but they can be so pushy. Anyway, nothing was said about it—guess they mean well."[21]

Mom soon changed her tune on that, around the time another church elder who was a mechanic sold me a very used Honda Civic, bright orange, that turned out to be held together with Bondo and duct tape. I got a few months' use out of it before it started falling apart. A salvage yard gave me thirty-five bucks to take it off my hands.

The piece-of-crap car Cookie's church elder sold me, swearing it would get me back and forth to college with no problem, should have been our first clue about her church. It was headed by a televangelist "known for taking an uncompromising stand on the word of God," according to a quarter-page ad he took out in *The Urbana Daily Citizen*, featuring a photo of himself with a sweeping Sonny Bono mustache.[22]

I had to take a third work-study job at college to replace the car. I mixed chemicals in the photojournalism lab, wrote press releases for the university, and did filing in the financial aid office—double- and triple-checking that my financial aid forms were in proper order.

THAT REPLACEMENT CAR WAS a blue fifteen-year-old VW Bug with a moonroof. Its battery under the backseat was held up by a piece of a cutting board my boyfriend wedged underneath for support. It had rust in spots, too, but it was reliable enough to get me through college graduation and partway through my first year of newspapering.

I don't remember whether Cookie ever commented on "The Moral Majority Is Neither" sticker I'd slapped on my back bumper. But it was 1986, and I'm sure the message rankled. If my sibling communications were deteriorating, America as a whole wasn't doing much better. The Federal Communications Commission appointed by Reagan would soon end the fairness doctrine, designed to protect the integrity of public information since the 1940s. With a brushstroke, the FCC gutted the rule that said stations had to present information honestly and fairly to balance out different points of view. That gutting paved the way for the "feminazi" rantings of Rush Limbaugh and people like Pat Buchanan and Newt Gingrich, the latter of whom urged his fellow conservatives to marry politics with Jerry Falwell's paternalistic white version of Christianity that was being gobbled up by the likes of Cookie and her Bondo-selling deacon friend. The goal was to demonize Democrats by calling them corrupt and dangerous, and to make "liberal" a word that scared the bejesus out of people like Mike Dukakis and Bill Clinton.

At the same time Reagan slashed the Pell Grant program, the anti-abortion activist Phyllis Schlafly was angrily protesting tax deductions for poor families, calling them "just an idea of liberal bureaucrats who want to redistribute wealth." It was the start of a full-on culture war as I traversed the suburbs of Columbus, Ohio, for my first reporting job, praying I'd make it to school board and city council meetings in my VW. Cookie's brand of Evangelicalism squared firmly with Schlafly and her ilk—and against people like me who believed women deserved to have full dominion over their bodies.

It was the dawn of misinformation, as the historian Heather Cox Richardson explains in her book *Democracy Awakening.* When the presidential candidate George H. W. Bush realized his relatively moderate patrician views were sinking him in the polls, he hired Nixon's former operative Lee Atwater and media adviser Roger Ailes to turn up the flames. They produced the infamous Willie Horton ad, a racist dog whistle that Atwater ended up apologizing for at the end of his life, describing it as electoral "manipulation" and "naked cruelty."

That ad laid "the groundwork for a new kind of right-wing television in which ideological propaganda would be filmed as if it were a news story, making it hard for viewers to tell the difference," Richardson writes. By the late 1980s, "Republicans had created an underclass of Americans increasingly falling behind economically. And, crucially, they had given that underclass someone to hate."[23]

In our family's case, that someone might turn out to be me.

# Seven

# STRANGERS

*When I took a picture of my niece Katie
to school for kindergarten show-and-tell,
I was the only aunt in my class. Cookie,
shown here in front of our house, was
eighteen when she had her.*

W hen my husband and I had kids in the 1990s, we joined a progressive, nondenominational Christian church called Unity, where we sang in the choir and went to Wednesday-night suppers. When Mom described our church positively to Cookie after one of her visits, Cookie told her that it sounded like a cult. "Pot, meet kettle," Mom said, reporting back to me.

In Cookie's church, men made all the decisions, people spoke in tongues, and no one questioned authority. Our church had a female minister and gay and Black people in positions of authority. At the end of every service, the congregation held hands and sang, "Let there be peace on Earth, and let it begin with me," as the children proceeded out from Sunday school.

In a letter to Terry a few years before, Mom described visiting her mother at an Urbana nursing home and spotting Cookie picketing with church friends and fellow abortion protesters at the Planned Parenthood across the street. "Guess she's into the abortion protesting again," Mom wrote. "I'm sure there's an appropriate quote to fit this but can't come up with it right off."[1] (Cookie doesn't remember ever protesting at a clinic.)

An older mother when she had me, Mom said that she'd never personally have an abortion, but she didn't believe it was right to ban the procedure. The year after Dad died, during my junior year of college, I had an abortion eight weeks into a surprise pregnancy. My boyfriend at the time, who was Catholic, reared in Urbana's management class, and in his first year of medical school, agreed with the decision, paid for the procedure, and went with me to a Columbus clinic that dreary November day. Birth-control pills had given me high blood pressure, so we used other protection. Accidents happen. I was twenty.

About a month later, the future doctor broke up with me, saying my abortion conflicted with his religious beliefs, even though rearing a child together was something he clearly had not wanted to do. He'd proposed no alternatives. Like most poor women with unintended pregnancies, I was entirely on my own.[2]

I was too ashamed about the abortion to tell Mom, and only recently did I even tell my husband. It occurred to me that our kids would not exist had I not made that choice in 1984. "Hell, *we* wouldn't exist," he said, and gave me a long, tight hug. "I'm sorry you've been carrying this for so long." In truth, having a child would have changed more than just my family's future. I would've had to quit college, move home, get a job, and rely on my soon-to-retire, overworked mom to help raise a baby. She might not have ever met up with her sweet future husband, Gene. My child would have grown up facing the same barriers I'd worked so hard to overcome.

Maybe my siblings would have made a different choice. But, as study after study about abortion has borne out, the ability to steer my reproductive life was vital to my social mobility, to my future ability to parent—and to my survival.[3] As Ruth Bader Ginsburg would later write, a woman's right to an abortion was nothing less than her "autonomy to determine her life's course, and thus to enjoy equal citizenship stature."[4]

But for the preachers and politicians who told my sister and millions of women what to think and whom to fear, agitating against *Roe v. Wade* would become the go-to tool for raising campaign funds for conservative politicians. It would also become a convenient way to control—and, eventually, to help radicalize—an electorate.

I WAS REPORTING IN GEORGIA in 1988 when the abuse allegations against Cookie's husband came to a head. There had long been complaints about his mistreatment from the girls. But Liza was now eleven, at the onset of puberty. She had never seen a penis before, she told me recently—until suddenly her stepdad shoved his in her face. She doesn't wish to describe what happened next, but it led her to a school guidance counselor who filed a police report. When I phoned the youngest girls' dad to tell him about it, he was stunned. When they went to live with him, I called the police and wrote a long letter to local officials, begging them to intervene. I reminded them that ministers, as mandatory reporters, are by law required to report allegations of child abuse and child sexual assault and urged them to investigate both the stepdad and the pastor.

A police officer I knew from home told me they were "looking into" pressing charges against Cookie's husband—nothing was ever filed—but they flat out refused to investigate the pastor.[5]

At the same time, the prosecutor Joseph Palmer, who was up for reelection, turned his zeal for justice elsewhere: overseeing a so-called decency panel that advocated for the abolishment of soft-core pornography being sold at a newsstand on Monument Square.[6] Without Palmer's blessing, Liza's complaints couldn't move forward, Johnny Evans, the investigating officer, told me.

"He used to be tough, but he's sold out," Evans said. "The system is so screwed up involving sexual abuse with kids. No one wants to do anything."[7]

When I called Palmer myself, he claimed he didn't remember the case, even though Evans had just brought it to him two days before.

I HATED THEM ALL—Palmer, the stepdad, and the pastor who introduced my sister to this creep. But I believed the pastor, who'd cozied up to Palmer as a leader on the prosecutor's "decency panel"—while driving around town in a brand-new Cadillac Seville—deserved a special place in hell. The prosecutor described their mutual fight for righteousness as "one battle in the long war against a disgusting foe— obscenity." He even took the battle to court, beseeching a municipal judge to order the magazines pulled because they "appeal to a shameful, morbid interest in sex."[8]

I was twenty-three when I laid out my case to city officials—two steaming pages, single-spaced, hammered out on a word processor with a font so square it was straight out of the OG computer game *Pong*. I'd forgotten about the letter, but ever the curator of my work, Mom had saved that too.

When I shared it with Liza recently, she was surprised. "I didn't realize you were that deep into things after that. I was stuck at Dad's in my own world." He was drinking again, the girls were fighting with their stepmom, and they would soon be sent to a children's home in yet another town, their fourth in as many years.

"Thank you," she texted. "U did a million times more than my own mother."

But we all felt so powerless at the time.

No one in our family had much capacity to talk about feelings, not even Mom and me, and we loved each other fiercely. But just as fiercely Mom and I also fought, usually over her criticisms of my clothes, hair, weight, or frequency of visits home. (She liked to waste time complaining about the length of my visits *while I was visiting*.) If I complained about her critiques, I was accused of being too sensitive.

We would cook away our fury or maybe hit a yard sale, and without ever discussing the thing that had landed us in the pickle, we'd make up. Usually. One spring during college, we got into an argument on the phone. Afterward, I wrote her a biting, over-the-top letter criticizing her lack of emotional support. Being a first-gen student was often painful, and I sometimes took my insecurities out on Mom.

A few days later I drove home for Easter. It was Good Friday, and she was working second shift when I arrived. On the kitchen table, she had thoughtfully left a large chocolate Easter egg to greet me, a pot of chili in the Crock-Pot, and a poem she'd typed on her garage-sale typewriter, titled "Easter Greeting to My Mean Daughter."

My relationship with Cookie had always been shallower, easier, and a lot less intense. She had an infectious laugh and could be hilarious, once driving us around Mom's neighborhood in Liza's convertible, blasting "I'm Too Sexy" on the stereo. We had visited over the decades at Mom's house—once a year, usually, around holidays—and

Your nasty letter really hurt
But over it I've got
I know you didn't mean it
You know I care a LOT

And so at Easter time let's try
To nicen up a lot
Remember I'm your "SuperMom"
And the only one you got!

And you are my special SuperKid
Like which there is no other
So Happy Easter to you Beth
            From your
                    Bitchy
                    Bitchy
                        Mother

            xxxoooxxx

*Poetic justice: Mom's "Easter Greeting to My Mean Daughter."*

we exchanged cards and small gifts.

But no one in the family ever mustered the language to talk in depth about Cookie's husband's abuse of her kids and the ripple effects it had on all of us. Or why she'd chosen to believe her husband's side of the story over her eleven-year-old daughter's.

Because of what he'd done to the girls, Cookie's husband knew he could never darken our fam-

*My niece Liza, eleven years my junior, at my parents' gravesite, with Mom's signature tattooed on her forearm.*

ily's doors. We were a united front, and he was dead to us. I honestly had no clue whether Cookie still remained committed to the church and husband she had chosen over her own daughter.

"He ruined my life," my niece Liza said. She thought about the abuse almost every day, she told me multiple times.

Early in their marriage, he had moved the family three hours away to Cleveland for a year, and Liza's older sister described him beating them on their first night in Cleveland because they used their hands to wipe pizza grease from their mouths. Later, he made them pull weeds in his vegetable garden for hours on end. When he forced the youngest to eat food she didn't like and she threw it up, he made her eat the vomit. (Cookie is the only one in our family who has no memory of that; the rest of us, including all her daughters, remember it as if it happened yesterday. "I remember him wanting them to clean their plates," Cookie said.) In their patriarchal church, the women ceded their parenting authority to the men, and it was years before we understood the extent of his cruelty. Terry referred to him as "the Nazi" in letters to Mom.

The shame felt like a permanent stain on all of us. It still vaguely does. And yet ignoring the elephant in the room or burying the damn thing in drugs, booze, religion, or food hadn't worked for anybody. When Mom called me in Georgia to tell me about the sexual abuse— she'd gotten a phone call from a guidance counselor at Liza's school— I promptly began having panic attacks. I was sweating profusely, couldn't catch my breath, couldn't even keep food down. I had to call in sick to work.

No one I knew in the mid-1980s talked about panic attacks—I'd never heard the phrase—but I literally believed I was dying and was relieved when a doctor said I wasn't. The attacks abated with medication and therapy from a psychiatrist I couldn't afford who said I was "carrying around too much baggage" from my family. At the time I thought it was bunk, but he was definitely onto something.

Throughout my late twenties and most of my thirties, my security blanket became my rock-solid husband. Recently, he reminded me that I also kept a single Xanax wrapped in foil that I carried with me at all times, my hedge against another panic attack.

You can't save your family, the psychiatrist had said. But if I learned to set healthy boundaries, I might be able to save myself.

THAT SOUNDED GOOD IN THEORY, but setting boundaries is a struggle, especially for class migrants. On Christmas Eve 1991, my husband and I were newly married and found ourselves driving around Dayton looking for Cookie's youngest daughter. She'd run away from her father's house, where she'd also been placed after the abuse came to light. I made several calls to her friends to triangulate her location to a local Burger King while the rest of the family seemed paralyzed, unable to step up to find the missing teen.

When we located her, we scooped her up and took her to my in-laws' suburban split-level in Indianapolis for the holiday. They welcomed her and scrambled to have presents wrapped for her under the tree by the next morning. She spent the next two days playing dolls with my husband's eleven-year-old niece. That Christmas I discovered that my mother-in-law, the granddaughter of German immigrants, wasn't always the most outwardly affectionate person but she was as dependable as they come.

A week later, my mother-in-law wrote in a letter, "I hope that somehow she can work things out. I even found myself thinking that she could finish growing up here . . . she seems like a sweet gal who needs some support and encouragement."[9]

My husband and I talked about taking her in, too, but we were in our mid-twenties and didn't think we could handle it. When she and Liza went to the veteran-run children's home instead, we felt equal parts guilt and relief. Boundaries can save, yes, but also boundaries suck.

When I told the psychologist Diana Zuckerman, who studies sexual abuse, about Liza losing not only her innocence but also her home, she said, "That is the worst of all worlds, really, because then you've been thrown away twice."

And to not be believed by her mother on top of it? "That's terrible," she said.[10]


FOR OUR FIRST INTERVIEW, Cookie made the forty-minute drive to meet me in Urbana in her minivan, using a walker to navigate the gravel driveway from the van to her oldest daughter's house. She was seventy-two, and her mobility was limited by arthritis in her knees. (She distrusts doctors, fears anesthesia, and refuses to have her knees replaced.) For two and a half hours, we talked, looked at old pictures, and read some of Mom's old letters aloud.

Like many midwesterners, she's not loquacious by nature, preferring a short text over a phone call and an online Scrabble game over a text, so I was stunned by her openness. It was the longest we'd spoken in decades.

She still laughed easily, too, like when she recalled renting a small house down the street from us in the late 1970s, between her second and her third marriages. Her backyard abutted the backyard of our dentist, who happened to be the uncle of the not-yet-famous actor Woody Harrelson, who was painting houses in Urbana and living with his aunt and uncle during his summer break from college. Woody stopped by our front porch shirtless once, with a rag in one hand and a can of turpentine in the other. He asked me to wipe the paint drippings off his back, which he couldn't reach—a scene Mom loved to recount, her eyes wide with feigned naughtiness. Woody was as bright and smiley then as he is on screen now, and he took a particular shine to Cookie's middle daughter.

"Who loves ya, Liza?" he would say, spinning her around like a ride at the county fair.

And five-year-old Liza, her preternaturally blue eyes glowing, would answer, "Woody loves me!"

At the beginning of our interview, Cookie asked if I'd ever run into Woody—the answer was no—and out toppled a story I'd never heard.

When she first joined the church and began hosting Bible study groups at her house, she invited Woody to join. He showed up at her prayer meeting wearing a T-shirt and shorts. A pair of really tight, really short shorts. Pure sex in paint-dappled Adidas.

Woody had no idea what he was getting himself into, Cookie remembered. "I don't think he stayed too long," she told me. "He kind of had his eyes on my girlfriend Cindy at the time." We cracked up.

---

THE NAME DONALD TRUMP didn't come up once in the interview. Cookie wanted to talk about the time I ran away from home at the age of four on my tricycle with our beagle mutt, Tessie—escaping to the only place I knew how to get to, the grocery store. She recalled finding me at Kroger staring longingly at the Popsicles and chatting up the butcher.

She lit up as she remembered taking me along to her last day of high school; I was five. "They said we could bring a brother or sister, and I wanted to show you off," she said, laughing. "You was so cute!"[11]

We compared our mutual shoplifting forays as teenagers: Cookie once stole steaks by tucking them inside the pockets of a reversible raincoat. A decade later, I got busted by a downtown merchant who accused me of stealing his jewelry—which he'd counted the moment I came into his store, rightfully clocking me as a hooligan—then made me empty my pockets. When he couldn't find his missing jewelry on me and I refused to speak, he let me go.

I rushed outside to expel the earrings I'd swiped . . . from my mouth. Scared straight, I decided my shoplifting days were over and gave away all my stolen jewelry the next morning to a classmate on the school bus. Cookie enjoyed my redemption story.

We guffawed at the memory of our oldest sister, Terry, the goody-goody one, getting caught sneaking into the Champaign County Fair. She was eighteen at the time and worked as a receptionist for a downtown optometrist. A sheriff's deputy tried to scare her straight, too, by taking her and a friend to the jail and lecturing them outside an unlocked cell before letting them go.

Weeks later, when Sheriff Stillings came in to pick up his new eyeglasses, Terry's boss casually asked him what kinds of crimes he'd been working lately, whereupon a crimson-faced Terry hid in the back of the office as the sheriff responded, "Well, you wouldn't believe the number of young ladies we've caught sneaking into the fair."

WHEN THE SUBJECT OF her marriage came up, I asked Cookie point-blank about the bad things her husband had done to her kids, especially Liza. My recorder was rolling, with her permission, and she didn't hesitate to answer.

"You know, I can't say that he did them or didn't. Those incidents that were reported, I was right there all the time, so I don't see how that could have happened."

"Liza's still very traumatized by it," I said.

"She really believes it?" Cookie asked.

It was all I could do to keep from screaming, but I checked myself. "She told me he ruined her life," I said.

Cookie looked down and sighed. She remembered calling on her pastor and his wife for advice. She remembered seeing them praying on their knees and looking up to her to say how much they trusted and approved of her husband, as if he were divinely blessed. "That was it," she said.

And so the crime, being both prosecutor sanctioned and pastor approved, was now buttoned up. All Cookie had to do, for the next forty years, was block it out.

"I'M PROUD OF HER," she said, after a long pause. With only a high school diploma from the children's home, Liza advanced to the management rung of an international digital marketing company. She taught herself computer coding and graphics and, eventually, worked her way up to managing a large team of people. Though she was unable to have children of her own, my niece helped her husband, who's ten years her senior, raise both his kids and grandkids—delighting in them, cheering at all their games, treating them as her own. She regularly sends me videos of them via text: her tall granddaughter playing center on the middle school basketball team, her grandson singing along with her in the car to Tyler Childers's "All Your'n." When her oldest granddaughter, Nya, was named to the Homecoming Court on her eighteenth birthday, we both squealed. (When the two of us took thirteen-year-old Nya to see *Hamilton* on Broadway, she burst into tears the moment she got her first glimpse of Times Square.)

Liza struggles with anxiety and copes by being almost manically organized about everything from her job to the number of calories she consumes and steps she takes. Not only do we share anxiety through our DNA—though ancestry.com has alternately matched us as sisters, cousins, and niece-and-aunt (we prefer the term "sister-cuz")—we also agree that *Schitt's Creek* is the funniest show ever made. Last year, when she reinjured an already bad shoulder and needed a bone graft to surgically repair it, she chortled, "I hope the donor gives me some anti-anxietal DNA."

She's a spreadsheet master who reads as constantly as her grandma did, consuming as many as six books a week on vacation. And she's as stubbornly apolitical as they come, to the point of refusing to vote. When I asked a mutual friend whether she'd help me talk Liza into voting in 2024, she said, "I don't think we could talk her into drinking a cup of coffee if she didn't want to."

Like Silas and like me, Liza had the grit to make her own support network when her family wasn't up to the task. As the trauma scholar Dr. Bessel van der Kolk, the author of *The Body Keeps the Score*, has said, when people were traumatized as children, shame becomes their predominant emotion. But those who are very lucky can partially hide their trauma in the safety of their talents.[12]

———

AFTER MOM'S DEATH, my siblings and I each received a fourth of her estate; it was modest by inheritance standards but a remarkable testimony to Gene's generosity and Mom's lifelong thrift. My brother bought a gleaming, like-new Ford F-150 with his. I used part of mine to take Liza on a two-week trip to England, Ireland, and Scotland as a celebration of Mom, who was Liza's favorite person on the planet. (The rest I set aside for mortgage down payments, when the time came, for our kids.) Liza was initially nervous about traveling internationally, asking me, "What are we taking for protection?"

"You mean travel insurance?" I asked.

My husband, listening to our conversation on speaker, mouthed the word "Condoms?"

Guns, Liza meant. When I explained that Europe is safer because their laws don't permit guns, she seemed to accept it, though her husband, an avid hunter, warned her repeatedly to "be mindful of your surroundings."

During the trip, I heard her telling him over the phone how safe and thriving the villages and cities felt compared with Ohio's, marveling at how friendly people were. "It's hard to describe it," she told him. "It's just *better* here." She was awed when her decade-long case of stress-related eczema on her arms cleared up in Ireland, practically overnight. "I just feel so . . . *at peace* here," she said.

She was picking up on something I'd noticed during my first trip to Ireland with my husband in 2003: Almost everyone we passed said hello; people drove much smaller cars; and because they walk so many places and eat fewer processed foods, they're in better physical shape. Trying to track down the modern-day version of my ancestors, my husband and I stopped people in Kilkenny to inquire about residents

*Liza and I toasted her grandma (my mom)
every time we had a drink on the trip.*

named Campion (my maternal grandmother's maiden name). They eagerly made introductions for us at places like Campion's pub and Campion Picture Framing. After a day of this and one very Guinness-soaked night, we explained that we had to be moving on because we'd already booked reservations for our next stay several hours away. But word had already spread far into the county as the frame-shop owner implored us in a thick brogue: "But I've already called ahead to me uncle Martin in Three Castles. He's expectin' ya."

Off we drove in the tiniest car possible to Three Castles, where Uncle Martin—who looked eerily like my mom's mom—met us warmly, then sent us packing to meet Uncle Tom in another hamlet even farther into the countryside. Martin had already called ahead to Tom, so he, too, was already expectin' us. I still don't know if we're related to the Campions of Kilkenny, but we had a blast trying to find out, and we left Ireland with a sense that it was not only friendlier than most small towns in America but healthier and safer too.

During my 2023 trip with Liza, she gravitated toward castles, cathedrals, and anything to do with history; we conversed using silly Scottish phrases from the TV show *Outlander* the whole trip. She drew the line at touring the Edinburgh Botanic Garden with me, saying that gardens triggered memories of her childhood abuse. "I just can't," she said.

We also visited Kilkenny, the likely home of my great-great-grandfather Patrick Campion. He'd fled the Irish potato famine in 1850, making his way to western Pennsylvania. By 1864 he was clutching a musket as a volunteer for the Pennsylvania Artillery's Fifth Regiment during the Civil War, a unit that fought in the Battle of Hanging Rock, a skirmish not fifteen minutes from my Virginia home.

In a photo of his unit from 1865, he is rail thin with chiseled cheeks; a canteen dangles from his wiry frame. Before they mustered out, the men had to properly rebury two thousand of the dead who'd been hastily interred after the Second Battle of Bull Run, then spend thirteen weeks building a stone obelisk at the battlefield's edge engraved with the words "In Memory of the Patriots." When he landed back in his adopted hometown of Bolivar, Pennsylvania, he worked as a night watchman for the railroad, had seven children, and lived to be seventy-four. A cousin who does genealogy found the photo and filled in many of the missing pieces of the Campion family history. "There is alcoholism all through our family tree," she said.[13]

Mom gobbled every bit of info I could find about her Irish ancestors, and the summer after my 2003 trip to Ireland I took her and her sister to see Patrick Campion's grave in western Pennsylvania.

Liza and I have texted and talked almost daily ever since our Irish trip. Sometimes we FaceTime at night to catch up while rolling matching jade facial massagers across our chins; she claims they help keep wrinkles at bay. Which I think would please Mom, who loved Liza deeply and marveled over how smart, strong, and funny she is. (Mom, too, had a thing about wrinkly necks, drawing a scarf atop hers on one particularly bad driver's license photo.) Liza once helped Mom buy a mattress for her guest bed—Mom being too cheap to pay for delivery, of course—only to watch it slide out the back of her husband's pickup truck in the middle of a busy intersection. Liza pulled over, stopped traffic, and single-handedly heaved the mattress over her head and back into the truck.

Liza was far closer to my mom than to Cookie. In her thirties, she had a replica of Mom's signature tattooed on her forearm. In Mom's sloped cursive, the tattoo said, "Love, Gramma XOXOXO."

As Mom's dementia worsened, she was bowled over by Liza's tattoo every time she noticed it, saying, "You still have that?"


COOKIE HATED THAT THEIR RELATIONSHIP had grown so distant. "I wish we were closer," she said. There was a lot she hated, it turned out, as she spoke freely about things she'd never told anyone in our family: namely, the isolation enforced by her controlling husband, her lack of agency, and the fact that she, as a disabled septuagenarian with limited mobility, couldn't even go to church. Her husband wasn't allowing it at the time, saying he feared she'd catch COVID. Like her diabetic son-in-law who turned down two transplants, Cookie had refused a COVID vaccine.

She feels sorry for her husband, who has health issues that are a by-product of working for decades on concrete factory floors. She described their marriage in symbiotic terms: She helped him operate the device that relieves his chronic condition, and he cooked, shopped, and cleaned for her. Asked if she loved him, she shrugged.

"You know, you lost a lot of your family because of him," I said gently.

"Well, that's true," she said. And then she told me something even sadder: "I think a lot, I just wish one of us would die already."

There would be a better reward coming in the afterlife, she believed. Cookie considered herself a righteous Christian warrior, a staunch defender of family values and the right to life. I saw her as a victim of trauma, toxic religiosity, and a broken masculinity that had manifested itself in helplessness and poor health, all of it colored by unspeakable shame.

In my more generous moments, I thought the truth might rest somewhere between our polar-opposite viewpoints. But mostly I sensed an ever-widening gulf between my sister and me, and it ran far deeper than politics. It was full of pain and loneliness, and I couldn't find a bridge.

As the interview wound down, Cookie asked about my kids. In what felt like a moment of shared vulnerability, I told my sister, "Max thinks you don't like him because he's gay."

"I love him, but I don't like that he's gay," she countered. "I pray for him."

And for the next five minutes, Cookie called upon the Old Testament to spew the most hurtful, stereotyping things about my productive, engaged twenty-nine-year-old son.

She wanted to know if I'd read the Scripture, from Leviticus, that said that a male "shall not lie with a male as with a woman; it is an abomination."

My son is not an abomination. I refused to dignify the question. She asked again.

"But, Cookie, he's happy!" I said. "Don't you want him to be happy?"

"I thought I was happy, too, when I was running around with every Tom, Dick, and Harry."

It didn't matter that he wasn't running around with every Tom, Dick, and Harry, or that his fiancé is a beautiful person with a great job, a loving family, and a big heart.

"God made man and woman for one another; that's the way it's supposed to be," she said. "The pastor explained it—"

"According to your theology," I said.

"According to the truth of God's word."

"According to what you think is the truth of God's word."

It hit me then that this was not the humble, empathetic, and respectful tone advised by my trauma-informed experts and rural-urban bridge builders. Until this moment, we had managed to map out some common ground—our pride for Liza, funny memories of Woody—but when it came to my kid, I was all adrenaline. My heart took over, and it was racing. My face turned red. I took a deep breath.

"Cookie, I'm getting mad," I said. "If we're going to have any connection at all, I think we can't talk about this." She nodded.

As I packed up to go, I thanked my sister for the visit. Calmly I said, "Well, I guess I won't invite you to the wedding."

She thanked me back, and just as calmly she said, "Well, I guess I wouldn't come."

NOT LONG AFTER THE INTERVIEW, I met Silas for lunch at Clark State. I was eager not only to hear about his latest developments at the college but also to tell him about my conversation with Cookie. We ate the usual (quesadillas), toured the welding facilities, and talked to his instructor, Blake Parrett, who was already hopeful that Silas would return to the studio one day to help him teach welding classes. He's that good.

It was midway through his first semester, and Silas had just quit McDonald's to join his mom and stepdad on the third shift of the car-parts factory where they work in Sunbury, just north of Columbus. He'd been hired for a robotic welding job, which his teacher viewed as a helpful adjunct to the precision hand welding he was learning in class, with opportunities for advancement once he earned his certification in May 2024. In the meantime, he'd have full medical benefits and earn $18 an hour and, theoretically, still have time for classes and homework during the day.

Somewhere in between, if the planets lined up, he might even get some sleep. That was the plan.

Legally, it was Elizabeth James who'd been hired by the factory, though Silas was about to start the process of changing his name. He told me the first thing he always tells job interviewers is this: "My name is Silas, and I'm trans. If you can't handle that, I'll work somewhere else. Have a nice day."

"Most people are like, 'No, that's fine,'" he said. "I'm very lucky that I haven't had any issues. Also, I pass pretty well."[14]

We both laughed at that, recalling our first meeting in Urbana at an Italian restaurant on the public square, earlier in the year. A drunk middle-aged man staggered out of the place at 5:00 p.m. and would not stop interrupting us, at one point sitting down at our outdoor table and demanding to know what we were talking about. A manager finally intervened, we moved inside, and the guy eventually left—but not before saying to me, "Come on, just hire him!" He thought I was interviewing Silas for a job.

As adult children of addicted people, Silas and I were both triggered by the man's slurring words and his hovering. "I was like, 'Dude, space! Put down the bottle!'" Silas remembered.

Still, we had noticed right away that, though drunk dude was making us both nervous, he did use the correct pronoun. Indeed, Silas now passed, and to be honest, now that we knew each other, I rarely gave his gender identity a thought.

I WAS STILL REELING from my Cookie interview, still wondering how my own sister could think of her nephew as an "abomination" instead of delighting in the memory of the little boy she had always known to be different from most. As a preschooler, he'd insisted on wearing red-ruby slippers to school and a matching cape I made, at his request, by whipstitching part of an old corduroy shirt of his dad's onto one of his turtlenecks.

"Did he get made fun of?" Cookie asked me, a bit of curiosity that felt like a momentary window of empathy.

Not until kindergarten, I told her, at which point he stopped dressing that way and commenced being an angry, sometimes sullen child with nervous tics that included chewing the hell out of his T-shirt collars.

"There was nothing he did or we did to make him this way," I explained. "It's just who he was from the get-go." When Max came out as gay during college, he stopped joining us on visits to Ohio; he told me he was afraid Cookie would say something rude to him, and he would have to "go off." During Mom's last week, he asked me over the phone, "If Grandma knew I was gay, do you think she would mind?"

I sputtered, "Of course she wouldn't." But I had no idea. They shared a rebel streak; he loved that she'd once taught him to gamble with nickels and dimes playing our family's favorite card game, oh hell. From her bedside, I texted him a snapshot from a photo album; he was three or four. The two of them were playing with a Playmobil castle she'd picked up for him at a yard sale. Max wore a headband he'd fashioned from a ribbon, taking on the role of princess. Folded into a miniature chair, Mom beamed.

WHEN I TOLD SILAS ABOUT COOKIE, he said his parents used to be homophobic, too. "My mom knew I was gay at four, and by nine she understood that I was trans, though she didn't know what exactly it was. But she knew I was not a girl."

At nine, he would break down crying to his mom, whom he described as "very, very Christian." He told her that he prayed to be straight, that he wished he felt like a girl. When she asked what he wanted to be as an adult, he didn't hesitate to respond, "I want to be a dad."

"She now thinks that God gave her me because she was homophobic, to show her that, like, 'It's not a choice.' She very well knows that none of this is a choice," Silas said.

It was so obvious to Silas's teachers who he was that when he told his eighth-grade principal he would not be wearing the requisite dress to his high school promotion ceremony, the principal responded, "I'm not going to make you." It was his first time wearing a suit.

This, in a town that just a decade before had canceled its long-standing Memorial Day Parade rather than allow the entry of an LGBTQ float. This seemed to me evidence that people's views can shift.

But it was soul-stirring stories—and genuine on-the-ground exposure to difference—that moved people to change their minds, not data, and certainly not lectures from professors, smug bureaucrats, or degree-toting little sisters.

THE SEISMIC CULTURAL SHIFTS happening across the nation and in the courts had seemed to occur slowly, then all at once—the Supreme Court's approval of gay marriage in 2015, for instance, or the demographic news that the United States will be a majority-minority country by the year 2042.[15] And while those shifts had even filtered down to parts of my conservative, 220-year-old hometown, they hadn't permeated everyone's perspectives, not by a long shot.

Were the mounting culture wars simply growing pains on our path to a multiethnic democracy championing human rights for all, or were we headed for a second civil war?

"I ask myself that question every day," said Lilliana Mason, the Johns Hopkins political scientist.

*Eight*

# TRIBALISM

*The U.S. and Ohio flags fly over Monument Square,*
*but Confederate flags can also be seen a few blocks away.*

I f you were to judge Urbana today by the tchotchke shops dotting its public square, you might think that everybody sends their kids to Ohio State University, wears a cross necklace, and drives a Ford F-150 when they're not out on their tractors. During my first reporting trip home, I nabbed a birdhouse that a local artisan had fashioned into a lamp. It had the look of something you'd see in a catalog for $400, and it seemed like the perfect representation of my hometown as I once knew it, in that it was as useful as it was lovely, and it only set me back fifty bucks.

In recent years and especially during COVID-19, newcomers began migrating to Urbana, pushing the population up slightly to around 11,500 people,[1] drawn by the town's relatively low housing prices, its attractive town square, and the fact that you can commute to both Dayton and Columbus in roughly an hour. The newcomers are responsible for much of the town's newfound outward vibrancy. On the square, there's now a brewery, a wine and tapas bar, and a Venezuelan restaurant. There are loft apartments you can rent with marble countertops and brick interior walls. A vacant furniture store is being turned into a co-working space up the street.

The square's flagship department store, Uhlman's, where I once bought clothes with my paper-route money, closed decades ago; it had been bought out by a chain not long after Walmart opened in Urbana in 1989.[2] But now Urbana has homegrown boutiques and local coffee shops, about which Urbana's mayor, Bill Bean, enthused, "We've got coffee out the ying-yang."

But as the drunk who crashed my interview with Silas demonstrated, it doesn't take long to bump into the town's darker side. Down the street from an Airbnb where I sometimes stayed, in a neighborhood of once-prominent Victorian homes, the vibe is a mash-up of home-tour elegance and DIY go-to-hell, as exemplified by a long narrow sign next to a front door that I mistook for one of those country-cute WELCOME signs, not unlike my birdhouse turned lamp. Instead, in homemade letters, this sign read,

F
U
C
K
O
F
F

A yard-sale sign I spotted captured the same zeitgeist in different language:

## COME BUY OUR SHIT. WE B BROKE.

ON OUR WORKING-CLASS WALNUT Street block, most homes now have security cameras perched along the porch rafters—including one with a motion-sensor recording that startled me as I walked past on the sidewalk, blaring, "You. Are. Being. Recorded." In a twist, our old house is now the nicest one on the block, with siding that doesn't rub off on your shirt and a front porch teeming with well-tended houseplants. Its current owner, a factory middle manager, refused to let me see the place after I asked him via letter, a response for which his wife later apologized. "My husband is paranoid about a stranger going through the house," she explained when I spotted her on the front porch and stopped to talk.

*My grandma Macy owned her home (left) and ours (right),
allowing my family to live in it rent-free for decades.*

The family finally let me peek inside but only months later, during a police ride-along I happened to be on when 911 operators took a call from my old address. On the street out front, an elderly neighbor riding a scooter had run into an errant manhole cover, tipped over, and needed help propping himself back up. The old kitchen had been thoroughly modernized, with appliances that don't require a match rubber-banded to a yardstick to operate them. In the living room, deer heads hung near the corner where Dad's recliner used to sit, where he'd thrashed me with the coat hanger.

The family's grown daughter still lives at home, along with her fiancé and two kids, not unlike when Cookie and the girls piled into our tiny abode. The residents were curious about the state of the house when I lived there. Were there roaches? (Yes, though my siblings insist they were "just water bugs.") Did you have to walk through the bedroom off the kitchen to get to the single bathroom? (Alas, again, yes.)

The daughter reacted enthusiastically when I pointed out my old bedroom in a lower front corner of the house, whispering that I'd lost my virginity there at the age of sixteen. "Same!" she said, pointing upstairs to her room.

When I asked what year she graduated from Urbana High, she said she'd been homeschooled by her mom, a housekeeper at nearby Urbana University before it shuttered in 2020. The closure had cost the region 150 jobs and resulted in a $30 million economic hit.[3] This, too, I discovered, figured into the town's shift away from a place that once heralded the blending of arts and literacy with scientific fact. Fear seemed to permeate the way Urbana residents conducted themselves, not just through the lenses of their home-security cameras but also in their K–12 schools.

A statewide policy of open enrollment, initiated in 1989, permitted scores of concerned Urbana parents—two busloads full, turns out—

to send their kids to the nearby village of West Liberty, an adjacent district with a more distinctly rural bent, fewer needy children, and a much higher graduation rate. Districts that lose kids via open enrollment also lose the state funding tied to those students.[4] Urbana parents even kept busing their kids to West Liberty after a 2017 school shooting took place at the high school there. No one died, but a classmate who tried to talk the seventeen-year-old shooter down was permanently disabled. "You have goodness in you," the classmate pleaded. "Let's pray together. Please stop."

"He shot him anyway," Urbana's police chief, Matt Lingrell, told me. The victim survived, but he's "still walking around with thirteen [inoperable] pellets in him."[5] A few months later, town leaders raffled off a rifle to raise money for West Liberty's Little League program.

Anticipating a shooting in one of Urbana's schools, Lingrell has begged leaders to let him add a second school resource officer to his stable, but the schools and city can't agree about which entity will pick up the tab, so the chief's proposal sits there, stalled. Right now, a single officer makes the ten-minute drive repeatedly each day between the primary and the high school buildings, responding to roughly 150 police incidents a year. Homicides and other violent crimes have tripled since Lingrell joined the force in 1984.

A former classmate advised me that Walmart was the one-stop shop for witnessing Urbana's demographic shift. A hospital CEO who commutes to Columbus, Shaun Muirhead, said, "You've got people shopping in their pajamas and yelling at their kids—*for crying!* I go to Walmart and I go, 'I come from here?'"[6]

The local historian John Bry said he regularly confronts parents cursing at their children. "I hear parents at Walmart telling their kids to 'shut the fuck up,' and I'll say to them, 'Dude, that is a three-year-old. Get your act together, or we'll go talk to the Urbana PD.'"[7] Bry's neighbor used to teach in Urbana schools, but the chaotic student behavior proved to be too much, and she, too, has since transferred to the rural enclave of West Liberty to teach.

Another old friend notices the downturn most on Friday afternoons, when kids who've been given free food for the weekends are seen sitting on the curb in front of school shoving it into their mouths as fast as they can, before their parents take it.[8]

PEOPLE WERE NOW SORTING themselves not just by geography but also according to some nebulous rubric that I couldn't quite read, whether it was those who'd shifted to homeschooling or were now sending their kids to West Liberty, where clubs like Future Farmers of America and 4-H were still popular. A local youth center employee told me she didn't mind working in Urbana, but she and her husband insisted on living in West Liberty because it was safer: Within a three-mile radius of her home in West Liberty, there were just three people on the convicted sex-offender registry. Within the same radius of the Urbana Youth Center, there were thirty.[9]

In Bry's telling, it had something to do with the racist rumblings of the old white guys seated at the Airport Café, a diner on the edge of town where you can watch small planes land in the airfield established long ago as the test field for Old Man Grimes. Not long ago, someone confronted Bry at the café over the Urbana Black Heritage Festival he helps organize, calling it "a bunch of Black Matters stuff."

WHEN I ASKED STEVEN CONN, a political scientist at nearby Miami University, to explain how the region turned from a runaway-slave haven to a place dotted with Confederate flags, he said the Stars and Bars have come to represent "a universal symbol of rebellion in some kind of low-rent way." With the declining power of unions and the concurrent rise of migrants from Kentucky and West Virginia, Conn described the shift as the "southernization of Ohio, which is why the hillbilly huckster JD Vance can run for Senate and beat the guy who represented everything Ohio used to be." He's talking about the Democratic former congressman Tim Ryan, the son and grandson of union steelworkers.

Vance beat Ryan handily, thanks in part to a last-minute $30 million contribution from a super PAC linked to the GOP Senate minority leader. Vance won Champaign County by a margin of 43 points. The venture capitalist Peter Thiel's $10 million contribution to Vance's campaign didn't hurt.[10]

Though he commutes more than an hour to the college town of Oxford, Ohio, Conn lives in the bright-blue bubble of Yellow Springs, home to Antioch College, a liberal enclave that was among the first schools to admit Blacks and designate women as full professors in the mid-nineteenth century. During trips home to see Mom, my husband and I used to ride our bikes to Yellow Springs for coffee; Mom's coffee was so weak you could almost see through it to Indiana.

We called it "cycling to the blue dot." As a teenage musician, Sasha, our youngest, sometimes busked on the upright bass in the middle of Yellow Springs—something my mom had never seen before and was miffed by. "But won't people think he's homeless?" she said. Though she insisted Yellow Springs was "weird," she loved having a beer in its Ye Olde Trail Tavern, the oldest bar in the state, also located on the old Underground Railroad path.

A town of thirty-seven hundred, Yellow Springs was now home to the comedian Dave Chappelle, an independent movie theater, a four-star restaurant, a vibrant public radio station, a worker-owned and award-winning newspaper, and a 1,125-acre nature preserve. But Conn conceded that as soon as he left the town's limits in the run-up to the Issue 1 vote to preserve the right to legal abortion, VOTE NO signs were everywhere he looked.

MY BROTHER-IN-LAW MIGHT HAVE teased me about his being "deplorable," but it was my hometown that imprinted lessons on me about justice, just as it nurtured my adoption of the journalist's creed to "comfort the afflicted and afflict the comfortable."

What happened to me was, Pam Bullard happened to me. It was 1972, and she was my first Black teacher, a second-grade style goddess who wore silver bangles on her wrist and taught us about the Black Panthers, Angela Davis, and Martin Luther King Jr. A graduate of Urbana High School and the historically Black Wilberforce University, she'd been Urbana High's first Black cheerleader as well as the first Black female on its Homecoming Court. She wore her hair in a perfect flip, like Diana Ross.

Despite the town's abolitionist heritage, growing up Black in 1960s Urbana, even as a middle-class person, was hard for Pamela Stokes Bullard (her last name is now Mack).

"I was like a token," she recalled. On away-game trips with the basketball team, she and the two Black players weren't permitted to eat in the same restaurants as their white counterparts, particularly in the western portion of the county. Her dad was a Wilberforce history professor, and her grandfather cut hair at a downtown Urbana barbershop. "He only cut white farmers' hair; that's how he made his money," she said.

The municipal pool where I lifeguarded was named in honor of her late uncle Wendell Stokes. He'd become the city's first Black councilman in the mid-1960s, after a Black teenager drowned in an unattended quarry pit—during a time when Blacks weren't permitted to go to the popular swimming hole, Muzzy Lake, and many never learned to swim.

While her family was considered Black royalty, Mrs. Bullard's dad made her register as a Republican when she turned eighteen because Urbana was Republican to its core. "He said, 'Vote any way you want, but you must register Republican'—he said it to protect me." A century after the Civil War, Blacks had just properly won the right to vote nationwide a few years before.

Before our first interview in 2023, Pamela Bullard Mack had a question she wanted to ask me. We hadn't spoken since 1972; she'd gone on to be a principal in another school district and, at seventy-five, was comfortably retired in a Dayton suburb. I tracked her down through a mutual friend on Facebook because I wanted to know more about my life-changing teacher and to thank her.

She didn't remember me exactly, but she had a hunch: "Were you the young child who had their mother buy them bracelets when you were in my class because I always wore bracelets?" The mom had grown tired of waking up to her kid's long hair tangled up in the bracelets and begged Mrs. Bullard to intervene.

I didn't remember that, but I told her about the bevy of bracelets I have long worn, for decades, on my left wrist. A month later, when I saw her for the first time in fifty years, we hugged and ceremonially clinked bracelets. She'd come to hear me speak about my latest book at the local library, long since relocated to a bigger building on the outskirts of town and, alas, no longer walkable. Judge Wilson and his wife, Linn, my favorite librarian, both retired and in their eighties, were there too.

In classic Urbana fashion, the judge already knew where I was staying that night, just as he had already gotten word that I was meeting old friends at Urbana Brewing on Monument Square afterward.

He'd recently had a stroke, and his speech was halting. Still, he managed to convey his feelings about my plans, reminding me that the Scioto Inn was so close to the brewery that I should just park my car there and walk the two blocks to the square, thereby avoiding any chance of ending up in his old court. His eyes twinkled when I asked him, "Judge, are you telling me not to drink and drive?" I walked to the brewery.

THERE IS A MOMENT that Pam Bullard Mack and I have never forgotten from her first year of teaching: When a student was heard saying the N-word, she stopped the day's lesson and went to her chalkboard. In giant capital letters, she wrote out the terrible word, every letter, and turned to the room.

"This word was used in my class," she said evenly. "And now we're going to have a conversation about it."

You could have heard a crayon hit the story-time rug.

"I taught Black history quietly," she recalled. "Nobody knew I was in that little room teaching you children how much alike you were, how much you had in common, and how to love each other."

When I admitted that my dad didn't like it when I came home from school talking about Martin Luther King, she said, "I bet he didn't. If [parents and administrators] would have found out all that I was teaching you, I probably would have lost my job!"

"You'd probably lose it today," I said.

When she went on maternity leave later that year, she was replaced by a student teacher from nearby Antioch College who went by a single name—Phoenix—and liked to travel around with her pet bird in a cage. Under the direction of Phoenix, our class wrote a local version of a book inspired by Shel Silverstein's *Giving Tree*, and nobody complained about the hippie teacher with the bird from the hippie school down the road.

Mrs. Bullard reminded me of the mirror she hung on the outside of her classroom door. Every day, as we filed in, we were supposed to look in it and tell ourselves one positive thing, even just "I am somebody."

"Some of them, they couldn't do it at first," she recalled.

She'd maintained ties with her oldest friend from Urbana, who was white, for many years, just as I have with Betty and Joy. But she'd been alarmed by the growing number of Confederate flags, a trend she blamed squarely on the presidency of Donald Trump, whom she referred to as "a monster" and "the devil walking on earth."[11]

Not long ago, a mutual Black friend of ours, Celesta Dunn, was out watering her flowers in front of her ranch house on Urbana's east end when a young man in an oversized pickup came to a stop on her busy street and screamed at her, using the same word Mrs. Bullard wrote on the board.[12] Racists had become emboldened by Trump, Celesta said, though being underestimated because of her blackness was a constant through line of her life in Urbana. A UHS guidance counselor once told Celesta that she wasn't "college material," even though her grades were top-notch, she starred in plays, and she won multiple debate-team honors. Now a retired executive assistant for the president of nearby Wittenberg University, Celesta quoted from memory a line of James Baldwin's from 1961: "To be a Negro in this country and to be relatively conscious is to be in a state of rage almost all of the time."[13]

"I haven't been shocked by anything racial since before I went to South Elementary," she said. "The talk these new parents have with their [Black] children in order to be [careful], that was a talk that wasn't even said out loud. That was like 'pass the butter.' You just understood because you were constantly denigrated because of your race."

Celesta had recently spotted an old friend, a woman she'd known for sixty years, at Walmart. "We were such old friends, we used to say, 'We grew up eating dirt.' And she refused to say hi to me. And this girl, she used to cheat off my homework, little blond thing."

But now, because Celesta sometimes makes pro-Democratic posts on Facebook, they no longer speak. She's lost about twenty friends because of politics.

Mrs. Bullard, too, had noticed shifts in her hometown—condemned houses, a homeless encampment on the edge of town. "My father owned three houses on Kenton Street; he rented them out; they were nice homes," she said. "But I can't even describe them now because they are so trashy, and it's horrible. My father would get up out of his grave if he knew. He just wouldn't believe it."


A BLOCK AWAY FROM the Man on the Monument, in the old library building where Mrs. Wilson once pointed me toward her favorite books, volunteers tutor at-risk kids from Urbana's schools, and retired teachers drill them on homework, help dropouts prepare for GED tests, and hand out toiletries and snacks. The same painted sign hangs over the front counter, saying, BOOKS ARE KEYS TO KNOWLEDGE.

The Urbana Youth Center survives mainly on donations, and the center's lack of governmental support weighs on its director, Justin Weller. A former Hillclimber football standout who, at twenty-seven, became an entrepreneur, Weller attempted to take on the good-old-boy network in 2019, running for mayor as an independent and losing—by just two hundred votes—to the longtime mayor, Bill Bean.

The town's leaders don't think much of Weller, because he tends to call things as he sees them: the four-year high school graduation rate of 81 percent, the soaring free and reduced lunch rate, the sky-high ACE scores. Only five of the eighty kids who attend the youth center come from two-parent households. Weller's critics argue that he runs the center too loosely, while others just don't know what to make of the former offensive lineman and star Hillclimber who's now married to a man. "Some think he's a groomer," Mr. Sapp, the band director, told me, referring to an accusation often leveled without justification against gay and trans people.

In the fall of 2023, Weller was counting on receiving the next installment of a $2.25 million grant that the youth center had been awarded from the State of Ohio to renovate and expand the old library turned youth center. Art Wills,

*After narrowly losing a mayoral election, Justin Weller opened the Urbana Youth Center.*

a project manager from the state, appeared at the center's ceremonial groundbreaking in August 2023. After a news article about the ceremony ran in *The Urbana Daily Citizen*, Weller was told the grant had been nixed because city leaders from the school board, mayor's office, and city council refused to write letters of support for the project. An exasperated official from the state told youth center volunteers, "We've never had a community turn away our money before."

As the retired math teacher and youth center volunteer April Jackson put it, "It's really hard to know the ins and outs of what's going on in our community and then have our leaders not see the issues, deny that the issues exist, and then work to defeat anybody trying to help or intervene."[14]

PROBABLY THE BEST DESCRIPTION of rising inequality in Urbana came from April's husband, a retired UHS history teacher and long-time coach, Lance Jackson, who seemed to be a modern-day Mrs.

*Retired UHS coach and teacher Lance Jackson helps at-risk students at the youth center, prepping them for GED tests, giving them rides to work, and teaching them employability skills.*

Bullard. A Weller supporter, Jackson spends most evenings at the youth center coaching dropouts for GED exams and helping them mentally keep their act together. He and his wife, April, moved to Urbana in 1985 just as I was moving away.

As Grimes switched names repeatedly and its new corporate owners lived who-knew-where, its employees dwindled from 1,400 in its postwar heyday to roughly 650. The middle class imploded in the wake of NAFTA, and those who could afford to leave Urbana left. Gradually, the Hillclimbers went from being mocked as farm kids and hicks—cheerleaders from a Columbus high school dressed in bibbed overalls at one of Jackson's first games, prancing onto the field with straw dangling from their mouths—to being taunted by opposing teams as "the thug school."

"By the time I left teaching in 2015, the middle-class group of kids had been gone for about five years, and we were left with just the top-performing kids from wealthier families and the lower-income struggling students," Jackson told me.[15] The dearth of middle-class kids made it harder for low-income kids to envision how they might get ahead, and guidance counselors no longer had the option of offering free four-year college via Pell Grants. "You had no one to point to for them to see where they might go." I thought of my high school friend Tonya (whose mom, Helen, made us lunch every day) and my dear friend Douggy, who drove everything I owned in his doctor dad's pickup truck when I moved to become a reporter in Georgia. Another hard-earned lesson from the first-gen files that no one taught me at college: I didn't know I could have asked my new boss for moving expenses. (Nobody from my family had ever moved out of state for a job; how would I know?)

Urbana was the perfect microcosm of what was happening in rural areas across the country. The unionized truck-making plant in nearby Springfield announced major layoffs, and Grimes went from operating three shifts to a skeleton crew. When the local paper mill downsized and relocated to Wisconsin, the company offered to help people move, but most declined, not wanting to leave relatives. The lucky ones landed at Honda in Marysville, while many ended up working fast-food jobs with poor benefits and halved wages.

Student test scores plummeted, and the graduation rate declined. According to the Jacksons and several other Urbana teachers I talked to, the tipping point came in 2010. That was the year school officials adopted a new assessment policy that turned homework from being required to optional, lowered the grading measurements from a 7-point to a 10-point scale, and allowed students who wanted to retake a test to do so without impacting their grade.

"They were trying to get the graduation rate up and improve the scores across the board, and what happened instead is everything got worse," Weller told me. "We moved to being okay with mediocrity but then being surprised when we don't even meet that bar." A UHS sophomore at the time, Weller took full advantage of the lighter workload but also told himself, "I'm not sure this is how life works."

The few who do leave for college rarely return home to live; the Jacksons cited just two young people among their daughters' friends who now make Urbana their home. "Once that goes on for a generation, you don't have enough families and kids who aspire to do that anymore, so the pot of college-going kids who want to be successful, or even just be college-prep ready—it just dwindles," Lance said.[16]

As he said this, it finally dawned on me that those billboards I'd wanted to erect on Urbana's Main Street, the ones informing poor kids about need-based financial aid, had been more of a pipe dream than I understood. Turning young people into happy, productive citizens couldn't just be fixed by Pell Grants, as I had naively once believed. What poor kids needed now more than anything, what our communities needed, was a robust and trauma-informed system of public education that prioritized mental health and met kids where they were—intellectually, physically, and emotionally.

When I met them, the Jacksons were considering moving to the northeastern Ohio blue dot of Oberlin, near their grown daughters, one of whom is gay and engaged. "When our daughter gets married to her wife, there are good friends here that we won't be able to invite because she'll 'rot in hell.'

"And I want to say, 'You've known her since she was three. She gave out towels and waters to girls on the basketball team. She's a beautiful, wonderful person. And now you're going to tell me how she needs to live her life to be happy or eternal damnation awaits?'" Lance said.

But the Jacksons are career public servants who also feel conflicted about moving away. They wrestle with whether it's better to stay, to try to educate people and open them up to new ideas—or, at the very least, not to hide the facts of their daughter's life. "How are we ever going to flip people to be accepting if we're not even talking about it?" Lance wanted to know. He wanted to talk to his longtime mentor, a septuagenarian who'd taught him how to coach, but the man made it clear that he believed gay people were an abomination.

"I can't say anything to him, because otherwise when he responded, I'd have to hit a seventy-five-year-old man!"

The Jacksons told me they'd grown so weary of the tribalistic, mean-spirited mindset among locals that they'd begun actively looking for property in Oberlin. "You watch, we'll all end up divvied up in districts based on our politics, just like *The Hunger Games*," Lance said.

THE CULTURAL ISSUES CLEAVING the nation seemed to take on an outsized presence in places like Urbana. As long as Monument Square looked cute, with coffee shops out the ying-yang, few in power felt pressure to address what was hiding in plain sight only a block away. By the fall of 2023, Mayor Bean was preparing to run for his fourth term, this time unopposed. And the largest civic gathering I found outside the football stadium was a combination prayer meeting and anti-abortion rally, where around seventy citizens sat and listened as a county commissioner told outright lies about the state's ballot amendment known as Issue 1.

Enshrining a woman's right to safe and legal abortion in the Ohio Constitution would gut parents' rights, such that a public school teacher would be allowed to take your child for a sex-change operation and you'd have no say in the matter, the Champaign County commissioner Nino Vitale claimed (needless to say falsely).

"We could have people coming into Ohio because abortion is so free and legal, and there's nothing you can do about it; we could be the abortion capital," he said, in a hyped-up cadence that ascended to a fever pitch. "The killing will be everywhere. And they are already selling body parts, and they make good money on it, unfortunately."

The crowd gasped. The crown on the reigning Champaign County Fair Queen bobbed as she nodded her head.

"Jeepers!" a woman near me kept repeating. No one from the newspaper reported on the event. Five weary Democrats huddled near the back but didn't speak.

When the votes were cast a few weeks later, Issue 1 passed state-wide with a 57 percent majority, owing mostly to the votes from Ohio's cities. In Champaign County, 58 percent voted no. As the law currently stands, a woman can have an abortion in Ohio through the twenty-second week of pregnancy, although Republican lawmakers moved immediately to undercut the majority voters' will.

Republicans have been competitive in Ohio for most of the state's history, but they've changed. "Thirty years ago the Republicans were middle-of-the-road, country-club conservatives," Conn, the political scientist, told me. "And now you have to be the most extreme person out there to win." When Reagan aligned with Jerry Falwell and other evangelicals, Republicans believed they'd be able to contain the fervor of white Christian nationalists. "But they couldn't keep the dog on the leash, and those folks eventually took over, which is how Trump executed a hostile takeover of the Republican Party." Because of gerrymandering, Ohio is practically a one-party state now, not unlike southern states during Jim Crow.

Conn, who's also served on school and economic development boards in western Ohio, believes the most successful rural leaders rise to power by appealing to single-issue voters. "I've had conservatives tell me they understand that Republican economic policies aren't good for them; they're not dumb, but it's this fixation on fetuses," Conn said of the realization among Republican politicians that abortion soapboxing is the surest path to power.

Beyond abortion, Conn struggled to understand why the nation's rural-urban divide has flared to such a fevered pitch. "With the Civil War, you get it; it's chattel slavery. But what's the existential crisis that's driving today's divide? The best I can come up with is that maybe it's the way information circulates now. The way in which you can separate yourself into totally separate epistemological universes."[17]

As he said this, my retired siblings were all home with Fox and Newsmax blaring in the background of their living rooms. Except for John, my eighty-three-year-old brother-in-law, who was spending the last part of 2023 battling pneumonia and COPD, moving between hospital and rehab facilities. His wife, my sister Terry, who was disabled by childhood polio and now uses an electric scooter, visited him most days in their handicapped-accessible van, often with the help of Liza or our brother, Tim. I helped, too, when I was in town.

During an earlier visit to their condo, John flipped between CBS ("to see what the liberals were up to") and the Christian Broadcasting Network in the living room, his oxygen tank tethered to him, while I talked to Terry in their kitchen. He'd never been religious before, but with his COPD worsening, John told me he'd decided to hedge his bets on Pat Robertson's version of the afterlife. He was a frugal person who made his own wine, yogurt, and almond milk to save money, and they'd only recently gotten a smartphone because Liza and I coordinated with the family to buy Terry one for Christmas. We worried that John might be offended by the gift, but all he wanted to know was who would pay the monthly bill. (My husband and I added Terry's phone to our family plan.)

But when John started mailing monthly donation checks to CBN and asked Terry to continue the practice after his death, I understood that more than just their media diets had changed.

As I said goodbye, Terry marveled at the Canadian wildfire smoke, which had descended on Ohio that week, coloring the sky orange. "What's with all this smoke?" she asked. "I've never seen anything like it before."

And for the second time, my rural-urban bridge training drifted out the haze-covered window as I snapped, "Terry, it's climate change!"

Whereupon she and John looked at each other and rolled their eyes. The next day I found the most basic, apolitical description of how rising temperatures were causing the surge in lightning strikes that spurred the Canadian wildfires—from CBS News, a network my sister and I had once watched together faithfully—and texted it to Terry, writing, "Love you, thanks for having me. I know we read different news, but here's CBS's take." She didn't respond.

THE DAY AFTER OHIOANS VOTED to legalize abortion through the twenty-second week, I made dinner for my friend Joy—a quiche with a homemade crust that was loaded with broccoli, heavy on the Gruyère. A picky eater, Joy had never tried quiche before, but she liked it so much she had seconds.

*Joy Ware Miller and I have been dear friends since the first day of kindergarten, but we can't discuss politics without one of us becoming insulted or exasperated.*

The marketing director of a local Christian radio station, she is also a lay minister and inspirational speaker and author who conducts workshops on grief and for years hosted a radio program called *Joy in the Morning* with a loyal following that included my sister Cookie. In 2005, she lost her thirteen-year-old son, Christopher, to sudden cardiac arrest on the basketball court of the Champaign County YMCA in Urbana.

Fifteen years later, as Mom

struggled to gasp her final breath, it was Joy who sat in her car outside Mom's nursing home, praying and sending me loving text messages. Mom never belonged to a church, but she knew and loved Joy, who'd given me hundreds of rides to school. As a gift for being a bridesmaid in her 1987 wedding, Joy made me a collage with a Proverbs quotation and a calligraphy note about trading back rubs while watching TV, a frequent Macy pastime we had passed on to her: *Back rubs brought us close. Friendship bound us together. I Love You. Joy.*

When I suggested to my siblings that Joy conduct Mom's graveside funeral, everyone agreed, and it was perfect. A bagpiper played as we gathered, I read a poem about grief that Mom had clipped from *The New Yorker* after our stepdad's death, and my husband and our youngest sang "Amazing Grace." It was the height of COVID, and only one relative—a great-nephew who came late to the service—refused to wear a mask.

Joy didn't flinch when my brother-in-law John recited Mom's favorite bawdy toast: "Here's to the girl who lives on the hill. She won't do it, but her sister will. Here's to her sister."

During dinner, Joy told me that it had been a very disappointing day for her community because women could now kill their babies after birth.

"Joy, that's not true," I said, aiming for an even tone.

"I'll send you a link," she said. Later, she claimed that George Floyd didn't die from having a police officer's knee pressed against his neck for nine minutes, and when I questioned the accuracy of that statement, another link was promised. But the links never came.

"I'm Black, but I'm not racially triggered," she said, decrying the "lack of home raising" she ascribed to Black Lives Matter activists in the wake of Floyd's murder. "Look, I know we don't agree on a lot of stuff, and that's okay because I love you enough to love you and not push myself," she said. At a restaurant during one of my earlier trips, when she challenged the integrity of mainstream news organizations like *The New York Times*, I tried to explain how thorough and rigorous the *Times*'s fact-checking department was: One fact-checker I worked with had managed to track down a homeless addicted person I'd interviewed who no longer had the same phone number; then she talked to him for an hour to confirm my account of his story. Another opinion piece received a solid ten hours of fact-checking; it was so in-depth it felt as if my brain had undergone a colonoscopy.

"Yeah, but who fact-checks the fact-checkers?!" Joy said, angry in a pitch I hadn't before heard from her. (She apologized later.) But when I said my back was hurting from the seven-hour drive from Virginia, she reached over at the restaurant and rubbed it for ten minutes while we chatted with Betty, and our mutual friend, Amy Puglia Hunter, in town from Atlanta, who stopped in to visit.

Joy believed a second civil war loomed, caused by a media that promoted falsehoods. "The false narratives are being so elevated, and we're in a tight situation in our culture where people want to create their own reality," she said.

We didn't agree on much, but Joy appreciated my cooking, and we reminisced about rides to school in the red Riviera her parents bought her when she turned sixteen. "You'd get in the car with your bacon sandwich and your softball gear with your hair still wet. You'd still be finishing your homework in the car. And I'd be like, 'That girl!' You were just . . . savvy. I grew up pretty protected and sheltered, but you were always like, 'Let's just do it!'" She was not the kind of kid who shoplifted earrings or drove through Dickie Pooh's, although once in first grade she pulled out my chair from underneath me as I sat. I hit the floor hard, and when I shrieked, she quickly clapped her hand over my mouth; her mom, a teacher who didn't tolerate shenanigans in her home or in the classroom, taught down the hallway, and Joy didn't want to be found out.

She'd recently heard that schoolchildren were being allowed to self-identify as cats, to the point of carrying litter boxes to school. I'd heard that one before at our cabin in rural Virginia, from a local handywoman hired to stain our deck. But I didn't realize it had become a mainstream-right notion about the daft ideas of woke liberals.[18] Joy knew I had two queer kids and seemed, if not exactly approving, then at least nonvocal about it, even inquiring about our eldest's wedding plans. To return the respect, I nodded without waffling when she asked me on a girls' trip to Florida with Betty, "Have you accepted Jesus Christ as your Lord and Savior?" even though it felt intrusive.

When I shook my head at the school litter boxes, Joy responded with a question: "How do you love past what you don't agree with or can't understand?" Neither of us had a link for that. But I was pretty sure the social media corporations making money off our divisions and anger didn't care if we loved each other or not.

# Nine

# RED-PILLED

During an early trip back to Urbana, I asked an old buddy to drive me around town. A retired firefighter and EMT, Dave Curnutte was voted class clown, as was I, and we were both athletes in our sports-crazed town. Both of us also hailed from poor families with tough, Grimes-working moms and drunk dads who sometimes stumbled into the family Christmas tree.

Curnutte (pronounced cur-NOOT) remembers his mom, Alice, helping him deliver newspapers on weekends in the snow wearing her only shoes, a pair of threadbare canvas sneakers. Curnutte's dad parked behind the baseball field and watched his son from his car with a twelve-pack on the floor. "He kept a coffee can with him to pee in," said Curnutte, a pitcher on our state-championship baseball team. "Whenever I struck somebody out, Mom would honk the horn."[1] His curveball was killer; his fastball clocked at ninety-two miles an hour.

His parents couldn't afford shoes for both basketball and school, so during that season he made do with a single pair of high-tops. On game days, the point guard, my old friend Mark Evans, quietly spiffed up Curnutte's shoes so they'd kinda-sorta match everyone else's.

In school, Curnutte was popular, lovable, and goofy, about the last person you'd expect to become a key class reunion organizer. But he was nostalgic for the camaraderie of his glory days, and he'd happily volunteered for much of the reunion grunt work. I attended all but the last, our fortieth, which I missed because of a work conflict.

It pained me to miss it, until I learned about all the feuding that went down. In the lead-up to the reunion, Curnutte had reposted several pro-Trump memes on the UHS class of 1982 Facebook page that Evans, who is biracial, considered racist, unleashing a torrent of comments pro and con. "Evans won't talk to me now," Curnutte said glumly. "He called me a white supremacist."

The Evans-Curnutte debacle was only the first shot fired on the class Facebook page. Things got so tense that Curnutte left the reunion planning committee after another classmate thought he was trying to silence her when, to hear Curnutte tell it, he accidentally bungled a Facebook Live planning session. "She made a death threat against me," he said. Peppering her comments with a glorious string of expletives, she hoped he'd choke on the barbecue that he'd arranged for everyone to eat.

As we drove around Urbana, Curnutte pointed out places where he'd administered Narcan to townspeople as an EMT, as well as the homes of fellow class members whom he described as QAnon conspiracists: One ran a local store; another worked as a nurse. His catcher buddy on the state-championship team had just gotten divorced from his wife, partly because of her online conspiracy compulsions.

Curnutte identified as conservative and backed Trump but considered QAnon too extreme. "I want to say, 'Are you guys smoking dope? Because if you're not, you ought to be!'"

The pre-reunion tensions grew so fierce that many regulars skipped it, including Curnutte and my dear friend Amy Puglia Hunter, who is white and married to a college basketball coach, Ron Hunter, who is Black.[2] (When their son, R.J., shot a three-pointer to win an NCAA March Madness game for Georgia State, his coach-dad became so excited that he fell off his coaching stool. The video of R.J.'s elegant jump shot, juxtaposed with Ron's courtside splatter, has been watched millions of times and spawned its own merch, including a Ron Hunter bobblehead that captures him mid-fall.)[3] Curnutte and the other jocks from our class love Amy—everybody does—but they are *crazy* about Ron, who is legit famous in the only area upon which red and blue townies are fully aligned: sports.

For thirty-five years, Amy and Ron have endured the slights of being an interracial couple in America—including once when a passerby screamed "white trash!" at her as she drove with her little kids in car seats. Among Black friends, their kids weren't considered "dark enough," relegating them to an in-between status where they "could move in all worlds and none at the same time," as she put it.

When old friends and relatives in Urbana backed Trump with enthusiasm, Amy took it personally. "You see people you thought you knew backing somebody so racist, sexist, homophobic, misogynistic, and xenophobic—and it's like, *Who really are they?*"

She was waffling about the last reunion so much that her daughter,

*Early in the project I had dinner with my first friends Joy Ware
Miller and Betty Sherman on Monument Square when our mutual
pal, Amy Puglia Hunter (far right), popped in for a visit.*

a psychologist, took her aside and said, "Why are you stewing about
going to this thing you're dreading? Just don't go!" For the first time,
Amy sat a class reunion out.

"I liked the world better before I was totally hip to cruelty being
the point," she told me. I reached out to Amy, a former school guidance counselor who lives in Atlanta and New Orleans and visits her
nonagenarian mother in Urbana most months, because she, more than
any other Urbana expat, had kept tabs on what was going on at home,
even as she and Ron moved from one city to the next for much of
his coaching career. The youngest of a large Italian American family—
her dad was a local bank executive and her mom a UHS guidance office secretary who helped me land my first Pell Grant—Amy was a top
student and a cheerleader from a family with a fabulous sense of mis-
chief. Double-jointed at the hips, she used to let us turn her into a party
trick: She'd cross her legs behind her head, pretzel-like, and allow us
to roll her around on the floor.

"I liked the people that I used to know when they were still the people I used to know," said Amy, who refuses to speak Trump's name. "I say to myself a lot regarding the former mango in chief, I say, 'I hope he was worth it,' because our hometown backs him, and we used to have all kinds of backgrounds that came together because we only had one high school, and we were there for it."[4]

Amy also fell out for a time with some of her relatives who claimed that the Sandy Hook shooting was fake and that Americans needed to "arm ourselves against our government," who believe that Obamacare equates to communism, and "yet they love Mr. Orange, who flirts with actual communist leaders?" Visiting her mom at the height of COVID, Amy refused to acknowledge a fellow cheerleader she'd known since kindergarten in the Kroger produce section, after reading social media posts in which she spouted the nonsense that leading Democratic politicians were pedophiles.

When I asked Amy how she'd responded to our classmate's hello, her blue eyes widened in mock alarm as she slid her hand over her nose, mimicking a face mask. "Not one fucking thing," she said. "I blinked. My sister Betsy was looking at me, like, 'God, you're such a bitch.'"

In early 2024, Amy volunteered on her next trip home to undertake some "oppo research," as she called it, on my behalf. (Our weeks home rarely coincided.) At Urbana Brewing, she met Curnutte and some other buddies in an informal planning session for a proposed forty-fifth reunion. At least that's what the fellas wanted to talk about. Amy made a plea to have a constructive conversation first about how the last reunion had gone off the rails.

"I'm like, 'Slow your roll, we've got some shit to work out,'" she recalled, reporting back.

And: "It's gone pretty tribal here."

And: "The thing about the orange one is that he didn't get the wall built, but he sure put up a lot of walls between us."

But that wasn't a conversation our old classmates wanted to have. Those gathered nervously tucked in their shirts, looked around the brewery, and talked about how poorly their high school sports injuries were aging—anything not to engage. Amy didn't push it, and at the end everybody hugged like the besties they used to be, and someone suggested that perhaps smaller, informal reunions might be the best route going forward.

Sports: safe. Beer: safer. A hard discussion about racism or the fragility of democracy: untouchable.

IN THE SUMMER OF 2023, I followed up with the other class reunion organizer, Terri Thompson, the alleged QAnoner, to fact-check Curnutte's claims. As his fellow class clown, I thought I knew bullshit when I heard it.

Did Terri honestly think the nation's levers of power were controlled by a cabal of Satan-worshipping pedophiles who milk an adrenaline-like substance from the bodies of children and drink it to stay young? Did she really believe that Joe Biden was dead and the president you saw on TV was really an actor with a face mask? That 9/11 was an inside job? If Biden really imbibed from a pedophiliac fountain of youth, why was he constantly hammered for looking so old?

In a 2022 national survey, 16 percent of Americans admitted to being QAnon devotees, and among Republicans that number was 25 percent.[5] (It's 14 percent among independents and 9 percent among Democrats.) In ruby-red Urbana, the numbers seemed higher. If you believed Curnutte, QAnon had infiltrated most of Urbana's east end.

Curnutte had not been wrong. Terri even sent me follow-up "proof," including photos of the supposedly fake Biden from CNN that were "taken from my own TV," she wrote. "Look at the neck where you can see the latex mask." She sent what looked to me like obviously doctored photos of the Obamas, which she believed proved Michelle was really Michael Obama. She included a video that she claimed showed the Arctic wasn't really melting, along with aerial photos from Guantánamo Bay that she believed confirmed that Donald Trump still operated as commander in chief under the faux-Biden presidency.

She sincerely believed this information would help and protect me. She was so breathless, so thoroughly convinced of the righteousness of her cause, that it felt like piling on to refute her every claim.

"Is there no chance you're wrong?" I asked, when I finally got a word in.

"No, no, no," she said.

"Or the videos have been doctored? Because, I'll be honest, it's like we're living in two different realities."

"No!"

We were at the Depot, a coffee shop featuring baked goods and sandwiches with a rare (for Urbana) display of subtle gay pride: A rainbow flag sticker adorned the cash register. When the owner stopped by our table to say hi, Terri offered that she had recently retired from her administrative assistant job and cut her health-insurance costs in half by switching from COBRA to CareSource, Ohio's version of Medicaid—without noting Obama's role in expanding it.

Following the QAnon playbook, Terri saw parallels between the modern-day world and the film *The Matrix*: "The blue pill and red pill? Blue is life goes on as you know it. And the red pill, you find out the truth. What I'm doing right now is red-pilling it. I'm sharing the truth with you so that life as you know it has now changed."[6]

She named nine of our schoolmates who meet regularly, sometimes gathering for dinner and wine but mostly online, to compare QAnon notes. An economic development worker in Urbana I'd interviewed a month before described leaving her church after noticing how many of her fellow parishioners had turned to QAnon. "A thousand percent they think the Florida school shooting was staged," Beth McCain said, of the 2018 shooting that killed seventeen people at Marjory Stoneman Douglas High School.[7] At the optometry office where she used to work, "people are completely comfortable saying the election was rigged because they just assume I believe it too, and there's no media here to contradict it."

But to hear it firsthand from Terri, a beloved sweetheart who used to own a downtown gift-basket shop called Terri's Touch, my jaw dropped. "I know," Terri said, halfway through her diatribe. "I thought it was crazy at first, too."

Lumping Tom Hanks, Oprah Winfrey, and Democrats generally together under the category of pedophiles had become just another pass-the-butter statement for people like Terri. Beyond them, she blamed our growing divisions on the media. When I asked about the myriad documented claims of fraud and sexual assault against Trump, she said, "He's not a perfect man by any means. I didn't even like him before. Then I found out all that he's done to save this nation and how the media has turned everybody against him."

She'd learned about the Great Awakening, as QAnoners call it, five years ago from a former Urbana schoolmate of ours who now lives in Florida. The friend posted something about it on Facebook with a provocative note: "Just you wait, there's a whole lot more you're going to be shocked about." A divorcée who lives alone, Terri reached out to our schoolmate privately, and within the span of a few days she was sucked into her friend's online maelstrom. She was as happy and as bubbly as I'd ever seen her.

With the decline in marriage and church attendance as well as in volunteerism and other forms of civic life, I wondered how much loneliness factored into the rise of the conspiratorial mindset.[8] It seemed sharpest among those who hadn't gone to college, where you're socialized to give facts that support your opinions. College is also the place where you get exposed to myriad kinds of people; I made my first Jewish friend at college (I knew of no Jews in Urbana) and befriended people who traveled abroad and joined the Peace Corps and other things I'd had little exposure to before. My college roommate, a math whiz and the daughter of a suburban-Toledo dentist, played cello in the university orchestra, subscribed to *The Atlantic* and *Harper's*, and had a wealthy aunt who regularly sent her "pizza and lipstick money"—all things I enjoyed and even benefited from (except when she talked out trigonometry problems in her sleep) but could not at all relate to.

Terri hadn't gone to college, but plenty of other conspiracy devotees I met in the region had.

"WHEN PEOPLE GET ONLINE, they're able to find more people who feel the way they do much more quickly than they used to, and they begin to think that rare behavior is ordinary," explained the New York University assistant provost Clay Shirky, a leading voice on the internet's impact. QAnon devotees are obsessed with pedophilia, Shirky said, "because they need a crime so heinous that people across the political spectrum can agree that 'those people are bad,' whereas if they accused them of the crime of not integrating African Americans into widespread society . . . some will think that's awful and some won't."

It's a rope-a-dope, not unlike rhetoric about Mexico paying for a border wall getting the biggest cheers at MAGA rallies. Even without a realistic immigration plan, blustery outrage is enough to light up an audience. It's politically advantageous to keep calling immigrants rapists, vermin, and inhuman.

Once people fear racial replacement, they become too distracted to think about the country's real struggles, like small towns suffering from trickle-down theories that have failed regular Americans for generations. Like the democracy-quashing seduction of online conspiracists and their full-on hatred of journalists who fact-check lies.

Outside the Depot, where I met Terri and many other Urbanans for interviews, I read and reread the historical marker erected to honor what transpired there on April 29, 1865. That night, a shrouded funeral train stopped in Urbana for fifteen minutes to present the body of President Abraham Lincoln, who was murdered by the white supremacist John Wilkes Booth six days after Robert E. Lee surrendered to Ulysses S. Grant, an Ohio native. About three thousand Urbanans—almost everyone in town—huddled in solidarity next to bonfires by the railroad tracks. Church bells pealed, and ten young women entered the train car to place flowers on Lincoln's bier. A chorus of forty people, Black and white, sang the hymn "Go to Thy Rest."[9]

During every visit to Urbana, I kept stopping to reread the plaque, trying for some connection of the disparate dots.

THE SINGLE THRIVING SOURCE of fact-based journalism I found anywhere near my Ohio hometown was a Columbus-based online news site called Ohio Capital Journal. Edited by a former Athens, Ohio, newspaper reporter named David DeWitt, the OCJ operates under the umbrella of the nationwide nonprofit States Newsroom, a network of correspondents in fifty states that investigates the impact of statehouse leaders' policies on people's lives. In five years, the OCJ's biggest stories have been about Ohio Republican lawmakers' continued gerrymandering even after voters passed anti-gerrymandering reform;[10] the largest political bribery scandal in Ohio history, in which the Speaker of the House and four others were paid millions in exchange for bailing out a nuclear power operator with taxpayer money;[11] and the Republican supermajority's unsuccessful efforts to block getting an abortion rights measure on the ballot by raising the threshold for passing constitutional amendments from a simple majority to 60 percent.[12]

"We are constantly trying to correct the misinformation going on," DeWitt said, through original reporting by veteran journalists (many of them hired by the OCJ after being laid off by legacy newspapers) and guest op-eds written by analysts, experts, and scholars. "We are described as left leaning, but I really feel we're just standing up for small-*d* democracy—not being left or right, just patriotic," DeWitt said.

"I have to still think that the majority of people are loving, sane, normal people who want a peaceful, comfortable, communal life." Indeed, surveys show that two-thirds of Americans are actually in between the extremes of either side; they're known as "the exhausted majority," the quiet and underreported middle ground, many of whom are avoiding news altogether.[13]

"But I worry about the psychosis going on that makes normal people want to tune out. That apathy is very dangerous, and if normal people don't participate, that allows the crazy people to run amok, even though they're not a majority," DeWitt said.[14] Just one in ten rural voters are classified as "rabble-rousers," the politically obsessed types who tend to dominate school board and town council meetings.[15]

WHEN I ASKED PEOPLE in Urbana if they read the Ohio Capital Journal online—which is free because it operates on grants and donations, without a paywall or advertisements—no one, save my former Urbana newspaper editor, had even heard of it.

When my friend Terri swore to me that Trump is "God anointed" and called members of my profession Satan-worshipping pedophiles,

I thought of the Canadian research psychologist Dr. Bruce Alexander, who is arguably the world's foremost authority on addiction. Asked recently to name the most harmful addiction out there, he didn't say alcohol, which kills nearly five hundred Americans a day; or fentanyl, an opioid that kills more than seventy thousand people a year, most of them in their prime; or even tobacco, which kills nearly half a million Americans a year.

No, Alexander cited right-wing conspiracies like QAnon, which he described as a fanatical mass devotion to political cult leaders like Adolf Hitler, Jair Bolsonaro, and Donald Trump.[16]

THE BROWN UNIVERSITY ASSOCIATE professor Stefanie Friedhoff, who studies information ecosystems, blamed not just misinformation for the rise in conspiratorial thinking but also the paucity of good local journalism; where it does exist, it's too often behind a paywall. She cited the excess of national information on free internet platforms like Facebook and YouTube, much of it conflicting, inaccurate, and out of date.

"You used to be able to call someone to find resources, but right now you can't even get a person on the phone," Friedhoff, a former journalist, said. "We're in a place technologically where there's so much information out there, but we don't yet have the tools to navigate it." A German immigrant, Friedhoff worries daily about the American slide into fascism. "My parents were raised by Nazis!" she said. "I have a strong sensibility to want to point out that people are not intrinsically evil."

The best strategy for overcoming misinformation around vaccine hesitancy, for instance, is to have a conversation with someone you already trust, Friedhoff says, "but that is hard to scale."

The Pulitzer-winning Appalachian author Barbara Kingsolver, whose *Demon Copperhead* chronicled the life of a country kid with trauma levels akin to Silas's, echoed Friedhoff's advice. "People take their truths from other people they trust; they don't use evidence to decide what's true," Kingsolver told me. But because national news is manufactured in cities, and rural people feel condescended to by city people, they've become so frustrated with a system that has proven itself impotent to correct problems that they think the only solution is to burn everything down.

"When people are living with a lot of trauma and poverty, it changes their thinking process; they see things more in black and white, all or nothing," she added. "My plea is for respect—to think about talking with people who disagree with you and carrying some respect into that conversation because nothing else will work."[17]

ON MY THIRD TRIP HOME, I met up with my ex-boyfriend Bill, whom I hadn't laid eyes on in thirty-eight years. During the Reagan years, in our western swath of Ohio, Bill was a recent graduate of Miami University and probably the most liberal person I knew. (He's the one who fixed my broken VW seat with the cutting board and gave me that "The Moral Majority Is Neither" sticker.) He went to Grateful Dead shows and planted herbs and vegetables, and for most of our yearlong courtship—long distance between Cincinnati, where he worked as a newspaper reporter, and my college town of Bowling Green—he wooed me by mail with scores of cartoons he'd drawn from his daily life that were quirky, self-deprecating, and full of joy.

When a mutual friend described watching Bill turn from an NPR-tote-bag-carrying Bernie Sanders supporter to someone on the far right who got most of his news from the Duran, a right-wing website based in Cyprus with known connections to Moscow spy agencies, I thought he had to be mistaken.[18] "I don't know how to describe it, but he suddenly just turned really . . . *angry*," the friend said. When I asked if he thought it was safe to meet with Bill in public, he said, "I think so."

For our first interview, Bill showed up in jeans and a sport coat, looking sharp. It was St. Patrick's Day, and he'd asked for an early dinner reservation—5:00 p.m.—because "the cops will probably be out" for the holiday, which confused me. The plan was to interview him about his shifting politics, not to get plastered.

As soon as he sat down, he said, "Sorry I was such a douchebag," referring to the end of our relationship. He'd cheated on me with a newspaper co-worker and, when I found out about it, broke up with me abruptly over the phone.

"Yeah, you were," I said. "But it's okay; I'm good." We laughed nervously.

He was sixty-one and presently single, after marrying the same woman twice. They were divorced and the parents of two grown kids when she died of cancer in 2020; he'd helped care for her at the end. He said he'd left journalism decades before for a job in the public sector but grew disillusioned with government's tendency toward waste and political corruption and retired early.

He owns a house in nearby Springfield, where he grows most of his own food with the goal of "decreasing my participation in the system, a system I realized is doomed to collapse like the Ponzi scheme it is."[19] He spends four to seven hours a day watching news on YouTube. When I asked whom he hung out with, he named his grown kids— "although my daughter thinks I'm a cultist," he said—and his next-door neighbor, Mike, a former Hells Angels member convicted of manslaughter many years ago but who actually, Bill insisted, is a very sweet guy. He had taken Bill in after part of his property was set on fire by a neighborhood fentanyl dealer. Mike had his back.

The reunion dinner stretched over three hours, and I mostly enjoyed it. The only awkward part came when, in the middle of describing his political conversion, he repeatedly steered the conversation back to Hillary Clinton. His hatred of her was over the top. He claimed she'd ordered the deposed Libyan strongman Muammar Qaddafi "raped up the ass with a bayonet and then laughed about it. She's a monster."

Indeed, Clinton had laughed on camera about Qaddafi's death to a CBS News reporter, saying, "We came, we saw, he died."[20] According to Human Rights Watch, it wasn't clear exactly how the Libyan dictator died, though the organization confirmed that Misrata-based militias wounded him with a bayonet in his buttocks, then pummeled him with kicks and blows. He was also shot in the head and abdomen.

When I offered that I hadn't read his version of the story in the national newspapers I read daily—*The New York Times* and *The Washington Post*—he smirked and said, "The *Times* is fully captured by the Democratic Party, whereas the *Post* is wholly owned by the CIA. They're going to tell you what those two groups want you to think." He hadn't trusted those papers since their failure to hold politicians to account for the false weapons of mass destruction claim in the buildup to the Iraq War. "Corporate media's job is to keep its audience smug in its bubble and to keep the nation divided over falsely framed issues," he said.

About the Iraq War mistakes, he wasn't wrong, of course. But it was strange to be sharing family stories in my favorite restaurant, only to be steered back to Qaddafi's brutal death time and again, something Bill returned to often in subsequent meetings. He was furious about Obamacare, saying his health-care premiums doubled in the wake of its passage. "It was all about getting poor people health care off the backs of the middle class," he said. He wanted nothing to do with it and hadn't had health insurance since he quit his last job. (If he had, he might have learned how lifesaving the ACA has been for the forty-five million low-wage Americans, including my musician kid, presently relying on it.)

But Bill's skepticism explained our 5:00 p.m. dinner reservation: He can't drive at night. His cataracts could be surgically removed, and he was thinking of paying cash for it, but he wasn't sure. The Democratic Party has totally sold out to the "deep state," he said, held hostage by warmongering, group-thinking globalists who believe they're smarter than everyone else when in reality their success and wealth are largely inherited or else ill-gotten off the labors of "regular-ass people" like him and Mike.

Because I remembered my trauma-informed advice to talk about more than politics, between visits we traded tips on gardening, and I brought him a seedling of my favorite heirloom tomato (a Berkeley green tie-dye variety), which he nurtured and sent me photographs of via text. He emailed detailed critiques about the left-wing sowing of gender dysphoria and of *The New York Times*'s 1619 Project, which he called an effort "to demonize Caucasians to foster further social polarization and disintegration."

In one seven-thousand-word email he jokingly called his manifesto (he'd titled it "The Road to Apostacy"), he described the harrowing effects of NAFTA on his hometown and state, which lost almost a third of its manufacturing jobs post-NAFTA.[21] Given that parts of Springfield now lie derelict, with escalating violent crime,[22] a 43 percent chronic absenteeism rate in the schools,[23] and one of the highest overdose rates in Ohio,[24] it was a fair point. Many of his theories contained chunks of truth that liberals like me are in the knee-jerk habit of dismissing out of hand.

Bill further soured on the Democratic Party when the Monica Lewinsky scandal broke, followed quickly by the U.S. military's bombing of Serbia, which he saw as a scheme meant to take American eyeballs off the sex-with-an-intern ball. After eight years of Obama ("a crushing disappointment"), he became a third-party independent, voting for Jill Stein in 2016. He hated that Obama had essentially reneged on a promise to change bankruptcy laws that would have helped struggling homeowners during the 2008 recession while bailing out big banks and carmakers, and Obama's support for unprecedented mergers in big tech and pharma.[25] About that, Bill wasn't wrong.

But his friends were furious about his support of Stein, calling it a vote for Donald Trump. A deacon at his church even invited Bill out for beers before the 2016 election, only to excoriate him for his planned vote. Bill joked that a mutual friend must have had a secret local influencers' meeting where someone said, "I need to unfriend [Bill]; some of his ideas aren't resonating within my echo chamber, and [the deacon] was like, 'Hold my latte.'" Other friends called him a fascist to his face. He left the church, dropped Facebook, and cut off connections with many old friends. No wonder he was angry.

Back then, he said, grabbing women by their genitals was among the most damning criticisms of Trump. "But he didn't say he did it; he just said he *could*. And he's right! . . . But Hillary got a guy sodomized to death and then laughed about it." While he found Trump's presidency "refreshing at first," he no longer thought of him as a capable leader. "But as failed as his presidency was, and as bad as he may be, he is nowhere near as bad as the lying, cheating, murdering political, bureaucratic, and media forces arrayed against him." Although QAnon intrigued him, Bill was skeptical about its leadership, theorizing that "it may have been taken over by DNC-adjacent and/or shadow government operatives, to keep Trump supporters politically inactive and make them look stupid at the same time as a bonus. . . . Still, like any 'good' psyop, there's a lot of truth nested in all that misdirection."

Near the end of our third dinner meeting, Bill ordered a third beer, then said he'd be paying for his own dinner and drinks this time, adding, "I can't accept *New York Times*–adjacent money." When I explained that I'm not a *Times* employee and that my book advances cover my work and travel expenses, he let me buy. Penguin Press: good. *The New York Times*: bad.

That night, he excused himself from the table three times to smoke his hand-rolled cigarettes outside. In my car, he accused me of going behind his back to interview his grown children about him— something I hadn't considered, let alone done. Another time, when I emailed a follow-up question about something I'd spotted in his living room, he turned testy and demanded to be able to "veto" what I wrote, harrumphing that I held all the power in this reporter-subject relationship. I'll admit he had a point; I'm the one writing this book, after all. But the respect had to extend both ways.

When I asked if he still drew cartoons—the daily journals he'd mailed to me by the scores—he didn't remember ever drawing them. I thought about his ex–Hells Angels BFF and the dark living room with its closed blinds and the item he forbade me to mention.

I don't know whether he's a cultist, as his daughter claims, but he is definitely not the joyful, free-spirited person I used to know. His ire was hair-trigger and, I would soon learn, white-hot.

THE ROAD TO APOSTASY looked to me like a murky dead end. The shifting status quo around inequality and race, the fear that America might become anything but a white Christian nation, had left many of my old friends searching for something profound and immeasurable. By 2023, Americans' trust in federal government was at an all-time low, having fallen from first place among G7 nations in 2006 (tied with Britain) to last place in 2023.[26]

Angus Deaton tried to pinpoint it when he said that too many middle-aged white Americans have "lost the narrative of their lives." But even the Nobel-winning economist couldn't quite nail the change, calling it "something like a loss of hope, a loss of expectations of progress."[27] And while studies show that rural people are generally more pessimistic about the future prospects of their communities, they also are less likely to want to move away, saying they prefer the slower pace and community connections of rural over suburban or urban living.[28] Place matters to them, a lot.

Playing on a tribal craving for community and belonging, conspiracies can be a balm for the part of the brain prone to storytelling, symbols, and self-deception. "Our brains were designed for an earlier time, for when we really needed the security of our tribe for survival, so as humans we tend to ignore stuff that interferes with our ability to believe our tribe is a secure place," said Tania Israel, the psychologist. "People with more resources and less chaos in their lives have a kind of privilege of being able to not fall so easily into prejudice and to rely more on rational thinking."[29]

When I told Amy about our hometown conspiracists, she shook her head. "They say time can heal all wounds, but I don't know." She wasn't hopeful she could ever have a real conversation with our classmates again, let alone a reconciliation. "And I don't know how else you get this done," she said. "Before, you had different ideologies, but you coexisted. In a country that has failed to really heal our racial wounds, all this stuff just feels so post–Civil War. Reconstruction was so botched that we just never got past that, ever."

After eight years of Obama, including the legalization of gay marriage, our hometown friends seemed to feel as if they were losing the Civil War all over again, even though our side had won. "Most hurt are those who live in regions depleted of good jobs and who also lack training for other good jobs, wherever they are," wrote the sociologist Arlie Russell Hochschild in her 2024 book, *Stolen Pride*. The left-behind find themselves trapped in what she calls "a pride paradox," a bootstrap mentality where they tend to blame themselves rather than the corporations and government laissez-faire that left them high and dry. "Doubly blocked, they become vulnerable to structural shame," and more apt to embrace authoritarians, the radical right, and the notion that it's okay to convert their shame to blame—of gays, immigrants, people of color, and liberals.[30]

Traveling back and forth between Ohio and my blue bubble in Roanoke, Virginia—where we still have a daily newspaper, albeit a diminished one, as well as two online journalism start-ups—I found it hard to square how information moved in my hometown among old friends and revered civic leaders. At a breakfast interview at the Farmer's Daughter, a restaurant where Urbana's decision-makers regularly hold court, Terry Howell, a seventy-four-year-old farmer and developer, said he didn't vote for Obama, but he supported him once he became president. He didn't think the Democrats or the media had extended that same courtesy to Donald Trump. "I know he's too emotional and too combative, but I think he was a great president," said Howell, who gets his news from YouTube, Fox, and Newsmax. A former Champaign County Chamber of Commerce president, Howell stopped watching the CBS affiliate out of Dayton a few years back "because it's controlled by the Democrats. And the Democratic Party has all been hijacked by Soros and other extremists."

His proof? A friend said so. His friend attended Trump's speech on January 6, 2021, "and he thinks Antifa staged it. He thinks the whole 'insurrection' thing is fishy. I think [Biden only won] because of ballot harvesting. Nobody likes a sore loser, but I don't think . . . it was right."

A local machine-shop owner agreed with Howell, claiming the January 6 violence was perpetrated by "three or four busloads of Antifa," hired protesters who were dressed like the insurrectionists and "organized to lead people" to break into the Capitol. "That's why Nancy [Pelosi] let people in," he said, falsely. He also believes it because a friend of his who went told him so, and the theory is widely accepted on the news sites he consumes.[31]

Howell, my ex, and my friend Terri are among what the sociologists Nicholas Jacobs and Daniel Shea call "deeply engaged" voters. Most rural people don't believe our political disagreements are so great that the United States should split into separate countries, "but among the deeply engaged, such a fantastical idea has majority support," the authors write in *The Rural Voter.*[32] The majority of them also believe that Democrats are operating a sex ring, that January 6 was peaceful, and that immigration occurs at the behest of a secretive government effort to replace white Americans.

Howell's family had recently invested in a new hotel venture on the south end of town. They'd sold off farmland, too, for the development of a custom fire-truck-making factory called Sutphen and were in the process of turning an old bank branch building into a combination medical office/coffee shop/massage therapy space. At the Urbana Country Club, another gathering spot for local decision-makers, Howell spearheaded the building of a new patio to complement the golf course designed years ago by the heralded homegrown course designer Pete Dye.

And yet Howell knew very little about the problems in Urbana City Schools, or the county's rising crime, or the employee absenteeism plaguing the region's factories, including at Sutphen, the one he'd helped recruit. In other words, he knew no one like Silas James, who had deep, firsthand experience with all of the above.


Midway through his second semester at Clark State, Silas was on his third job and fourth clunker car, crossing his fingers that he'd be able to make it to work and school without another starter fritzing out. The factory job he'd been so hopeful about a few months before had ended after just six weeks, when he was fired for leaving the assembly line abruptly due to sickness. (He told his boss he was sick but didn't ask permission to leave.) Silas kicked himself for not communicating better, though the truth is he hated the job, which turned out to have nothing to do with welding, as was promised. His boss required mandatory overtime to the tune of sixty-hour workweeks, partly to make up the gap in production caused by the worker shortage.

Within a week of his dismissal, Silas landed a full-time automotive technician job at Walmart that paid roughly the same amount, with benefits, and was much closer to home and therefore easier on his latest car, a twenty-year-old Honda Accord with 211,000 miles.

For his Walmart interview, he wore black pants, a white collared shirt, and a quarter-zip sweater after consulting his favorite fashion maven, "David M. Sapp, director of bands." They were still meeting for lunch, though not as often. "I miss wearing my [drum major] uniform; it made me feel important," Silas told me one day after welding class. "Band was my second home; really, it was sometimes my first home. It was the only consistent thing in my life." But Toni, his Clark State mentor, had begun to fill in where Mr. Sapp left off—interpreting class assignments as needed, furnishing gas cards from a college fund when money was tight, and encouraging Silas when he said things like "I'm truly scared that I will never own a house."

"I think you will," Toni said. "Because of your work ethic; I see the path. I'm 100 percent confident that you will own a house if you want to," she said.

"Actually, I want to own multiple houses and rent some out; I want to dabble in everything," he said. Silas had dreamed of owning a house since the age of nine, the year his grandmother passed away and his parents were in and out of jail. He was twelve when the family lost its Marysville house to eviction and moved to Urbana with one of his

*Silas on the stoop of the Marysville home he shared with his mother and siblings as he commuted to Clark State and worked full-time.*

mom's relatives. One Wednesday during that period, his mom left for a "treatment appointment" and never returned. Back in jail, she left him with the Urbana relative who went on to molest him for three years.

"Stability is the only thing I've ever really wanted," he explained to Toni.

"That's why I like the business degree on top of the welding certificate for you," she said. He could weld full-time and manage property on the side.

His mom had recently regained full custody of his younger half-siblings, and Silas's new boyfriend of three months, Max Spencer, had moved into the family's rental house, too. When I marveled at the fast pace of change in his life and the sheer amount of drama—including a lost wallet, a car wreck (that totaled his third vehicle of the school year), a minor concussion, getting fired, and a recent diagnosis of high-functioning autism to add to his less recent diagnosis of full-blown

*Silas met his boyfriend, Max Spencer, online, and
the relationship moved fast: Max soon dropped out
of college to move in with Silas and his family.*

bipolar disorder—he smiled. That had all happened just in the past
couple weeks. He was about to turn nineteen.

The poverty scholars Sendhil Mullainathan and Eldar Shafir refer
to the kinds of nonstop interruptions of plans Silas experienced as a
"bandwidth tax," calculating that being poor reduces a person's cog-
nitive capacity more than going a full night without sleep. People pre-
occupied with poverty "have less mind to give to the rest of life," they
write in *Scarcity: Why Having Too Little Means So Much.*[33]

"I don't like it, but I'm used to it," Silas said of the constant changes.
His mom was planning to leave his stepdad, necessitating more complications and yet another family move. They were pondering a move
to Yellow Springs, the über-liberal enclave.

"I'd like to actually find comfort in the boring things, for once."
Silas was figuring out more ways to hide his trauma in his talents, I
could tell, but the trauma was still there, still peeking out. And his
bandwidth was broader than so many of his peers'.

## PART III

# SHOWING UP

*Natalie Yoder shows youth center students how to use a weed trimmer behind a vacant property they were cleaning up.*

*Ten*

# INTERVENTIONS

*Attendance officer Brooke Perry pays house calls
to the homes of children who chronically don't show
up to school. Her schedule was often overwhelming.*

O utside a pristine Champaign County farmhouse, the long
driveway was cordoned off by a thick chain. A sign next to
it let me and Brooke Perry know exactly where we stood: IF
YOU CAN READ THIS, YOU ARE IN RANGE. The words fit inside the shape
of a bull's-eye.

Brooke, the county's school attendance and homeless liaison, drove
past the house slowly in her Ford Flex, parked at a nearby intersection, and called 911. She'd been to this peaceful-looking farm before,
a two-story home surrounded by hundred-year-old shade trees, dairy
barns, and soybean fields. Her job took her from one end of the

county to the other, from students' homes to schools to courtrooms. In a county with five school districts, her task was to respond to the same problem that Urbana's factories were having: People weren't showing up. In five years, she'd put 115,000 miles on her car.

It was Brooke, forty-six, who'd made sure Urbana schools provided Silas transportation during his extended period of homelessness, even when he was technically sleeping on couches in another county. Shadowing Brooke during my trips home, I began to think of her as the mobile helper of last resort. No day was anything like the one before. The district needed about ten of her.

WHILE WE WAITED FOR deputies to arrive, Brooke explained, "The last time I was here, they sent out six dogs after me. It's nice to have protection. Not to get you involved with this, but this is my daily life. I think, 'What if they start shooting? What are you gonna do?' I'm a damn sitting duck."[1]

The farm family identifies as "sovereign citizens," part of a fringe movement of people who are virulently antigovernment; some experts believe sovereign groups recruit among QAnon followers.[2] The movement is spreading, according to the Southern Poverty Law Center, which counted ninety-three aligned groups across the United States in 2023 and roughly 300,000 gun-toting adherents.[3] Sovereign citizens oppose taxation and refuse to participate in anything government related—including paying speeding tickets or sending their children to public schools. "They don't believe in police officers, but they spend our money and use our roads," said Urbana's police chief, Matt Lingrell. He showed me a video of one sovereign citizen who'd made himself known in a Champaign County courtroom hearing over a property dispute. The man was brawling on the floor with one of Lingrell's officers, a bailiff, and a probation officer.[4]

Brooke's task today is to deliver a second official notice explaining that, by law, the parents in the farmhouse are required to fill out a form if they want to homeschool their two teenagers. Civil arrest warrants for the farm couple, including for failure to appear in court, had been issued for several years in a row, but arrests were never made. I would soon learn why.

Until recently, Ohio parents had to submit detailed lesson plans for approval from the district before they could homeschool their children, but in the spring of 2023 the Ohio state legislature passed a Republican-championed law that gutted the guidelines. The form is now a simple one-pager with no instructional plans or textbook lists required. No longer is a certified assessor or retired teacher required to sign off on the plan. A mother from the nearby Graham Local School District handed Brooke a homemade version of the form she'd scrawled on a Post-it note. But the sovereign family won't even do that.

"They just inform us now, and we can't even ask questions," Urbana's superintendent, Charles Thiel, told me. "Some families really work hard at homeschooling. But this new law makes it so the parent who doesn't want to hear from the school about Johnny being a bad kid or missing school can say to us, 'I don't care; I'll just pull my kid out.'" And it all falls under the political rubric of "parents' rights."

IN THE PAST SIX YEARS, the number of Urbana's homeschoolers has doubled.[5] It's a nationwide trend that scholars say crosses lines of geography and demographics: Homeschooling is now the fastest-growing form of education in the United States. At the moment, Thiel's district was down 115 current students to homeschooling, and another 145 to charter schools (mostly Catholic), for an annual state-revenue hit to his budget of $1.14 million.

To attract schoolkids who don't attend church, an Ohio-based religious-education program called LifeWise Academy was further blurring the line between church and state. For the 2023–24 school year in Urbana, LifeWise pulled fifty-five first and second graders out of school to bus them to a nearby church—as long as it wasn't during a core subject—for what the group described as "Bible-based character instruction."

Now operating in three hundred schools in a dozen states, LifeWise appeals to conservatives fighting what they see as liberal indoctrination in public schools. Donald Trump increasingly kowtowed to this anti-public-ed crowd, promising Moms for Liberty that he would "liberate our children from the Marxist lunatics and perverts who have infested our educational system."[6]

LifeWise participants wear matching red T-shirts, and many students are enticed to join by peers who return to their classrooms and describe getting ice cream, candy, and prizes for religious-themed games.[7] "The drive to end public education as we know it is just part of a political movement that seeks to transform the defining institutions of democracy in America," writes the journalist Katherine Stewart in her book *The Power Worshippers: Inside the Dangerous Rise of Religious Nationalism*.[8] (The book was adapted into a documentary called *God & Country* that was so scary to my teacher-husband that he had to get up and leave the room partway through watching it.)

The goal of the Christian nationalists heading the movement is to break down democracy, using voter suppression and gerrymandering as well as reframing Scripture to cast aspersions on minorities, gays, and the poor, who should only be helped via churches, in their telling. Stewart argues that we underestimate the wealthy leading the drive for authoritarianism at our own peril. Those people exploit their base as a means of controlling all of us.

Superintendent Thiel said that LifeWise, approved by the school board in a 3–2 vote, hadn't caused problems, though he noted that participants do miss morning sessions where staff teach social-emotional learning and intervene with struggling students. This, at a time when reports of student depression and suicide attempts are at an all-time high.[9] More than a third of twelfth graders had skipped two or more days of school in the past four months and/or had below a C average.

Heather Tiefenthaler, the local Democratic Party chair, decried Life-Wise as another route for conservatives to rally against LGBTQ inclusion, library books they find objectionable, and the teaching of racial history in America. She'd formed a committee to halt the expansion of LifeWise to more grades, which was presently being considered. "We have to fight back," she said.[10]

In 2024, two Republican lawmakers in the statehouse introduced a bill that would not just allow groups like LifeWise to pull kids out of school for religious teachings but actually *require* religious-based instruction in all schools.[11] Oklahoma had already passed such a law; Texas would soon follow.[12] "Perhaps, in a show of fairness, these state officials could mandate the teaching of algebra in churches," one critic quipped.[13]

Nationwide, such laws are often

*Heather Tiefenthaler, the local Democratic chair, worried about violence in the run-up to the 2024 presidential election.*

penned and championed by the American Legislative Exchange Council, or ALEC, a nonprofit supported by the Koch brothers and other wealthy scions, including fossil-fuel and for-profit prison executives as well as some members of the Sackler family, whose OxyContin painkiller was the taproot of America's opioid crisis. Among other initiatives, ALEC seeks to privatize education, strengthen gerrymandering, and champion voter suppression by generating model laws for state legislatures.[14] ALEC pushed red states to pass nearly eighty laws restricting what teachers could say about race, sexual orientation, and gender identification, according to a 2024 analysis by *The Washington Post*.[15]

Coupled with an open-enrollment policy where many parents now send their kids to adjacent rural districts with better scores and higher graduation rates—"we joke that West Liberty is the Harvard of Champaign County," Thiel said—pulling students out of public school propels a vicious cycle that weakens already distressed schools. The long game, as predicted by the philosopher Kenneth Conklin: "The easiest way to break apart a society long-term without using violence is to establish separate educational systems for the groups to be broken apart."[16]

But violence wasn't off the table, either, as my time with Brooke would soon demonstrate.

THIEL BLAMED URBANA'S HIGH DROPOUT and absentee rates on the fact that the region's vocational school, Ohio Hi-Point Career Center, had grown more selective, to the extent that many students who might have once gone to Hi-Point now stay in Urbana. "School is not their thing; they're the ones who are dropping out," Thiel, a former vocational instructor, said of those students who aren't admitted to Hi-Point because they are credit deficient due to poor grades and/or attendance.[17]

*Urbana residents Denise Collins and relatives cheer as
Jonathan Collins accepts a welding diploma from Ohio Hi-Point,
a vocational school that has grown more selective in recent years.*

Hi-Point disputed Thiel's take, as did every local educator I talked
to, all of whom believed Thiel was trying to shift blame from his own
leadership deficiencies. Hi-Point's increased selectivity was actually
part of the state's efforts to correct a decades-long dearth in vocational
education, the spokeswoman Kelsey Webb insisted, to enhance work-
based training so students could earn living wages in their home communities. Hi-Point offers certifications in fields including cosmetology,
construction, graphic design, nursing, corrections, and firefighting.
"Schools are no longer just pushing four-year college degrees," Webb
told me. "We're now treating each option—enlistment, enrollment [in
college], and employment—with the same amount of respect."[18]

But Hi-Point students must be on track to graduate with their
class, an out-of-reach requirement for Urbana's low-achieving students
who'd been passed along for years. Just one of every three cosmetology
applicants was admitted for the 2023–24 school year. Roughly half of
Urbana's Hi-Point applicants were accepted for the 2024–25 school

year;[19] a third were denied because of credit deficiencies. According to an Ohio Department of Education rubric called the School Report Card, only 24.8 percent of Urbana's 2022–23 seniors were deemed prepared for college, career, workforce, or military enlistment.[20] West Liberty's readiness score was at 52.7 percent, not exactly a ringing endorsement for my region's so-called Harvard but more than double Urbana's score.

As EIGHTY THOUSAND FACTORIES shuttered post-NAFTA and Pell's purchasing power plummeted, vocational training—already viewed as the stepchild of America's K–12 system—fell even further behind. "NAFTA put a nail in the coffin of anyone who thought they were going to make Whirlpool refrigerators and have a union job making $70,000 a year," said Jo Blondin, the president of Clark State and a national leader in vocational education. "My generation and the younger generations saw what happened to our parents, and we decided over my dead body will I work in a technical field because it's going to move to China or Mexico." Four-year colleges wrongly lobbied against the notion of free community college long after it became clear that government should put more emphasis on funding nurses over art historians, she added.[21]

And yet the vast majority of public funding still gets funneled "toward the half [of students] who are focused on four-year college degrees," said Robert Lerman, an American University and Urban Institute economist. Making community college tuition-free, as Obama proposed in 2015, would help correct the workforce shortage, and it would have given those rightfully ticked-off workers whose jobs disappeared a place to land in the knowledge economy. But in the same intransigent, Republican-led Congresses that refused to let Obama nominate a Supreme Court jurist or allow Biden to pass a bipartisan border-reform package, the idea went nowhere. Making Pell Grants allowable for short-term job-training certificates, a bill put forth repeatedly by the Virginia senator Tim Kaine beginning in 2017, would have also gone a long way toward helping the displaced become stakeholders in their own lives.[22] (The bill, which now has bipartisan support, would have made it possible for Silas to use part of his grant to actually get to campus.)[23]

"Government is starting to be more responsive to the non-college track, but the thing that's missing is a vision of scale," said Lerman, who praised long-established apprenticeship programs in Germany, Switzerland, Canada, and Australia.[24] In the United States, the fervor surrounding standardized tests had the effect of sounding egalitarian without providing equal opportunity for children who learn best by doing rather than by rote memorization.

*Justin Dobie, twenty-three, started working at a carbide technology factory in Urbana while in high school and became a full-time employee after graduation. Now married with two young kids, he's glad he didn't go to college—which would have put him in significant debt—though he may attend later in life.*

The academic rigor via testing movement had grown out of the 1983 educational reform report *A Nation at Risk*, doubled down under President George W. Bush's No Child Left Behind Act, and ended up kneecapping vocational education—making it damn near impossible for employers to find future plumbers, electricians, or machinists in many places.

Jeff Helman, a second-generation Champaign County tool-and-machine factory owner, was dumbfounded when nearly two-thirds of his business evaporated after China joined the World Trade Organization in 2001. He'll never forget losing a $2 million bid for a job to a Chinese company that had bid only $600,000—less than it would have cost Helman to buy the materials.

"That's supposed to be illegal according to the WTO rules China agreed to," I observed.

"It didn't matter," he said. Like the third-generation furniture scion I wrote about in *Factory Man*, you had to be extremely wealthy just to petition the government to initiate an anti-dumping case. (And usually, it's the lawyers who end up benefiting most.)

Helman's Rosewood Machine and Tool shrank from employing a hundred people to forty. The business held on by becoming smaller and nimbler, specializing in higher-skilled design work and more automation for customers, supplying auto parts to Honda and other automakers.

Helman courts prospective employees by saying to them, "If you work for me for four years, you'll make more than a college graduate, and the only debt you'll have is your house and your car." New hires earn $25 to $30 an hour, depending on their math skills and mechanical aptitude, plus benefits.

But those students are hard to come by, and Helman has to rely on his sister-in-law, who teaches at Graham High, to alert him about the rare student who might make a good fit. In his experience, the best employees are always farm kids, teens who are used to doing chores in the predawn, just as Helman, now sixty-three, once did.

"If you want to get a degree in medieval French art, fine, go do it. But you're probably going to end up working at Walmart because that degree's not going to pay your college debt. Colleges should be held accountable for that," Helman said angrily.

With the gutting of shop classes, Helman's family business was left with no feeder programs to prepare high school students for becoming machinists and few grads who knew enough geometry to be trainable on the job. "But I bet they know their pronouns," Helman said derisively. His vitriol seemed to be his only balm.[25]

It was late summer, and the presidential election of 2024 was heating up. Biden had just dropped out, and Helman predicted Kamala Harris would be the winner—but only because the Democrats would act duplicitously to make it so. "The process will be hacked somehow," he predicted. "The Democrats have a plan, but it'll be a cheat. That's how Biden got elected."

When I pressed him by asking, "You mean you think the machines will be rigged?" he said, "Not necessarily, but the process is being hacked somehow."

I didn't abide Helman's misplaced hate or conspiratorial thinking, but I'd been embedded in rural Ohio for a year and a half by now, so none of it came as a shock.

A few weeks before, a casual exchange with the ex-boyfriend turned unexpectedly heated when I reached out to set up a fact-checking interview. To demonstrate I was trying to get his point of view, I attached a memo written by a friend, Anthony Flaccavento, who runs the nonprofit Rural Urban Bridge Initiative, which trains people how to communicate across the divides.

I'd imagined that Anthony's analysis of rural resentment would land well with my ex, from the bad trade deals that made the rich

*The 2024 Champaign County Fair was held just as President Joe Biden dropped out of the race. Local Dems scrambled to update their signs and were easily outnumbered at the fair by Trump supporters.*

richer and smugger and people like Jeff Helman poorer and angrier, to the hollowing out of small-town America, to Clinton's and Obama's deregulation of Wall Street, to the elite's dismissal of "yesterday's occupations."

"The end result is widespread anger and resentment, essentially a rebellion against government, major institutions, liberal elites, the professional class, and all of their affectations; they believe that the system is too broken, too rigged to be reformed and needs to be burned down so we can start over," Flaccavento concluded. "The result is Trumpism."

But I underestimated the ire of my ex. We had been having a pleasant email exchange about our gardens and our grown kids. He marveled at the volunteer ornamental gourds taking over his raised beds, leftovers from seeds I'd given him the year before. "I did such a good job taking care of a buddy's chickens while he was on vacation that he let me keep the keys to the coop so I can bring them kitchen scraps!" he wrote. "They're so cute. Ducks too!"

But half an hour later, after reading Flaccavento's memo, he was furious.

"Burn it down?!? Are you and your smirking lying friend fucking kidding me?!? You guys continue to lie to people, but fewer people are being fooled by your wordplay bullshit every day. . . . You can dupe Americans, but the rest of the world sees you for what you are. Your team! Your fucking people! BLM and antifa! They spent a whole summer burning stuff down, destroying homes, and minority-owned business and outright killing at least twenty-three people, and you say WE want to burn it all down?!? Fuck you. You people are fucking liars. I can't be nice about it no more. . . .

"There will be blood in the streets and that's not a threat, that's just an observation of how the policies you support have devastated Europe. And I think it's what you fuckers want."

Message received. I backed off.

———

MEANWHILE, my cop buddy Chad Seeberg had been advising me to buy a gun. I'd never touched a gun, let alone owned one, but as election temperatures flared and AMMO FOR SALE signs appeared on the windows of my local hardware store, I found myself awkwardly polling friends and acquaintances about the necessity of it.

By and large, urban dwellers, including my husband, thought I was being paranoid. But just as adamantly, friends from suburbs and rural areas couldn't believe I wasn't already strapped up, including a contractor buddy who told me exactly what kind to buy. "If I were you, Beth, I'd get me a .38." My friend Rick, a retired court psychologist and Vietnam vet, recommended a Mossberg 590 pump-action shotgun— "for home defense, you want the short barrel for maneuverability," he said—but his had been on back order for more than a year.

In retrospect, the bull's-eye greeting me and Brooke at the sovereign citizens' farm now seemed as revelatory as it was alarming. We could read the warnings all right, and we were maybe even in range.

*Eleven*

# MEDIATION

*The Champaign County Republican Party tent at the 2024 fair. Supporters were eagerly awaiting a visit from Congressman Jim Jordan, only to learn he couldn't make the stop.*

Ninety minutes north of Urbana, a neo-Nazi network was discovered to be operating a twenty-five-hundred-member online "Dissident Homeschool" promoting white supremacy and openly embracing Adolf Hitler, peppering its lessons with homophobic, racist, and antisemitic slurs.[1] Ohio education officials and the leader of Ohio Homeschooling Parents condemned the group.[2]

Most of Urbana's homeschooling parents weren't doing it for religious or political reasons, according to Brooke Perry, but rather because "they're afraid [of getting truancy] charges, so they pull their students. Some of that is addiction related, or it's just the laziness of parents deciding they don't want to get up in the mornings with these kids."

When I sent her a news story about an abused fourteen-year-old West Virginia homeschooler who was found dead on her bathroom floor "emaciated to a skeletal state,"[3] Brooke said, "This is my biggest fear for a homeschooled child."

BROOKE AND OTHER EDUCATORS had no idea what was going on inside the homes of families who homeschooled their kids, including the sovereign citizens who'd sent their dogs out to attack her.[4] As we waited for sheriff's deputies to arrive at their farm, Brooke was too scared to knock on the door. By law she wasn't allowed to leave the notice in the family's mailbox. A deputy called to say he was on the way and reminded Brooke to stay put where she was—well out of shooting range. "We're not going to go through the gate this time," he told her. "[We're] afraid he'll go ballistic and start shooting. Worst case: He's so unstable and sovereign that he could shoot himself and shoot the kids."

Fifteen minutes later, the deputy and his colleague arrived in separate cruisers. After a brief huddle, they stood by for protection as Brooke got out of her car in front of the gate and, leaning on her cane for support, affixed the form to the chain. At Brooke's request, I stood outside her car and took a picture for documentation on her phone. She thanked the deputies, and we left to track down the next of the school no-shows on that day's list. Relieved not to have met the dogs, we were both ruffled by the *Little House on the Prairie*-meets-Waco vibe.

If teachers had turned into counselors and social workers during my forty years away from Urbana, the truancy officer's job had morphed into a full-contact occupation.

THE CANE WAS A HOLDOVER from an on-the-job bus accident in 2017 that almost killed Brooke. Back then she was also working part-time as a bus aide, wrangling students who attended the region's school for emotionally disturbed children. A suicidal driver under the influence of meth and marijuana purposely crossed over the centerline of U.S. 68 and smashed head-on into the bus Brooke was riding in. (No students were on the bus at the time; the driver was also injured, though not as badly as Brooke.)

While the perpetrator is serving eight years in prison for aggravated vehicular assault, Brooke suffers from a painful condition called spinal stenosis, causing her to walk gingerly and rely on a cane—which comes in handy when people sic their dogs on her. Her hands itch constantly from the nerve damage, and she gets regular counseling for her accident-related PTSD. During our first interview, just before the 2023–24 school year, she was about to have her 567th accident-related medical appointment and her seventh surgery.

Still, she remained upbeat and relentless about her work, taking calls at night and offering whatever supports she could. When grandparents or parents argued with unruly kids, she listened patiently to both sides before coaxing students to return to school with her, often walking them into a counselor's office when they arrived. As a reward for one student who'd dramatically improved her attendance, Brooke took the girl to a Comic Con gathering in Columbus she'd been desperate to attend—on a Saturday, on Brooke's dime. "I try to give 100 percent and not be judgmental; that's the biggest thing that shuts these families down," she said.[5]

A FORMER OHIO DEPARTMENT OF EDUCATION official stressed that schools should meet students where they are, intervening earlier and empowering them to test only when they're ready. "It's like when you're giving a swimming test; you don't do it until they actually know how to swim," Steve Gratz said.[6]

School leaders are resigned to the fact that too many teens "are waiting around either to become famous or to fall off the face of the earth," writes the child development professor Robert Halpern. "A great quantity of youthful idealism, energy, imagination, questioning, pushing at boundaries has no place to go."[7]

That void is both a destroyer of human potential and a pedagogical disconnect. "Sameness is not equality," Robert Lerman said. "If you try to make learning processes the same for everybody, you're doomed to inequality because people learn in different ways."[8] In Maryland, Lerman was helping design an apprenticeship program to funnel 45 percent of that state's high school graduates into apprenticeships offered in collaboration with employers and community colleges.

I thought of my brother, Tim, a high school dropout turned GED holder who'd created his own apprenticeship program—teaching himself computer-aided design on a bootlegged copy of the program in a single weekend (if I may brag). He worked his way up through the ranks of a Japanese automaker, from which he recently retired after winning several innovation awards from the company. When he heard I was making only $16,000 a year at my first newspaper job in 1986, he said, "You went to college for that?"

I thought of my mom, who read multiple books every week but never earned more than $8,000 a year. Not long ago, I stumbled on her report cards from the 1930s and early 1940s—straight A's. In her

*My brother, Tim, circa 1973, eventually got his GED
and worked his tail off, earning one promotion after
another. "I got this one because I knew how to use
a tractor," he said, of the early mechanic job.*

mid-eighties, she could still flawlessly recite a few Shakespeare son-
nets and the Gettysburg Address.

Jo Blondin, the Clark State president, used to believe it would take
years for the country to recover from the pandemic's learning losses,
but now, lacking the intensive English and math recovery programs
necessary to help kids work at grade level, she's not sure recovery is
even possible without drastic measures. To counter policies that snub
critical blue-collar professions, "we should be paying child-care workers, mental health and addiction workers, and educators a real salary,"
Blondin said. "I'll never understand people being okay with this massive transfer of wealth that's created so many billionaires while being
content with $15-an-hour child-care workers."

She cited Ohio's impotent implementation of a little-known federal program called SNAP Employment and Training, where unemployed and underemployed people who already get food stamps can qualify for extra dollars for education and training. Ohio bureaucrats were more interested in enforcing the program's work-requirement rules rather than providing services to help needy students like Silas and Maddie. As a result, 73 percent of the state's funds for it went to policing the rules, with the remainder trickling down to the wraparound services for which the program had been designed.[9]

Why? "Because Ohio doesn't want to be seen as a blue state," Blondin said.

She'd just presided over the first graduating class of a bachelor's program called Addiction and Integrated Treatment Studies. After being thwarted by state officials, "I called the higher-ed chancellor and said, 'This has been denied twice. People are dying. There's more [opioid funding] than we can say grace over. Do you want this on your hands?'"

UHS DOES HAVE A single advanced manufacturing class, thanks to the work of Christina Flowers—she who teaches "how to human" and other problem-solving skills. She'd recently added health-care internships and manufacturing boot-camp programs to encourage students who are both trade- and college-bound to work in Urbana or to return home after college. Flowers also secured driving-instruction grants for low-income students because the school no longer provides driver's ed. She'd gathered data showing that car wrecks were up substantially among young Urbana drivers like Silas, who couldn't afford the cost of driver's ed lessons.

Flowers personally drove some of the kids home from their driver's ed classes. "If you're just a teacher these days, you're missing the boat," she said. Flowers, too, worried about the new homeschooling law. "For many kids, school is their only safe environment; it's their place to get lunch. I'm concerned about the parents who are just using it as a way to hide out."[10]

Rural districts like Urbana's may be more underfunded than many, but research shows that such high-touch interventions are key to turning absenteeism around—more flexibility, less standardized testing, in other words. "One of the things schools can do, which none of our other institutions are as well poised to do, is to create an equitable access point for supports and services," said Catharine Biddle, a University of Maine sociologist and rural education scholar. Small school divisions may be even better than urban districts at attacking local issues collaboratively because parents, teachers, and administrators tend to already know each other.

In rural Maine, Biddle's team designed a resiliency-building program called Some Day: Students were randomly assigned a day where they alone got to choose something that made them happy to be at school. Administrators were initially skeptical, assuming the kids would demand things that were too cumbersome or too expensive, but the students mostly wanted reasonable, achievable things: A fifth-grade girl asked to help teach kindergarten for a day. Another wanted a day where she got to share the same lunch period as her younger sibling. A boy wished to spend a little time eating M&M's while sitting in the principal's chair. A student with a dying pet wanted her class to celebrate her dog, and with her teacher's help she made a slideshow they presented to the class. She even had a school memorial service before the dog's death, which morphed into a school-wide project with a wall set aside to highlight all students' pet pictures. "It became an instant place of community," Biddle said. "When the kids had trouble regulating their emotions, they could walk to the pet wall. We saw attendance, especially for kids who were habitually truant, almost double. And the ideas were entirely theirs."[11]

In 2022, an estimated 26 percent of public school students nationwide were chronically absent (defined as missing more than eighteen days), a 15 percent increase from before the pandemic. In poorer districts, the rate had more than doubled.[12] A research consortium at the University of Chicago charged with helping Chicago Public Schools increase its graduation rate meticulously tracked absenteeism among its ninth graders and intervened with social supports. Teachers, counselors, and social workers met often to discuss which students were absent and why, then addressed their specific attendance barriers, rather than waiting for an absence threshold to build or for students to come to them.

As attendance rallied, the district's graduation rate surged from 50 percent to 84 percent. The chief takeaway was not unlike that of Biddle in rural Maine: Far more predictive than test scores, it was the students' *feelings* about how they were treated at school that most boosted success, said Elaine Allensworth, director of the university's Consortium on School Research.

"Too often schools will say [of attendance], 'It's on the parents; we can't do anything about it.' But if a student really loves school and wants to be there, they're much more likely to make it work," Allensworth told me.[13]

Across the nation, programs like Allensworth's and Biddle's were innovative and evidence based. But, lacking national or statewide frameworks for educating young people and preparing them for well-paying jobs, they were scattershot at best.

In Champaign County, Graham Elementary had a forward-thinking principal who met weekly with Brooke to nip absenteeism before it became chronic. Once a week, they spent an hour jointly reviewing the progress of every flagged student on a projector screen, then following up by mail and phone and if necessary via the courts. But administrators at Graham Middle and High Schools declined to adopt the same methods, deeming them too much work, and Urbana's counselors and administrators were too overwhelmed with behavioral problems to adopt the practice, Brooke said.

AT PRESENT, Brooke was tracking six homeless kids—two were living at a shelter in Urbana, the other four in motels—and around eighteen students who were already deemed chronically absent. It was only a month into the school year.

By the beginning of the second semester, on our fourth ride-along, Brooke's chronic absenteeism list had tripled. On a chilly January day, Urbana schools reported 160 absences. Asked how many were legitimately sick, Brooke guessed 30. Twenty-seven percent of the district's students were now deemed chronically absent, down from 40 percent two years earlier during the height of COVID.[14]

Later that morning, Brooke mediated a shouting match between a mother and her angry sixteen-year-old. After taking her to the high school, Brooke personally escorted the student to the school counselor, whom the girl had never met. Earlier in the week, Brooke helped an Urbana family find housing after their landlord jacked the rent up from $600 to $1,300 with almost no warning.

Why did they hike up the rent so much?

"Because they can," she said. The dearth of housing was a national issue that affected all income levels in Urbana; a Presbyterian minister had recently turned down a job because she couldn't find a suitable house to buy in the region, and two development projects for new construction on the city's outskirts were stalled, ostensibly due to high interest rates.[15] But poor people, as usual, felt the brunt of the housing shortage. The police chief, Matt Lingrell, was increasingly getting calls about Urbana's homeless, including a woman who pooped and peed on and near the benches on Monument Square.

The mother of a police dispatcher and the wife of a small automotive shop owner, Brooke knew more about trauma and poverty in Urbana than anyone else I met. Ten years into the job, she remains the only school employee who regularly interacts with students and parents inside their homes. She's knocked on doors to find parents overdosed ("I can't get Mommy to wake up"), diapers that haven't been changed in days, and an elementary schooler walking on her tiptoes because she was being horrifically abused by her mother's boyfriend. Brooke called police after seeing the girl walk in agony and clocking empty Vaseline jars lying strewn about the trailer.

"Honey, are you okay?" Brooke asked her, and fighting back tears, the girl stammered, "I'm fine." The girl now lives with a friend from church and attends the school for emotionally disturbed students. Mom's boyfriend is in prison.

"If you saw the conditions they live in, you get immediately why going to school is the last thing on their minds," Brooke said.

*Boys play football as a neighbor keeps a dog at bay along a tightly spaced block of Court Street near Monument Square.*

# MEDIATION

————

A TYPICAL SCHOOL YEAR has Brooke checking on truancy concerns for eight hundred kids in Champaign County, three-fourths of them in Urbana. She buys them alarm clocks, coaxes them to shower and lay their clothes out the night before, and sets up interventions between guidance counselors, administrators, teachers, and parents. According to Ohio's new attendance law, an intervention plan must be created with weekly check-ins for three months. The approach works to improve attendance for roughly 80 percent of the county's absentee students.

For those who still won't attend, another 60-day diversion program run by the family court kicks in with the goal of correcting the problem before "unruly youth" charges are filed. "So, that's 150 days," Judge Lori Reisinger told me, sighing. "The school year is only 180. By the time they end up in court, it's almost summer, and the school year's over." She knew of no family court judges who liked the new law. "We get the cases too late," she said. She was working on securing funding to hire a court mediator who could intervene earlier, as a few other Ohio districts have done.

"When you were in school, was there any idea that school was optional?" the judge asked me.

No, I said, remembering how sad I was when a fourth-grade case of chicken pox ruined my perfect-attendance record.

"What we're left with is either no parental support or complete helicoptering where their children can do nothing wrong," Reisinger said.[16]

BROOKE NEVER SAW the helicoptering side. Seventy percent of her regulars live with grandparents, aunts and uncles, or older siblings. In the spring of 2024, she spent weeks helping a widowed seventy-four-year-old grandma whom I'll call Shirley who was spending her retirement raising a one-year-old grandson and an eleven-year-old granddaughter, after thirty-eight years of working on factory floors. The girl, whom I'll call Lindsey, desperately wanted to live with her dad, a meth user the courts forbade her to visit. (Her mom was in jail.)

"Brooke, I started today trying to get her up at 6:00 a.m., and every half hour I begged her to get up and go," Shirley said of Lindsey. "I don't know what to do." When we arrived at their house at 10:30 a.m., Brooke listened intently to the grandmother's story while Lindsey snoozed in her bedroom. It was Brooke's second visit to the woman's tidy ranch house, which was a fifteen-minute car ride from town—the middle of nowhere for a sixth grader who desperately wants to hang out with friends.

"Yesterday, she cussed me all morning long," Shirley told Brooke. "I asked for her phone because she wouldn't get up, and she said, 'I'm not gonna give you my fucking phone, you bitch.'" The girl had thrown the recycling bin at her, smacked her in the face, and threatened to kill her.

When we walked back to Lindsey's bedroom, Shirley said, "There's people here to see you."

"Oh, Jesus," Lindsey said, rolling over in bed.

Brooke asked if she wanted to talk about why she doesn't want to go to school, and Lindsey declined. "It's against the law not to go to school," Brooke said, calmly. "Your grandmother is doing the best she can."

Lindsey agreed to ride to school with Brooke, who asked her to get dressed quickly.

In his living room Pack 'n Play, the baby slept through the drama, his arms thrown out like goalposts. "He's so easy. You just have to feed him, love him, he's so happy," Shirley said.

A pit bull named Blue who also belonged to Shirley's son barked wildly from the next room, but the baby slept through that, too.

In Brooke's car, Lindsey said she desperately wants to live with her dad.

"Does he have a drug problem?" Brooke asked gently.

"Yeah."

"That's hard," Brooke said.

On my next visit, Brooke said Lindsey was doing better. But Child Protective Services was now also involved—Brooke wasn't permitted to tell me why—and Shirley had recently missed a hearing when she couldn't find a sitter for the baby.

A month later, when Brooke returned to Shirley's house to take Lindsey to school for the fourth time, Brooke told the girl she didn't have time that day to wait for her to put on her makeup; her no-show list was long.

Lindsey turned her makeup mirror on anyway. Brooke unplugged the cord. Things escalated.

Lindsey punched Brooke with her fists and her shoe. While Shirley ran into the living room to call 911, Brooke and Lindsey tussled on the bedroom floor, and Brooke tried to protect the baby—who was awake this visit and toddling in and out of the bedroom.

As police escorted Lindsey out in handcuffs, she tried to shoulder check Brooke. "I'd never had her even be disrespectful to me before," Brooke told me later.

Assault charges were filed, along with drug-possession charges for a marijuana vape pen found in the girl's purse. Lindsey was expelled for the year after spending a night in juvenile detention. Shirley was beside herself, Brooke said.

She texted me photos of her toe, which was broken, and her bruised neck and jaw. A week later, Brooke's back pain grew so intense that she had to have emergency disc surgery.

LATER THAT SPRING, Brooke was concerned about another UHS student I'd gotten to know in my reporting, Maddie Allen, the student who had planned to ride her bike to college from her mom's trailer park—ninety minutes one way—even in winter. A senior, Maddie was seventeen and had been an honor roll student and on track to use the same Clark State scholarship that Silas had been awarded, but she had missed so much school that she was now in danger of not graduating.

"When I was in sixth grade, I was molested by a very close family friend," she wrote in an English class paper she shared with me. "I didn't tell anyone out of fear that nobody would believe me, and because I didn't want to be the reason a family got torn apart." When she told her mother that she was addictively cutting herself because of the abuse, her mom got Maddie into therapy and kicked out the offender. When Maddie wrote the paper, it had been seven months since she'd last cut herself.

*Maddie, in the lunch line at UHS, was often tardy or absent during her senior year, but her teachers and counselors rearranged her schedule and checked in often. "I really hope she can get it together!" one told me.*

But by March, her English teacher, Cassie Cress, was growing worried. Maddie had begun twitching in class, her head jerking uncontrollably. The school nurse thought maybe she was faking it, but her mom insisted the Tourette's-like movements were trauma induced, and Cress believed it too. Her moments were so sudden, almost violent, no way it was an act.

Maddie had recently moved out of her mom's trailer when the person who'd abused her moved back in, partly because her mom needed help paying rent. That April, Maddie was staying in a roach-infested motel suite on the outskirts of town with a friend from school and six of the friend's relatives. It was stressful, she told me, and she was trying to line up calmer, cleaner accommodations with another friend.

And yet, like Silas, Maddie still managed to participate in extracurricular activities and work her Burger King job after school. She talked on the phone daily to her mom, who still took her to school and picked her up from work many days. Once Maddie left the trailer, her tics subsided, and her grades improved, despite her being tardy many days. (A counselor had already adjusted her schedule to later hours, after Maddie's doctor confirmed that she had a diagnosed sleep disorder.)

Maddie had recently volunteered to crew the UHS spring musical, *Guys and Dolls*. "She was the most helpful person among them," Cress said. "When all the other kids deserted us to go to the cast party, Maddie stayed and helped us clean up."

She hoped to get a degree at Clark State in its new addiction studies program. Her heroin-addicted father had moved from the streets of Dayton, where he was living when we met, to the regional jail. Maddie's mom planned to teach her to drive that summer, once she turned eighteen. When she said, "My goal now is to buy a car so I can get to Clark State," I was relieved she'd given up on the cycling-to-Springfield idea.

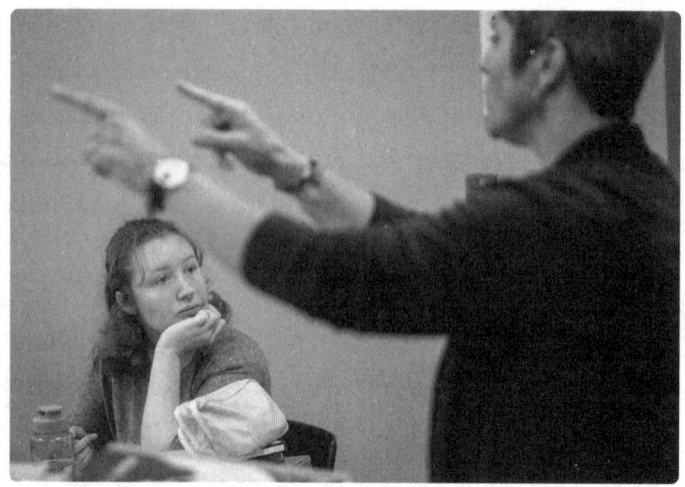

*English teacher Cassie Cress told me of Maddie:*
*"She's a deep thinker and a very good writer."*

She wanted to write a thank-you letter to her English teacher, Ms. Cress, for being so supportive to her, even when she turned her papers in late and sometimes not at all. "Honestly, it's kind of shocking that I even graduated," she said.[17]

THAT MONTH, in my Airbnb down the street from UHS, I convened a group of teachers, retired and still working, to talk about the changes I'd observed in the schools—the dumbed-down grading scale, declining enrollments, the dearth of vocational training, and poor attendance rates.[18] I invited my two favorite former English teachers, who'd retired long ago. They were joined by Cress, the recent retirees Lance and April Jackson, and my old classmate Amy Hunter, also a retired teacher. Before the gathering, Maddie stopped by after school for a catch-up interview and ended up helping me bake brownies for the meeting.

The teachers tried not to revert to knee-jerk nostalgia, the old

"Back in my day . . ." But the older ones were gobsmacked by the younger teachers' reports, especially when Cress spoke of a student she'd recently caught watching *Better Call Saul* on his cell phone, which he'd hidden between his body and his school-provided Chromebook. On a good day, he told her, he could watch six to seven episodes.

"I have to say to them, 'Hey, it's me! *I'm the show!*'" Cress said. It said something about the addictive nature of cell phones that their Silicon Valley inventors didn't want their own children having them.[19] Two months later, Ohio's governor, Mike DeWine, signed a bill limiting cell phone use in schools, and Urbana soon joined the nationwide wave of districts banning the devices.

The retired teachers found it hard to comprehend how the graduation rate dropped twelve points in a decade, or why 30 percent of the freshman class now failed English. The words "oh my God" were uttered repeatedly among the older teachers, who were still active in the town but had no clue. One said, "When I was growing up, the school and the library were my refuge."

Monument Square looked more charming than it had in decades, but with no real media presence to document what was happening beyond the pretty facades, the professional class in Urbana was left to rely on press releases, which now made up most of the newspaper's content. And nobody fact-checked those.

The retired math teacher April Jackson suggested that Urbana create in-school health clinics with a nurse practitioner and counselors, as some of its surrounding districts, including West Liberty, have done. When her husband, Lance, proposed that the best teachers teach the lowest-performing students—an idea that has gained traction among researchers[20]—my former English teacher interjected: "Then you take away my reason for living!"

Margaret Tabor, my sophomore and junior year English teacher, was the first woman I knew to use the "Ms." prefix. I believed Ms.

Tabor to be the epitome of sophistication, and in the Urbana of the early 1980s she kind of was. She decorated her classroom with fresh flowers tucked into Perrier bottles and brought literature alive by dressing like a witch and bringing in special effects that mimicked thunder as she taught *Macbeth*. She assigned homework that was creative and personally meaningful—the kind of work you could disappear into for hours and it was as if no time had gone by at all, including the illustrated booklet of favorite quotations I have carted around with me, brittle though it now is, through a dozen moves.

"Which of these programs could struggling school systems, like Urbana, implement?" Tabor asked me, assignment-like, in a follow-up message. I assured her I was researching that question.

"Good," she said. "I had a vision of you being run out of town by irate villagers, a scenario that does not have to occur!"

EXES AND IRATE VILLAGERS weren't my only concerns. The Curnutte-Evans kerfuffle appeared to be coming to a head again as our class of 1982 pals arranged a second get-together at Urbana Brewing the night after my teacher powwow.

Mark Evans was still mad at our hometown, especially after attending a recent Black History Month event about the 1897 lynching in Urbana. It was the same incident he'd tried to highlight during Urbana's inaugural Juneteenth festival in 2022 but was shut down when organizers deemed it too touchy. In subtle protest, his sister, Meridith a professional singer, performed Billie Holiday's version of "Strange Fruit" at the event.

"It was our first Juneteenth, and we wanted both Blacks and whites to feel included," said the co-organizer Scott Reeves, an educator who was working on a book about the lynching of Charles "Click" Mitch-

*My classmate Mark Evans has spent decades paying
tribute to his ancestors, especially Underground Railroad
organizers and indigenous tribespeople.*

ell, his distant ancestor. "We were fearful of something like Charlottes-
ville where the Proud Boys showed up, and we didn't want to give any
credence to that."[21]

My friend Joy Ware Miller moderated the panel, which included
Reeves as well as three white historians and teachers. "We're looking
for transformational community change from the inside out," Joy told
the crowd. Another Black event organizer added, "We're not here to
point a finger, or to defend; we want to talk about reconciliation." I
was seated next to Evans, who sighed loudly and rolled his eyes.

For the next hour, the panel described how in 1897 a lynch mob of
Urbanans had ripped Mitchell, a twenty-three-year-old hotel porter,
out of the local jail, after a prominent woman whose family owned the
*Champaign Democrat* newspaper claimed he raped her. A front-page
headline quoted her shouting, "Hang him! Hang him!" Very minimal
investigation was done into the woman's accusations before a lynch

*The Man on the Monument is the centerpiece of Urbana, erected in the city center to pay homage to the region's Union soldier dead.*

mob gathered and quickly grew to a thousand Champaign Countians, many of them armed and some carrying dynamite.

The sheriff telegrammed the Ohio governor for help, but the governor declined, leaving forty local militiamen to protect the peace. Urbana's mayor and the sheriff ended up fleeing for their lives.

In a hail of gunfire, two men were killed as the crowd rushed the jail, beat Mitchell with bats and sledgehammers, then strung him from a tree. The next morning, the crowd displayed Mitchell's body in a pine box on the courthouse lawn—directly across from the Man on the Monument, the Union soldier statue. As *The New York Times* reported, "Threats of getting and burning [Mitchell's body] were freely made. Before being removed from the Court House yard, relic hunters had nearly cut the coat off the dead man. Every button was gone, and even his shoes and stockings were taken off and carried away."[22]

For more than an hour, people of all classes paraded by to peer inside the pine box. Mitchell's family was too frightened to claim his body.

"The men taking part in it made no attempt to disguise themselves," a Columbus reporter wrote. "But it is not known who did the work, and the person who attempts to find out will get himself into serious trouble."[23]

MARK'S FATHER, JOHNNY EVANS, a retired Urbana police officer—the same one who'd investigated my niece's abuse—sat behind us at the Healing Histories event and muttered loudly, "This is a farce." He, too, was a distant descendant of Click Mitchell. Decades before, Johnny had undertaken his own research on the lynching after discovering a picture of the gawking onlookers in a book—including some whose descendants were still living in Urbana, he was pretty sure. Then he interviewed elder Black Urbanans who were alive when the lynching occurred.

"Oh, honey, that ain't true; they were seeing each other secretly," one church elder told him, of the rape allegation. Others confirmed that the relationship between Mitchell and the newspaper owner was consensual, and when they were discovered by her adult sons, "she hung him out to dry."

But that critical piece of information wasn't mentioned until the end of the program, and only after Mark asked a pointed question about the "illicit affair." By that point, Mark's dad had already stormed out. The whole thing infuriated Johnny Evans, including the fact that the old fire department dog Queenie has a marker at the Urbana cemetery but Click Mitchell still lies there in an unmarked grave.

DESPITE THEIR ONGOING BEEF, that spring Curnutte phoned Evans to invite him to the brewery mini-reunion, even though he was still hurt by Evans's calling him a white supremacist over his support of Trump. About thirty of us gathered, including several people of color, with classmates traveling from as far away as Georgia, Florida, Michigan, and Louisiana. Beers were slung, pizzas consumed, and if anything of substance was uttered, I missed it.

Curnutte was happy afterward, though he struggled to understand why Evans remained so obsessed with racism. "It would be nice when we do get together to talk about just life . . . or how we as friends are doing instead of always talking about his findings," Curnutte said, including Evans's recent revelation that he and Curnutte shared some of the same Native American ancestry. "I miss the old friend Mark!" Curnutte said. "You know what I mean?"

I understood what he was saying, but I also knew that Curnutte and I had never been forbidden to date someone we loved because of

*An amateur historian, Mark Evans spearheaded the
installation of a national historical marker to honor the area's
contribution to the Underground Railroad. "I got so many
pains about this town," he told me, tearfully.*

our skin color. We never had a grandmother who refused to give us a
hug. Neither of us was born to parents who struggled to marry because it wasn't legal. Both of us had correctly viewed the Evanses,
with their backyard swimming pool and their widely respected (and
sober) police officer dad, as being better off than our own families.
But we never knew about the jobs lost or the mortgage loans rejected.
We'd never seen the trash that racist vandals threw into the family's
pool. We didn't know what we didn't know.

Our "old friend Mark" could no longer abide stifling such painful
topics; he'd kept them bottled up for too long. "If I'm an example of a
white mother and a Black dad, and I can function just like you can,
then I know there's nothing wrong with me," he said. His research
had become a compulsion because "I have to find out who I am. To
make sure I know I'm not inferior."

Evans had spent more than a decade reading, interviewing scholars,
and presenting original research at conferences on the Underground

Railroad as well as the Shawnee Nation. He had the support of the National Park Service to erect another marker in nearby Bellefontaine, and to elevate the Urbana one he'd already shepherded into part of the new National Underground Railroad Network to Freedom, in conjunction with America's 250th anniversary.

But three years in, local officials were slow to respond, and his lifelong friends and teammates didn't want to hear about it, let alone intervene on his behalf. "They are still playing deflection games," Mark wrote to me. "It's all very discouraging." (The city did approve the new national designation on the last possible day.)

Gone was the grace that had once prompted him to shine Curnutte's basketball shoes before games, and for Curnutte to be moved by the gesture decades later.

*Twelve*

# ASCENSION

*My sister Terry, the new family matriarch,*
*lives in the same condo complex where*
*our mom spent her final years.*

I n late April 2024, I drove home for my brother-in-law's celebration of life. John, eighty-three, had passed away three months before from complications related to COPD. My oldest sister, Terry, was seventy-five and had never lived alone; I stopped in frequently during John's illness to help during my trips home. Terry was exhausted, battling overworked rehabilitation nurses, Medicare administrators, and Veterans Administration admissions people who could never find a bed. She visited him almost daily in her electric scooter, driving to the hospital or rehab center in her handicapped-accessible van.

Our niece Liza checked on her constantly, and Tim helped, too, spending entire days at John's bedside with her. The neighbors in their condo association also rallied, visiting her daily, dropping off food, helping with tasks.

Seeing my sister's daily life up close for the first time in decades, I worried about her ability to function on her own. She didn't own a debit card because John had believed they were too easily hacked, and the credit cards that were solely in his name were immediately canceled when he died.

The night after John's death, I spotted Terry's bedroom light on after midnight; neither one of us could sleep. I suggested we polish off the peanut-butter-chocolate pie a neighbor had dropped off. Sitting in her bed, we talked late into the night.

Terry recounted meeting John in a bar on Monument Square when she was thirty-one and still living at home. John's company had sent him to Urbana to install robotic cranes for a Grimes warehouse. When he asked her out for dinner, Terry was just tipsy enough to blurt out, "I'm tired of hiding my arm. I'm handicapped. There!" she said, pulling her left arm out from under her sweater. It was skinnier than her right, scarred from surgeries, and bent at the elbow. She told him about the polio she'd contracted at eighteen months. In her early thirties, she still walked unassisted but with a slight limp.

The story reminded me of a conversation I'd had with an old classmate of Terry's who described watching her struggle on their first day of school to push her cafeteria tray through the lunch line and open her milk carton with one arm. When the friend rushed over to help, Terry thanked her, but by the next day she'd figured out how to do it by herself. They became dear friends and fellow honor roll students. At their UHS graduation procession in 1967, Celesta Dunn remembered a favorite former teacher of theirs crying as she watched a student limp down the high school hill. From a football field away, the woman immediately clocked who it was. "When I think of your sister, I think of her coming down the hill at graduation like, 'I got this,'" she said.[1]

Dunn, whose mother cooked at the Urbana Country Club and kept house for many of Urbana's farm and factory owners, majored in journalism at Kent State. Terry graduated from high school with honors but stayed home, worked in an optometry office, and helped Mom pay the bills—until she ran into the cute guy with the beard. Within a span of two months, Terry shocked us all by getting on a plane for the first time in her life and flying across the country to live with John, then working in Houston. She and Mom wrote letters to each other almost every day.

Having never heard the meet-cute story before, I wondered about John's reaction when Terry explained her handicap. "I just asked you for dinner, not to marry me," he deadpanned.

"I thought he looked like Kris Kristofferson," Terry said. A Southern California homeowner and staunch Reagan Republican, John was rich by Macy standards. He had a job we didn't understand, traveling the country and sometimes going to Europe. He spoke Spanish and was an early technology adopter and tinkerer, making his own 3-D printer before anyone had heard of such a thing.

Dad thought he had to be CIA. When they married eighteen months later, we all thought Terry won the lottery. Though she volunteered for local libraries and neighborhood groups, she never worked full-time for pay again.

"We've had a nice life, haven't we?" John said a week before his death. And it was true. I wouldn't describe either one of them as feminists, but they'd had a healthy, loving long marriage that was mostly egalitarian—the first one I'd witnessed up close.

In 1982, the year after Terry and John married, I was a college freshman and only two weeks into my first semester when a campus cop stopped me and several friends walking at night between parties and carrying 3.2 percent beer around in whatever the 1982 version was of a red Solo cup. My official charge was open container, and the punishment was a visit to the academic dean's office plus an $85 fine that might as well have been $1 million.

My work-study jobs hadn't yet materialized, and I didn't have the money. Mom was working full-time and nursing a dying husband, and I knew she'd flip if I phoned for help. Waylaid by the thing that had stymied generations of my family—alcohol—I thought my college career was over before I'd taken my first test.

In a state of panic, I reached out to Terry, who was then living in San Diego with John. "She called here all hysterical," Terry wrote in a letter to Mom, immediately outing me.[2] But she mailed a check for my fine right away.

For the next forty years, John never failed to skewer me about my late-night freak-out call—"collect!" he'd say, with a sarcastic jab. It made me cringe to have that low moment, as silly as it was, lorded over me, including in front of my kids. It didn't feel playful; it felt mean.

Two years before he died, it finally occurred to me to interrupt the umpteenth retelling of the great Solo cup debacle: "Hey, John, did I ever pay you back?"

I wasn't sure if I had, honestly. But I knew that John, who tracked every penny of every dime, would remember.

"You did," he said.

"Well, then, do you think we could stop talking about it?"
"Sure," he said, and shrugged. He never brought it up again.


THE DAY AFTER the late-night pie, I drove Terry to the funeral home. John was scheduled to be cremated later in the week, and she wanted to say goodbye a final time. Ever the firstborn child (bossy) as well as a consummate worrier, she wanted to make sure they were cremating the right guy.

She also wanted to pick out a marble urn for his ashes—blue to match his eyes and the Pacific Ocean, which John used to sail in a boat he'd named after his mother: *Bessie Mae.* His body was barely cold, and already Terry was defying his last wish, which was for his cremains to be held in a cheap plastic box, not a $450 urn.

As John's COPD had worsened and his heart function declined, he became tethered to an oxygen tank and turned borderline paranoid. Noting the increased number of tornadoes and severe storms blowing through the Miami valley region where they live just south of Urbana, he advised Terry to sell their condo and buy a duplex built into a hillside after his death. She could live on one side and Liza on the other, though he still refused to acknowledge climate change. A brain scan showed significant decline. One day in the hospital, he inexplicably spoke Spanish to everyone he encountered, something he hadn't done since the 1960s. Another day, he told his nurses that he was president of the hospital. Terry asked if she could be vice president, and he said sure. "Our office is right in there," he said, pointing to the bathroom door.

But having no debit or credit cards in her name would unintentionally and briefly leave Terry—who has to be extra careful when she transfers in and out of her van (when she falls, she almost always breaks a bone)—with no way to place a grocery store order for delivery. After

Liza and I explained the merits of bank fraud protection the week of John's death, Terry made appointments to establish her own line of credit and got a debit card, too.

She was already reverting to the independent girl Celesta remembered, buying what she wanted and running errands on her own, although Liza often tracks her location via the iPhone the family got her.

IN A BACK ROOM of the funeral home, I stood a couple feet behind Terry to give her some space. She cried and kissed him and wished him "safe home." Seeing him there, covered in a blanket, I remembered how he'd doted on my sister and spent much of his retirement taking care of our widowed mom, who was not always appreciative of his efforts to "fix the damn computer" or her TV remote when the near-daily snags were most certainly caused by operator error.

Only now did it occur to me that from his needling me about being "deplorable" to recounting my Solo cup calamity, maybe sarcasm was the only way John knew how to connect with me. As I started a career and family of my own, maybe it was simply his way of reminding me that he had been there for me when eighty-five bucks meant everything in the world.

ON OUR WAY BACK from the funeral home, Terry and I decided to visit Mom's grave. She hadn't seen it since Mom's burial in 2020, though Liza and I had decorated it the year before. For as long as I can remember, every female Macy within a day's drive was expected to help Mom plant flowers in late May and spruce up the extended-family graves, a tradition the old people in the family called Decoration Day (that holiday was eventually replaced by the establishment of Memorial Day). In a family Polaroid from 1965, Grandma Macy stands hunched by her parents' graves, trying to keep toddler me, clad in a frilly dress from the store where she worked, away from the flowers and dirt.

In her later years, Mom never failed to mug for the camera on Decoration Day, her arms held high over her future headstone, which had Dad's date of birth and death on one side and hers on the other, her death date still blank. In 2010, the year I was a Nieman fellow, she wore her HARVARD MOM sweatshirt for the annual ritual she jokingly referred to as the taking of her "ascension picture."

*Mom hams for her 2010 "ascension photo" after refilling planters at our relatives' graves, including by Dad's headstone—her future resting place. Photo by Beth Macy.*

Now, on a drizzly January day, I steered my sister's van into the cemetery and toward the top of a hill next to our family's row. But when I pulled Terry's wheelchair from the backseat and set it up, it sank into the wet ground as soon as she sat down. I tried pushing her up the hill to Mom's grave. I turned the chair around and tried pulling her instead. We were getting soaked, and the wheelchair wouldn't budge.

"Do you think we could just drive to it?" Terry asked.

It would be a tight squeeze, off road, between two narrow rows of headstones. We'd be in big trouble if we got caught turfing on our ancestors' graves, clipping the headstones of strangers, or leaving tracks in the grass. I'd have to back up to get us out of there, and I'm notoriously bad at driving in reverse. (When I finally bought my first brand-new car at the age of forty-five, I promptly backed it into a brick carport column.)

The van wheels spun in the mud. But slowly we made our way up the hill, passing first Grandma Macy and then Mom's mom. By the time we arrived at our parents' headstone, the rain had picked up. Terry looked at me, smiled for the first time in days, and said, "Oh, Mom would love this!"

Only the dead were there to witness the spectacle of our exit.

JOHN'S CELEBRATION OF LIFE was held at their local VFW, a few towns away from Urbana. They'd been regular diners there for years, especially on cabbage roll night. My siblings would all be in attendance, including Cookie, whom I hadn't seen or spoken to since our tense interview six months before. Our youngest child, Sasha, the traveling musician, hustled in from a gig in Pittsburgh to play music at Terry's request. I am pretty sure that Sasha is the only nonbinary person ever to perform at a VFW hall wearing a floral Alfred Dunner blazer that used to belong to their grandma. Sasha had spent the four-hour car ride memorizing John Denver's "Leaving on a Jet Plane," one of John's favorite songs. They also played one of Terry's favorites, the Beatles' "Come Together," the first song Sasha learned on the electric bass, an instrument Mom pitched in to help us buy.

My brother, Tim, who'd re-friended me about a year before on Facebook, was there too. Tim and his wife knew no other nonbinary people, but in the fall of 2023 the couple had driven seven hours to watch Sasha's band, Palmyra, play a Virginia show. When he asked me, "Does he still date girls?" it was an honest question asked in a caring, curious tone. "They're dating a young woman now, yes," I said, adding that I, too, had trouble sometimes remembering to use the right pronouns. He'd recently astonished us by RSVP'ing yes to our son Max's upcoming wedding. On Facebook, Tim was now a Palmyra superfan.

We had always bonded over talking about our work. During a conversation at a brewery near his house in nearby Bellefontaine, a waitress who knew him by name handed me a menu and said, "You the author?" When I asked how she knew, she nodded to Tim and said, "He brags on you."

The feeling was mutual. With nothing more than his GED and a few community college classes, Tim

*Nine years my senior, my brother, Tim, said his first memory of me was "waiting in the driveway for them to bring you home from the hospital. I was so excited."*

had worked his way up from automotive-store clerk to mechanic to engineer for Honda Research & Development, tasked with building a crash-test dummy site and designing safety-testing implements and airbags before his retirement in 2022—and making way more money than I ever earned at a newspaper. He was a rare person who could do the hand labor of stitching and welding as well as designing elaborate test fixtures on the computer and building them to spec.

He can make or fix just about anything. Once, when the accelerator cable on my VW Bug snapped, stranding me on the side of a highway, Tim described over the phone how to tie a rope to the engine so I could operate the gas pedal by hand until I got to his house, whereupon he replaced the broken cable.

He spends his retirement tinkering in his barn, fishing and camping, helping his wife hunt morels, and mowing the acres surrounding their countryside home with his tractor. On another trip to visit us in Virginia in 2023—their first visit since Trump's election in 2016—they brought their fishing rods and showed me how to fish again, something I hadn't done since childhood visits to Muzzy Lake. Luck was with us that day as we hauled in several trout and bluegill (though we threw them back, something Mom would have thought foolish), and the only time politics showed up was when Tim offered that he was planning to vote for RFK Jr.

Which, not my cup of worms, but fair enough. I held my tongue. After spending more time together than we had in a decade, we were both working to not be offended by what we couldn't understand.

I no longer posted what he'd once labeled "liberal shit" on my Facebook page; the momentary hit of dopamine wasn't worth the comment drama it often provoked from the hometown crowd. Besides, research shows that deeply engaged voters don't typically change their minds when confronted with opposing views; most dig in their heels instead.[3] What works better is having nonjudgmental conversations, a technique social scientists call deep canvassing, which actually does work but isn't easy to scale. (Also, the people who most need deep canvassing are the least likely to seek it or agree to it.)

In my family, a better solution seemed to be standing knee-deep in a mountain creek with my brother, the gentle clickety-whir of our fishing lines sailing under the trees. Before he left for home, Tim fixed one of our toilets.

WE'D NEVER SERIOUSLY TALKED about our childhoods before. About how, as Dad's alcoholism progressed, he grew meaner and less reliable. Or about the time, around the age of twelve, Tim went to the bank to discover that his savings account had been wiped out of

$300—something I couldn't imagine our mom doing, though Tim thought she'd acted out of desperation to keep our heat from being turned off.

When he was fourteen, Tim ran away from home, hitchhiking to Indiana with a friend. He'd had an explosive argument with Dad, during which a hungover Dad picked him up by the neck and held him against the wall, choking him. His crime? Tim was refusing, on a near-daily basis, to get up in the morning for school. He hated school, as noted by his teachers, who wrote on his report cards that he "stares too much" and "talks too much."

"I never understood that; I don't talk much," Tim told me. "I have a little stammer; sometimes it's hard to get my words out. But I quit talking altogether after they wrote that." When his girlfriend got pregnant when he was sixteen, he dropped out of UHS, rented a little house a few blocks away from ours, and went to work at an auto-parts store in Urbana. It was his first of four marriages.

I was only seven when he left home, but I remember mornings when Tim stared into space at the edge of his bed when he was supposed to be getting ready for school. First, it would provoke Mom's ire, and then, much louder and more dramatically, it provoked Dad's. We'd all beg him to get up, but Tim just sat there in his underwear, staring at the wall.

When he was diagnosed with a moderate form of epilepsy in his late teens, we finally had the language to

*I was closest to my brother, Tim, in age and disposition. But our relationship frayed for a time during Trump's first presidency.*

explain what might have happened to the sunny boy who used to do a song-and-dance routine with his older sisters and proudly paraded me around the neighborhood in my stroller.

He described his mini-seizures as "almost like an out-of-body experience." He zoned out once while driving and wrecked with his young son in the car. (They were both okay. Now, with regular medication, he keeps the seizures at bay.)

Only with the diagnosis did Mom recall that his behavior had changed not long after a neighborhood kid threw a brick out of a second-story window and hit a seven-year-old Tim, who was playing in the back alley, on the front of his head. He fell backward and onto a rock, striking the back of his head and causing a serious concussion.[4] "I remember him coming in all bloody," Terry said. "It was awful."

Asked what Mom did in response to the head wound, Tim said they didn't go to the hospital. Instead, in a fit of indignation, "she marched me over to Billy Bean's house and made his mom clean me up!"

Billy Bean—a.k.a. the longtime Urbana mayor Bill Bean, who was then around twelve. Tim had no idea I was scheduled to interview the mayor in a few days, just as I didn't know the fabled brick lobber, long referred to as "the mean kid around the corner," had been Bill Bean.

When I asked Bean if he remembered the incident—I seriously doubt anyone could forget my mom shouting at the front door with a bloody kid at her side—he stammered and paused. "Well . . . huh . . . I could have," he said. "But, God, I don't remember that. I don't blame your mom being pissed; I'd have been pissed too."[5]

AT THE VFW, my husband arranged for Terry's favorite video of John—of him skydiving on his seventy-second birthday—to play on a loop. Our cousin Barry, a former missionary, flew in from Minnesota and delivered an opening prayer. I told the Solo cup story at Terry's request, and she told the meet-cute story. Tim, still a classic introvert—he had purposely missed his own surprise fifty-fifth birthday party at Honda—said a few words about how close he and John had been after Terry and John moved back to Ohio, sharing rides to work and going out for beers. Cookie recalled the time she was about to drive to a revival in Tennessee with a church friend and John unexpectedly slipped her a wad of cash. Her son-in-law Troy, the one who'd turned down two transplants, was there and looking wan. He was now on home dialysis and so desperate to get better that he'd recently put his name back on the transplant list—even if the donor had had a COVID vaccine.

Cookie and I didn't have a lot to say to each other, but when I asked how she was, she sighed. Her husband's health was now in rapid decline, but she said he refused to even discuss moving out of their two-story rental and into a single-story home. I'd recently spent a day shadowing Cheryl Wears, a community paramedic/nurse in Urbana, whose job is to help older people live more safely in their homes or transition to home-health or residential care. Cookie brightened when I told her about Cheryl, whose family used to take me camping when we were kids, and said she'd talk to her.

Seated in her wheelchair, she thanked me for all I'd done to help Terry these past several months. "I wish I could have done more," she said.

But when I texted her Cheryl's contact information the following week, Cookie shut the idea down immediately, saying she'd changed her mind. It bewildered me that she was too scared to push for what she wanted at the risk of her own safety and health.

When I told Silas about Cookie's reaction, he coaxed me into a more generous take. "Sometimes you're in a situation so long you get used to it, and you feel like there is no other way of life," he said. "Sometimes you even think you did something to put yourself there, so why try to get yourself out?"

He'd just turned nineteen, was managing a Taco Bell at night, and was on the verge of getting his welding certificate. And now here he was, counseling me. And it helped.

When Terry hugged me goodbye, she sent me off with a portion of John's ashes. Liza and I had marching orders to sprinkle them in the Chesapeake Bay during the weekend of Max's wedding in Annapolis, Maryland.

The day before the ceremony, Liza and I huddled on the beach at Cape St. Claire, and over the phone Terry wished the cute guy at the bar "fair winds and following seas," an old sailor's blessing. It wasn't the ideal body of water for her California baby, but I sprinkled the cremains while Terry did what she usually does and told him exactly what to do: "Now, John, I want you to go out and find the Atlantic and take a right," she said, over the cell phone speaker. "Then hang another right at the Panama Canal, then go north, and you'll be in the Pacific.

"Bon voyage," she said, her voice cracking.

"You are loved."

Terry said she considered coming to the wedding but decided the travel would be too hard on her back. But Liza flew in, and Tim and his wife made the eight-hour drive. There were only three members of my family in attendance compared with twenty from my husband's extended clan, including his niece and her wife, but my small contingent meant the world.

It felt as if Mom were there, too, as Sasha, resplendent in a scalloped tulle jacket I'd lent to them—beige to match the other of Max's attendants, only one of whom was straight—delivered their grandma's signature bawdy toast: "Here's to the girl who lives on the hill. She won't do it, but her sister will. Here's to her sister."

*Thirteen*

# GENIALITY

*Young 4-H'ers prepare to show their hogs
at the 2024 Champaign County Fair.*

Around the time President Biden dropped out of the race, Trump was shot at a campaign rally, and JD Vance, the not-quite-hillbilly reared just down the road, became Trump's vice presidential candidate, the Champaign County Agricultural Society prepared for its 183rd annual fair, the same one my sister Terry got caught sneaking into in 1969. The fair was vintage Mayberry long before *The Andy Griffith Show* existed, with its devotion to youth farming and agricultural innovation. Since its founding in 1841, back when talk centered on the merits of all-metal plows and modern grain-reaping machines, thousands have gathered annually over the course of an August week with the purpose of partaking in "genial social interactions," as a local historian put it.[1]

Livestock queens are crowned; ribbons awarded for craft and home-making best in shows (my friend Betty still holds the record for winning the most sewing ribbons and rosettes). A midway cuts through the center with carnival rides, games of chance, and the requisite fried food. At night, people crowd the grandstands to watch harness races, a tractor pull, and a rodeo. Among the biggest draws is the calf and pig scramble contest, a kind of musical chairs for livestock where 4-H teens win a free animal to raise and sell at the next year's fair, as long as they're among the first to wrestle a beast into muddy submission—pigs for the girls, calves for the boys.

In 1913, my grandma Macy, a winsome teenager gussied up in a floral dress and a wide-brimmed hat, sat for a souvenir postcard portrait taken at the Champaign County Fair. The descendant of a country-store owner, small-scale farmers, and at least one of those Champaign County Union soldiers, she sat with her friend in the front seat of an

*At the same fairgrounds where generations of my family enjoyed the Champaign County Fair, the 2024 tractor pull competition drew an enthusiastic crowd.*

*My grandma, Lessie Ethel Macy (right),*
*sat with her friend for a souvenir*
*fair portrait in 1913.*

open-air roadster in what must have been among the county's first automobiles. On the back of the postcard, she wrote her name and her friend's name in pencil, using the same curlicued cursive she taught me when I was four.

Decades later, I made my way around the same fairgrounds, playing "The Star-Spangled Banner" and pep-rally songs with Robert K. Martin's high school band. In college, I wrote some of my first newspaper stories about which kids were showing and shearing the finest sheep. In all fairness to Terry, my friends and I snuck into the fair, too, learning precisely where to hop the fence—on the cornfield side at the edge of town, so we wouldn't be caught. Mayor Bean said he'd done the same.

Then as now, working-class townies stuck mainly to the midway while the farm kids, in their flannel shirts and boots that cost more than Mom made in a week, hung out along the perimeter in the livestock and 4-H buildings. Thus, with the exception of my stint on the sheep beat, farming seemed like both a throwback and a mystery, though many of us townies took our first bitter sips of alcohol in the backseat of someone's car while cruising past rutted fields that had been handed down for generations, some via Revolutionary War land grants.

We stopped occasionally to pee in the corn rows or engage in hijinks, like tipping over a sleeping cow. Even as the number of family farms shrank and individual acreages ballooned, fair season remained the pinnacle of the year in Urbana, a time when people of all ages, jobs, and backgrounds gathered to ride the Tilt-A-Whirl or the Gravitron, eat funnel cakes, and cheer their farm-reared brethren as they wrestled lard-slicked pigs, and everyone prepared to meet the shiny new school year.

At first glance, the 2024 fair wasn't so different from my experience of it four decades before, not counting the modern landscape of tattooed limbs or the newfangled cheese curds imported from Wisconsin. But my first stroll around the fairgrounds turned up some surprising features in the most anodyne corners.

It wasn't just that the emcee of the pig and calf scramble, a local farmer, interjected his politics over the loudspeaker—"An eight-year-old could run the country better than who we have!"—to thunderous applause from the crowd. "We have to take our country back!"

Or that, on the fair's second day, an off-duty police chief from nearby St. Paris refused not to open carry his gun, in violation of the fair board's posted "no weapons allowed."[2] When he repeatedly declined to place his gun in his vehicle, deputies arrested him and took him to jail, where he was booked on charges of criminal trespassing and obstructing official business.

Or that, shortly after news of his arrest broke, three members of the

*Farm culture has long permeated the historic Champaign County Fair. During the 2024 pig scramble, a local farm girl wrestled one into submission, winning a sow to raise and show at the next year's fair.*

group Ohio Gun Owners came to the fair toting guns of their own, along with a selfie stick, provoking the same response from sheriff's deputies. Their goal was to record what they viewed as the debasement of their Second Amendment rights, leave immediately, and then, in their own words, "get lawyered up." They would legally challenge the fairgrounds' firearms ban, believing that it violated their right to carry guns in a public space. Whether or not the Agricultural Society, formed in 1838, was technically owned by the county, as the gun-rights people argued, or whether it was owned privately by a nonprofit board, as the county prosecutor claimed, would be a matter for the courts.

On Facebook Live the next day, the executive director of Ohio Gun Owners, Chris Dorr, clad in a T-shirt that read ATF IS GAY, encouraged his members to call the fair board to point out that Ohio Revised Code 9.68 allows open carry in most public spaces. "When the sheriff is . . . ordering this off-duty police officer to put his firearm back in his vehicle, the only proper American response is, 'You can kiss my lily-white ass,'" Dorr told his 190,000 followers.

As the presidential election season heated up, Dorr posted regular advice to the group, including

*Eat Red Meat.*

*Exercise Daily.*

*Buy Ammo.*

*Train w/Friends.*

*Repeat.*

I remembered the postcard of my fair-going grandma Macy, who was so genial I never once heard her cuss. If she errantly dropped a glass on the floor, "fiddlesticks" seemed to do the trick. She would've wilted at the notion of middled-aged men carrying guns near children at the Coke Bottle Pitch and ammo-ing up for the apocalypse.

And, by the way, 39 percent of Americans now believe we are "living in the end times," according to a Pew Research Center report.[3] What the fiddlesticks.

DOWN A MAIN DRAG OF THE FAIRGROUNDS, the Champaign County Democrats huddled beside the local Republicans' tent. The Dems had just bought a used shed from the Republicans to store their belongings for the event. The sale had been neighborly, even if the Republicans did a little bragging about having outgrown theirs.

With little more than a week's notice, the Democratic Party chair, Heather Tiefenthaler, was working nonstop to switch out the Biden-Harris memorabilia to Harris-Walz, crafting buttons in the local library's fabrication lab that featured a comma, followed by "La." Her roster of sixty active volunteers, heavy on retired teachers and librarians, had recently gathered signatures for the "Citizens Not Politicians" proposal that would place a statewide anti-gerrymandering amendment on the November ballot. I'd recently run into two retired teachers gathering signatures in an uptown antiques mall.

On Urbana's Monument Square, Tiefenthaler had finally secured space for a Democratic headquarters, after buttering up the landlord with flowers. It had taken four months to find someone who would rent to her; all the others she queried refused or doubled the rate when they learned whom she represented.

As we spoke, seated on furniture she'd hauled in from her home, Tiefenthaler jumped when a passing vehicle on the square backfired. On edge about the upcoming election, she told me she took small comfort, as a former school secretary, in having had active-shooter training. On the fair's first day, she'd tried to have a conversation with a man who stopped to shout at her about Biden causing high gas and cereal prices. When Tiefenthaler tried to explain that General Mills doesn't seek presidential permission to raise the prices on Cinnamon Toast Crunch, he walked backward away from her with his arms raised, as if fleeing a bear. So much for deep canvassing.

*Local Democratic Party chair Heather Tiefenthaler (left) chats with Urbana mayor Bill Bean, a Republican, under the Democrats' tent at the 2024 Champaign County Fair.*

*Charlie Brown (right), the brother of Ohio Senator Sherrod Brown,
works the crowd at a dinner fundraiser Tiefenthaler organized
before the 2024 election. Brown, a Cleveland-based progressive
Democrat, lost his long-held seat to Trump-aligned businessman
Bernie Moreno, whose win helped turn the Senate red.*

The following week she worked on a local fundraising dinner that raised $20,000 for the reelection of Senator Sherrod Brown, who was in a nail-biter of a race against the Cleveland luxury car dealer Bernie Moreno. Mitch McConnell's super PAC donated $83 million toward Moreno's TV ads, part of an effort to flip the Senate red.[4] While rural Democrats raised money for Brown and Governor Mike DeWine decried Issue 1, the anti-gerrymandering amendment, local vandals stole many of Tiefenthaler's new Harris-Walz signs.

Nationwide, Harris was now ahead of Trump in some polls, though memories were fresh of Trump's 2016 win despite most polling to the contrary. "I do think we should expect violence, and I don't know how to prepare," Tiefenthaler told me, adding that police officers in her Mechanicsburg hometown had already planted Trump signs in their lawns and flew Appeal to Heaven flags, symbolizing Christian nationalism. If she called them in an emergency, she wondered, would they even show? My friend Chad, the police captain, said the same.

Tiefenthaler found herself wondering, "Will the violence come to small towns like ours or be relegated to big cities?" Nationwide, 11.5 percent of white evangelicals and 17.7 percent of white weekly church-goers now fell into the top quartile of people who supported political violence, Christian nationalist beliefs, and support for QAnon, according to the political science professor David Buckley. They numbered in the millions, and a whole lot of them owned guns, multiple guns.[5] Sixty percent of Republicans falsely believed that undocumented immigrants were illegally voting en masse, a theory experts have connected to racist massacres in El Paso, Buffalo, and Pittsburgh that targeted Hispanic, Black, and Jewish people, respectively.[6]

When I reached back out to Lilliana Mason, the Johns Hopkins political scientist, her latest data showed a record 60 percent of Americans now approved of political violence if the other party initiates it, up from 40 percent four years before. "Republicans who think Trump won in 2020 are expecting way more violence and chaos than anybody else," Mason said. "They believe, more than anyone, that America is close to a civil war. They're very concerned about misinformation, and, in their minds, they believe the rest of the country has been lied to."[7]

From our class reunion organizer to my dearest, oldest friend to my once-ultra-liberal ex-boyfriend—I could now attach faces as well as feelings to Mason's data.

Too few Americans understood how deeply Christian extremists had infiltrated the Republican Party, using anti-abortion, anti-immigration, and anti-trans appeals to cement their political power. And they're organized. As the Faith and Freedom Coalition founder, Ralph Reed, described his group's in-depth efforts to turn North Carolina from blue to red, "We put voter guides in your churches, we were in your text messages, and we didn't stop till you voted. . . . [W]e had 147 different data points we tracked."[8] By the fall of 2024, the

Faith and Freedom Coalition was handing out thirty million pieces of literature in 125,000 churches, spending $62 million to register and turn out evangelical voters.[9]

Many national journalists were slow to touch this aspect of the story, fearing they'd be accused of religious bigotry or intolerance of Christianity or even just paranoia, Mason said. "The actual sense of alarm? I haven't seen it," she added.

The exception was Jeff Sharlet, who wrote the siren-ringing 2023 book *The Undertow: Scenes from a Slow Civil War.* Sharlet had recently told the podcaster Marc Maron that he blamed journalism's gatekeepers—specifically, those in New York—for being reluctant to expose the country's creeping state of fascism. (The word wouldn't become part of the news-cycle conversation until the election's final weeks.) Most were living, Sharlet believed, in a kind of "delusional bubble."[10] Meanwhile, in rural America, journalism was almost extinct; by the end of 2024, the United States was on pace to lose one-third of all newspapers and two-thirds of local journalists.[11]

"We talk about systemic racism, misogyny, and LGBTQ rights, but we don't talk enough about how, for fifty years now, this strange evangelical-slash-Catholic movement has been trying to infiltrate the government and turn our country into a religious nation," Mason said. "We've never faced it in any kind of organized way or even said out loud that it exists!"

More than a year after our first interview, Mason now had this to say: "Back then I was thinking, we're in the bumpy part of the road, and if we ever made real progress, there would always be backlash. The question now is, do we make it through?"

When I reached out to him, Sharlet was pessimistic enough to point out that, as we spoke, he happened to be driving through a town in Maine called Gilead. Having been threatened multiple times because of his dispatches from the front lines of fascism, he told me the notion of my getting a gun was a terrible idea; he himself owned an antique shotgun but kept no ammunition, or "freedom seeds," as his detractors call it.

A writing professor at Dartmouth, Sharlet hadn't reported for nearly a year and worried that in the interim he'd been "absorbed into the bubble of living in a college town. . . . But you're validating my doomism, thank you," he said, half joking. Some of his Ivy League colleagues were so far to the left that they blasted *The New York Times* for being "in bed with Trump," about which we both thought, *Come on.*

"There is open disdain here for any of the suffering in our [rural] region, [and when you point out the suffering,] it's seen as a provincial elevation of whiteness." Nonetheless, he reminded me, we are called to keep reporting facts and to hold steadfastly to our ideals, politics, and beliefs "despite the disdain and contempt from enemies and friends and allies."[12]

A year and a half into my home-going project, I was getting whiplash. Where I live, friends filled with the newfound joy of candidate Harris didn't believe me when I described my hometown. They were, I had to agree with Sharlet, living in Kamala la-la land.

At a gathering in the college town of Lexington, Virginia, for a mutual friend's book release, the celebrated photographer Sally Mann told me that Democrats had never done anything worthy of provoking the ire of the right. I told her about my trips home, including the ammo-buying activists. I suggested that maybe she was too insulated to understand the utter rage provoked by globalization, Christian nationalism, and widespread rural despair—and how truly nihilistic the American experiment seemed to be turning. We argued for a bit, and she pushed back hard, as if she didn't believe me. Finally, I threw up my arms and sputtered out the rawest description I could manage on the spot: *Hurt dogs bite.*

A few days later, Sally sent me an email: "Your news from Ohio disturbed me enough to galvanize me into action." She'd just signed up to volunteer with her local Democrats.[13]

INSIDE THE FAIRGROUNDS' Merchants Building, a local pregnancy and family life center featured pamphlets and plastic models of newborn-sized fetuses on its tables. Nearby, LifeWise proponents were signing up more kids for school-day Bible instruction. Urbana City Schools was now on the cusp of expanding LifeWise from two to eight grades, and LifeWise organizers from Graham schools were recruiting heavily, too.

In her ongoing how-to-human campaign, Chris Flowers hoped to reach more students as well, steering them toward trade certifications and local factory work. On behalf of the region's hard-up employers, she passed out branded Post-it notes, stress balls, pens, and tote bags. We were visiting next to her table when Silas showed up to meet us with his boyfriend, Max.

It had been seventeen months since Flowers first introduced us, a time when Silas's school mentors and teachers predicted that clawing his way into a calmer, middle-class life would be an anguished quest. He was now on his sixth job since we'd met, on the management track at an O'Reilly Auto Parts store in Marysville. The 2006 Honda he was driving had been his fifth car of the year; he and Max had bought it jointly. Their short-term loan was almost paid off, and the car was still running strong, as was their partnership, it seemed. The couple wore matching tattoos on their collarbones, each in the other's handwriting, featuring lyrics from a song by System of a Down. Max's said, "If you go, I wanna go with you." And Silas's featured the next line of the song: "If you die, I wanna die with you." (They got the idea from Tik-Tok.) Silas had aced the coursework for his welding certificate, winning a campus award for a welded art piece he'd fashioned for Max in the shop—a metal flower.

But things weren't very calm at home. His stepdad had been released from jail, and the mood was tense. "Is that not a good situation?" Flowers asked.

"I cannot stand that man," Silas said. "He screams at the kids, and they're only like three and four!" Their parents were back on CPS watch for the younger two children as well as for Silas's teenage siblings, who were born with methamphetamine in their systems. The family used to joke that when the police department happened to relocate its headquarters down the street from their Marysville house, it was so they could be closer to their work, Silas told me. He worried a lot about his fifteen-year-old brother, whose doctor thought he might have borderline personality disorder.

With the incentive bonus Silas was soon to receive from Clark State for completing his welding course, he and Max now planned to get a place of their own somewhere between Marysville and Columbus. Silas would not be taking a welding job right away, he told us. He'd also postponed his long-standing plan to continue his education at Clark State, decisions that discouraged me and Flowers and his team of Urbana supporters.

"But you have such a gift as a welder!" Flowers said. She'd recently met his Clark State professor, who'd raved about Silas's welding chops. When Silas countered that he was making $17 an hour as an assistant manager at O'Reilly's plus benefits, she said, "With welding, you can start at $22 an hour. And here's an idea: You can work welding, and they'll actually *pay you* to go to college." It reminded me of the long letters I used to write to Liza, begging her to go to college, telling her about Pell Grants, offering to help her fill out the paperwork. (She got into a local community college but ultimately opted to work and move in with her boyfriend, now her husband, instead.)

Silas shook his head. After all the hurdles he'd faced in completing the program—after the suicide attempt and the initial dropping out, after the flat tires and loose starter wires—he couldn't quite articulate (or didn't want to explain) what was keeping him from pursuing his dream career. He muttered something about not liking the repetitive nature of factory work and hating mandatory overtime. He raved about his cheerful store colleagues and his new manager, who hadn't even realized he was trans until he told her.

But that wasn't the whole story, we could tell.

"You know I'm going to keep bugging you, right?" Flowers said sweetly.

"I do," he said.

Clad in a Green Day T-shirt, he hugged Mrs. Flowers and showed her his latest tattoos, including some he'd personally inked. He seemed in good spirits, excited about an upcoming punk concert in Columbus. He planned to help Mr. Sapp with homecoming again if he could get the time off work.

*Christina Flowers, one of many teachers who suggested I interview Silas, encouraged him to return to college as they caught up about his post-UHS life at the 2024 Champaign County Fair.*

As he and Max left the building holding hands, Flowers and I sighed. I thought of his wise take on Cookie's predicament a month earlier: Traumatized people often cling to what little security they have. The monster they know.

A year earlier, Cassie Cress, his English teacher, had predicted Silas would have to physically separate from his family or "they would keep dragging him down." Mr. Sapp, who'd placed Silas's chances of finishing the program at fifty-fifty, now worried that Silas was self-medicating with marijuana and was too afraid of failing a welding-job drug test. Silas told me later that he smoked weed (but not when the kids were around) and disagreed with Mr. Sapp's take.

Maybe, I suggested to Flowers, moving out of his mom and step-dad's house really was the North Star among the constellation of his present problems. "He needs to separate from the toxicity in his life," Flowers said, nodding.

But she would keep sending him notices about welding jobs. She wasn't letting go yet.

# Fourteen

# GRACE

*"Chaos Coach," says a nameplate in Natalie Yoder's
office at the Urbana Youth Center, where she directs
after-school programming, helps pick up students from
Urbana's schools, and teaches myriad life lessons.*

Down the row from Mrs. Flowers at the county fair, the Urbana Youth Center program director, Natalie Yoder, was trying to recruit kids for the center's after-school tutoring, GED, and life skills programs. She loved touting her most recent grad, the one she'd most closely mentored. A young woman with autism spectrum disorder, Grace Slagle had been so beaten down when they met that she typically spent entire school days with her head slumped on her desk. Outside school, Grace escaped into fantasy novels at the youth center and drew made-up creatures on her laptop. Before Grace dropped out of UHS, joining the one in five Urbana students who don't graduate in four years, she was living with her parents in a cheap motel in Springfield, along with multiple siblings, dogs, and cats. Grace slept on the motel floor, wedged between a bed and the window.

As a mandated child-abuse reporter, Natalie had turned in Grace's family for suspected abuse a few years before. The teen ended up spending seven months in the custody of relatives, but after six months CPS workers returned her to her parents.

"Natalie, I can't go back to that hotel," Grace visited the youth center to confide. "I can't take it."

She was eighteen at the time, so Natalie offered, "Do you want to come home with me?" Natalie was already a certified foster mom, having raised a teenager who would soon graduate from Hi-Point's cosmetology program; a previous foster dad had raped the girl, and Natalie's house was her twenty-seventh home.

"God is good," Natalie told me. "You know that quote, 'To much has been given, much is expected'? I thought, how can I keep all my good fortune to myself?"

Thus began Grace's yearlong tutorial at Natalie's on how to human: A new day means new socks. You don't have to always wear black. Here's how to place and pay for an order at Taco Bell. Don't forget to take your meds and your iron supplements. No need to take food from the garbage when you can help yourself to what's in the fridge.

When Natalie couldn't understand why Grace only slept *atop* the guest-bed comforter, Grace said she'd never slept with sheets on a bed before. It had been months since she'd even slept on a bed.

When they first met, Natalie was sure Grace would end up homeless and living under a bridge somewhere. When I asked the same question of Grace, she said casually, "I thought I'd be dead of suicide or living on the streets."[1] Though she was a senior when she dropped out of UHS, she was so credit deficient that technically she was still a freshman.

The first time I arranged to interview Grace in early 2024, Natalie found her hiding in a closet, too scared to talk to a stranger. We gave her more time to get used to the idea, and when I came back the following month, she appeared. When I asked Grace to show me her artwork—she liked to make up animal composites, including a husky/wolf named Diyan—she warmed up quickly.

"I hated school so much—the bullying," Grace said. "I was failing school not because I was stupid but because I hated it.

"Apparently," she added, her hazel eyes crinkling over a Cheshire grin, "I'm actually quite smart!"

After passing her GED in three months and graduating from the youth center's life skills program—the first of the center's kids to complete both components—Grace landed a job as a school bus aide. Lance Jackson, the retired teacher and one of the center's main tutors, taught her how to drive, and center volunteers all rallied to prep her for the hardest and final portion of the test—math—which she had to take twice.

By late summer, Grace was living independently for the first time and riding her bike to work. She'd rented an airy studio apartment on Monument Square in a building with an *elevator*, which she deemed quite fancy. Her couch wobbled when I sat down on it, and the two plants in her window—she'd given them both names—were a bit spindly.

But the place was all hers for $650 a month, which she could afford. That is, until the third month, when her mother begged to borrow $700, and Grace was powerless to say no, even though it made her late on her rent. "The hills and valleys, always, but we believe it keeps trending up," the youth center director, Justin Weller, explained.[2]

*Grace Slagle doubts she'd be alive today if not for the life-coaching of Urbana Youth Center program director Natalie Yoder, who took her into her home when she was eighteen. Grace now lives independently in an uptown Urbana apartment and has both her GED and a job.*

Grace vowed to set firmer boundaries after she caught up on her rent. She asked her supervisor for more hours at work, which was a miracle considering that she hadn't been able to summon the nerve to make a phone call to a stranger just two years before, and that was only because Natalie strong-armed Grace into it by sweetening the deal. If Grace would make the call, Natalie would also do a hard thing: She would tell a guy she knew that she had feelings for him. Grace made the call, Natalie told her crush, and thirteen months later Grace wore a black suit to Natalie's wedding, adding a white turtleneck to the mix.

Around the Champaign County Fair, success stories like Grace's were rare as a five-legged lamb. The misinformation swirling around Weller had become so heated that a civic leader accosted Natalie inside the Merchants Building and said, "You know your boss is gay, don't you? He even has plans to install showers in there for the young boys!"

Yes and yes, Natalie said, calmly, explaining that the center's planned expansion called for single-user showers because many students don't have access to basic hygiene facilities.

To which the woman snapped, "I can't believe you call yourself a Christian!" The woman, whose children I went to school with, was a longtime factory owner in her nineties, Catholic, and somewhere to the right of Tucker Carlson. Her daughter's the one who took her kids out of school for the January 6 insurrection, and her son-in-law's the county commissioner who told a public gathering that women would soon be killing their babies after birth. When I asked him later to explain why the post-birth killing wasn't happening after the Ohio amendment to protect the right to abortion went into effect, Nino Vitale told me, "Give it seven to ten years."

WHEN CITY LEADERS BLOCKED the remainder of the youth center's $2.25 million grant for the planned expansion—money already approved by the state, $750,000 of which had already been disbursed—Weller filed a federal civil rights and equal protection lawsuit against several of them, including Mayor Bean, his councilwoman wife, the city manager, and a new school board member, Taylor Armstrong. In the filing, Weller accused Armstrong of killing the grant by way of his connections to a Republican statehouse representative. Armstrong works as the rep's aide, and in his motion to dismiss, he vehemently disputed Weller's claims. (Later, a judge ruled Armstrong's name be stricken from the suit.)

The Urbana-Weller beef dated back to Weller's earlier campaign for mayor, the complaint noted, and included the unlawful removal of some of Weller's campaign signs by the city, its lack of support for the youth center, and its demolition of a building that Weller and his business partner bought to renovate. "An abhorrent and defamatory rumor was spread that Justin had established the Youth Center not out of altruism or civic duty, but rather as a front for his own financial gain and as a means to groom the Defendant Urbana's youth sexually," the filing alleged. Of Weller's efforts to develop low-income housing as well as to give teens work experience in construction, the filing noted that "disparaging rumors spread that Justin was coercing the students of the Urbana Youth Center into slave labor for his own personal gain." I'd heard all those rumors and more.

But this is what I saw, not counting the miracle of Grace: Weller paid the students $15 an hour, while Lance Jackson, the retired social studies teacher, gave them rides to work and supervised them, demonstrating demolition, carpentry, dump hauling, and basic work ethics, like staying on-site until the job's done. The work pays more than McDonald's, students must maintain a C average, and if their grades dip below the cutoff, they're required to join Jackson at a study table.

Halfway through the last school year, Jackson told me, one student ended up living with his grandmother: "He used to smoke dope with his dad. Mom couldn't control him, so Mom put a dog [shock] collar on him so when he tried to leave out the window or the door, she zapped him." During the center's first year, a student marveled while emptying a box of cereal from the center's food pantry, stunned to discover a world in which cereal could be roach-free.

Beyond helping students unpack such trauma, Jackson fills out back-to-school and financial aid forms they can't count on their parents or guardians to do. Such scenarios remained beyond the grasp of Urbana's leadership class, most of whom had still never set foot in the place.

"Urbana is basically the country club and the ghetto, and neither

*Middle schoolers (from left) Megan Allender, Kenley Buckler, Hayden Rogan, and Isabella Williams play a game of slapjack at the Urbana Youth Center.*

group has any idea that the other group exists," said Dave Uhl, who is Justin's partner in redevelopment projects and a school board member for Graham schools, his alma mater. Uhl started the business, now called Urbana Tomorrow, in his mid-forties, following a first career managing international supply chains across the globe. When he bought the company in 2021, he was astonished by how hard it was to find a business's most basic unit: employees. The young men he did hire required step-by-step instructions on how to read a tape measure, operate a vacuum cleaner, use a hammer, and arrive at work on time. At school board meetings, he noticed that Graham High's graduating class had shrunk by about a third, not unlike Urbana's.

It wasn't just fundamental skills the young workers were missing. "They lacked a desire," Uhl said. "If it were me, I would think, 'If I can get a job, I can get the hell out of the shithole life I've got,' but they don't even have that desire. Because they don't know there's something different out there."

It was October 2024, and Uhl seemed fine talking about the changes, and then suddenly he began to cry. "We lost our compassion

for humanity," he said. "We being America. We being a nation of immigrants that seem to be angry and hate everything."

UHL DIDN'T LOVE the idea of Weller's federal lawsuit against the city
and its leadership. The company had already spent more than $80,000
in legal fees on it, and Uhl worried it would further fray his relationships with the city and county administrators he had to work with
regularly. But he stood behind Weller and hoped the lawsuit "just
may be the thing that breaks [the funding stalemate] loose and begins
to shift the topic of conversation to 'What are we going to do about
these kids?'"[3]

In 2023, the head of the county's mental health services board had
zeroed out what was the youth center's only public funding, explaining to me that Weller didn't set enough boundaries. "I think Justin
has the best intentions in the world," Adam Sorensen said. "But it's a
vulnerable population, and there are ethical trainings about how to
work with at-risk youth."[4] In a follow-up interview, Sorensen claimed
the center represented a duplication of services that better-trained social service workers should have been performing instead—but unlike youth center workers, they don't work evening hours.

John Bry, the local historian, said he backed off from supporting Weller during his mayoral campaign because Weller, who'd run
against Bean as an independent, was too far left. Bry, who is also gay,
subscribed no untoward motives to Weller, just that "he was throwing
out stats and programs that the modern Urbanan can't resonate with."

In my first interview with Mayor Bean, more than a year before the
legal filing, he was deeply suspicious of the youth center. "Who oversees the place, what agency? Are they certified? No. They keep coming to us wanting money, but this should be part of the school

system!"[5] After Weller's legal filing, Bean refused to discuss Weller or the youth center.

Back in February 2024, as a courtesy, Weller invited Taylor Armstrong to his office to let him know the lawsuit was forthcoming and that he would be named in it. He'd hoped Armstrong might reconsider his stance on the youth center, maybe even help get the grant back on the table. As Weller saw it, most Urbana politicians were at the tail end of their careers, whereas Armstrong was twenty-four and Weller twenty-eight. Neither was going away anytime soon.

"My thinking was, if there's any hope of us being amicable or at least arriving at an agreement that neither of us loves but we can move productively away from, I want to know I've exhausted that before I permanently make an enemy of this person," Weller said.

It didn't work. As Armstrong stood to leave, he shook his head, saying he hoped Weller would reconsider. "If you don't, you'll end up six feet under when this is all over with," Armstrong said, according to the legal filing. Armstrong said he could not discuss the case.

Months earlier, Weller and his husband, a nurse, were so tired of battling the powers that be that they planned to leave Urbana for good. But when the grant was rescinded, Weller decided to stay put. In high school, he'd played left offensive tackle on the Hillclimbers' last undefeated football team. Weller attended Xavier University, a small historically Black college where he majored in psychology and political science.

"He's still the left tackle," said his dad, Tim Weller, pointing out that the left tackle's job is to protect a right-handed quarterback, like the star player in *The Blind Side*. "Only now he's protecting the kids."

To make payroll and keep the lights on, Weller shored up funding from a foundation in Dayton, first a $45,000 grant and then $100,000. A new family donor was in the works, along with grants from a local

*Fresh from a painting job, nineteen-year-old Hunter Smith*
*sets goals with Urbana Youth Center director, Justin Weller,*
*before heading to his GED tutoring session at the center.*

church and one from a Fraternal Order of Eagles group. Not everyone in town opposed the youth center, just as—my well-off childhood
friends kept reminding me—not every student struggled as much as
Silas, Maddie, and Grace.

By the week of the fair, Grace numbered among three youth center
students who'd passed both their GED and the center's life skills
course. At least forty kids who came to the center for tutoring had
graduated from UHS. Eighty kids would soon show up for after-
school homework help, food, clothes, work training, and other how-
to-human help.

"I grew up hunting, but I'm not somebody who ever felt like I
needed to own a gun," Weller told me. But after the Armstrong threat,
Weller and his husband went out and bought two firearms.[6]

MADDIE ALLEN, the youth center kid with the same scholarship as
Silas but no way to get to Clark State, made plans that summer to ap-

ply for Mrs. Flowers's discounted driver's ed. But three weeks before her community college classes were due to start, she hadn't filled out the paperwork and still had no idea how she would get the eighteen miles south to Springfield for her classes. Her older brother was trying to buy "a beater with a heater" that he offered to share. It was possible she could get a job at Aldi and ride both to work and to school with her mom. But nothing was arranged, all of which seemed to worry me more than it did Maddie.

The next time I checked in, Maddie had taken a second job at a Walmart in Springfield, across the street from the vape shop where her mom works, and was taking her Clark State classes online, which was fine until JD Vance began spreading lies about Springfield's Haitian immigrants eating pets, which Trump amplified a few days later during the 2024 presidential debate. Before Maddie knew it, colleges, schools, and hospitals in Springfield were besieged by bomb threats, Proud Boys marched in Springfield's streets, and Governor Mike DeWine, a Republican, sent in state troopers to quell potential violence and refuted the rumors. Some people, older folks who showed up at Maddie's Burger King counter, checked to make sure she was not serving them dog.

In one news story, I watched as Bill, my ex, his once shorn hair and neat attire now replaced with a chest-length gray beard and long hair, complained to a crowded city commission meeting about the sudden influx of fifteen to twenty thousand Haitians on his home turf. It was stressing the community, he said, causing jumps in rents, insurance rates, and reckless driving incidents, including an unlicensed Haitian driver who hit a school bus and killed an eleven-year-old boy in 2023.

In a story for *PBS News Hour*, Bill was identified as a former journalist and an operator of a Facebook group called Stop the Influx into Springfield, Ohio. "Our concerns don't have anything to do with racism," he said. "But they want to make it sound like a race issue so they can demonize us and ignore our concerns."[7] Bill's group had valid criticisms, particularly about untrained and unlicensed drivers and the impact of so many newcomers on school and health-care services.

Sandwiched between MAGA-hat wearers, an angry-looking Bill was also featured in a front-page *Springfield News-Sun* photograph at a town hall meeting moderated by a leader from Moms for Liberty. A reporter friend covering the Haitian pushback said the whole town was panicked and on edge. If Trump ended up coming to Springfield, "that will be the match, and they will light fire to the city," my friend said. "I feel this is just the next step (Jan. 6 the first) that will culminate with violent imposition of Trump to power."[8] She asked me not to use her name because she feared retribution from the Stop the Influx group.

The CEO of Springfield's McGregor Metal, the company contracting with Clark State to train its Haitian employees, had praised his Haitian workers in national news reports. But he was now, following credible death threats, being coached by FBI agents and security experts to arm and protect himself. "We're being hunted like animals," his wife told *The New York Times.*[9] Even his eighty-year-old mother received hateful calls.

A sheriff in another Ohio county suggested that people with Harris yard signs should have their addresses recorded so that the immigrants could be sent to live with them.[10] Some Urbanans, including the police chief, worried the Haitians would feel so unwelcome in Springfield that they'd move to Urbana next. And though he personally didn't have any Haitian employees, Jeff Helman, the Rosewood factory owner, told me falsely that the Haitian factory workers operating in the region defecated publicly while working on the factory lines.

MEANWHILE, between school and her new Walmart job, Maddie was still working the counter at Urbana's Burger King, still giving homeless people larger-than-allowed portions of free "senior coffee." One of her co-workers, in her thirties and the mother of five kids she'd lost custody of, was presently homeless, sleeping atop the benches on Monument Square. Maddie was still saving to buy a car but kept lending money out to people at work or blowing her paychecks impulsively on "stupid stuff." I'd seen Silas do the same thing, and in my twenties I'd acted similarly—buying clothes I didn't need, just because, finally, I could—until I met my skinflint, middle-class husband, who deserves a lot of the credit for the fact that we are miraculously, gloriously debt-free.

"The rule about money and poverty is, 'If you ask me for some and I have it, I have to share,'" explained Ruby Payne, a nationally known educational consultant and poverty scholar based in Texas. "When you're poor, your decisions are based on survival, relationships, and entertainment."

I thought of the punk show Max and Silas had recently gone to in Columbus. Silas lost his car key in the mosh pit and broke his glasses. (They found the key but had to pay $1,000 to replace the glasses.)

"The way you stay alive is through people," Payne added. "In poverty time, two weeks is an eternity; it's so far down the road that you discount it because, by the time you get there, you'll just ask somebody else for help."[11]

Between her two jobs, going to counseling, and her full-time classes, Maddie was juggling a lot. She was still living at her friend's house on a beautiful Champaign County mini-farm. After showing me her shoddy trailer a year before and the roach-ridden motel where she'd lived in the interim, she couldn't wait for me to see her new digs.

"You're gonna be like '*whoa*' when you see it!" she said cheerfully. "They got all the appliances that beep and make the fancy noises. It's *crazy*." As we drove down her hosts' tree-lined road to their farm, which Maddie happily helps tend, including washing chicken eggs and feeding the pigs, she beamed. "Do you see what I mean? From a trailer to *this*?!"

Her friend's mom was canning the tomatoes she'd grown when we arrived. When I asked why her family had taken in Maddie six months before, she shrugged and said matter-of-factly, "She needed stability. And we have the space."

TWENTY MINUTES SOUTH, the mayor of Springfield, a centrist Republican, had recently awakened to a throng of swastika flag-carrying neo-Nazis protesting on his front lawn.[12] During one of my last visits home, my friend Betty's mom, Kim, brought up the thoroughly disproved pet-eating debacle as we ate a delicious dinner she'd prepared for us of tofu, rice, and kimchi. She lives catty-cornered from Betty and her husband, just down the road from a grandson who mows her lawn, on a quiet country road hemmed in by soybean and cornfields. It's lovely.

In her eighties, Kim still goes to work daily at the family business. She has a brilliant brain for finance and is such a taskmaster that Betty frequently warns people elsewhere in the company with a text that says "Kimchi coming!" when her mom is en route.

Everyone at the dinner table, myself included, had benefited from Trump's hefty tax cuts. During a post-dinner card game, Kim trembled as she described her belief that the Springfield Haitians would literally invade her property if Trump lost.

"I'm very scared," Kim said.

"Mom, that's enough!" Betty said.

In recent years, Betty and I had what I understood to be an unspoken policy of maintaining our six-decade friendship by not discussing politics. I had intuited that Betty, recently named to the board of a local bank—she's the region's first woman and first minority to hold such a position—did not want to be interviewed for my project, though she and her husband kindly offered their guest suite to me on many visits, feeding me and sending me off with produce from their garden and a nearby orchard and eggs from her daughter's free-range chickens. (Kim gave me her homemade kimchi and, never one to pussyfoot around the truth, a box of Korean face masks that she swore would help tame my wrinkles.)

During a girls' trip with Betty and Joy to Kim's beach condo two years before, Betty taught me how to make Kim's kimchi, slicing the vegetables precisely, and how to measure water for rice the way her mother does—by laying a hand in the rice until the water reaches your first knuckle. But the first thing Joy said when they picked me up at the airport was, "What happens in Florida stays in Florida," which meant no taking notes for your book.

Halfway through my project, Betty asked why I was so focused on kids like Silas and Maddie rather than the students in Urbana who were thriving. Then she remembered: The goal had been to write about the challenges facing a modern-day me.

"Yeah, but you were exceptional," Betty said, arguing that Silas wasn't a fair substitute. I'd gone from feral to fairly capable, and Betty believed my transition was born of a kind of superior intelligence. She admired my hustle, watching me put in long workdays after making the seven-hour drive to Ohio on a bursitis-inflamed hip.

But I had never been an exceptional kid. I wasted a lot of time watching *I Dream of Jeannie* and *M\*A\*S\*H*. A solid A minus/B plus student, with a slightly above-average ACT, I behaved badly at times, broke laws, drank more than the daughter of an alcoholic should, and sometimes mouthed off to teachers I didn't like and to my parents, none of which ever occurred to Betty to do.

Of the two of us, Silas was the exceptional one. My home life was no picnic, but if you overlaid a map of my childhood trauma onto

Silas's, it would maybe cover his pinkie finger. I'd left poverty behind in another era, back when it was enough to have a gritty mom, a grandma who spoiled me with unconditional love and lawn-mowing money, and a political class that used to not view the education of poor kids as a threat to their own grip on wealth and power, on the betterment of their own kids. That had been the point in choosing him as a stand-in for a young me.

Betty had never been to the Urbana Youth Center, not since the building housed the town library—the same building where our Grimes-toiling mothers introduced us when we were four. Back then her family lived in one half of the duplex next door, in the exact spot where Grace figured out how to pass her GED.

THAT WEEK, COOKIE'S HUSBAND developed a bedsore that wouldn't heal, and his cellulitis turned into a full-body blood infection. And yet he stubbornly refused to go to the hospital because he couldn't get himself dressed and didn't want EMTs to see him in that state. In town at the time, I offered to drive over to their house and help, and a very rattled Cookie asked, "What could you do?"

It was a fair question. I muttered something about being pretty strong, and she said he'd still be too heavy for me to lift. Having not laid eyes on him in almost forty years, I had no idea. Considering our distant relationship, I had never imagined becoming so involved in Cookie's world as to contemplate the potential mixing of body fluids.

Turned out, I didn't need to. Our bossy big sister, in language that she later apologized for, told Cookie to "grow a pair!" and call 911, and finally Cookie did. After having refused the help of the community paramedic Cheryl Wears, Cookie also reached out to her, finally. Wears met them at the hospital and ended up facilitating the ongoing transfers between hospital and rehab centers to treat his persistent infections.

With the help of some friends from church, Cookie bought a one-story condo in Urbana using the couple's retirement funds and what was left of her inheritance from Mom. From his hospital bed, her husband relented about moving to a one-story home and finally, Cookie said, apologized "for being such an ass."

It was my sister's first time being a homeowner, her first time navigating a move alone, her first time buying homeowner's insurance (which Wears also helped her arrange). It was the first momentous decision she'd made on her own in four decades.

My niece Liza and I were still talking most days and planning another trip, this time to the Grand Canyon. She hoped her abusive stepdad would "die a slow, painful death!" she told me. She found the language to tell some of our relatives what a betrayal it was when they asked her to forgive and forget, and even when they spoke his name in front of her. And she thanked me for never not believing her.

Sasha, my musician kid, now wore an oversized hoodie over their preferred concert wear when their band stopped to fuel up on the road. The latest trans kid to be beaten to death, fourteen-year-old Pauly Likens, had become the nineteenth trans or gender-expansive person to be murdered—or at least the nineteenth we knew of—that year. (Such violence is often unreported or misreported.) Pauly's dismembered body was found in a reservoir in western Pennsylvania, close to where our Irish ancestors first settled.[13]

And though Aunt Cookie probably thought Sasha was following

their older brother to hell, I was touched when Sasha nonetheless offered to drive with me to Ohio to help my sister move. It was not the gesture of some muscly Jesus who'd strut into my hometown fair toting an AR-15. It was an offer straight out of a chapter of Luke: *To whom much is given, much is expected.*

Liza bristled at our plans because it indirectly helped her stepdad. But she also knew it was hard to ignore a sister in crisis when she had so little agency and I had so much.

Two days later, just before Sasha and I were due to drive to Ohio, Cookie said she no longer needed us, explaining that her grandsons, her youngest daughter, and church friends were taking care of it. I'd be lying if I said we weren't relieved. Cookie, too, I'm sure.

Two weeks later, for fact-checking purposes—and because I'd told her at the start she'd have a chance to respond to what I'd written—I called to read Cookie her section of this book. Ten minutes in, I could hear her begin to hyperventilate. Having the story repeated back to her, she said at the end of an hour-long conversation, was "making me sick to my stomach."

She was so stunned by my account it was as if she had never given me the two-and-a-half-hour interview; as if we had never openly addressed Liza's account of her splintered childhood, even though I'd recorded it all, with her permission, on my phone. She cried and asked me what to do. She said her pastor had told her not to believe Liza, that it would be best for everyone if the family simply never brought it up again. That the pastor and his wife had been praying about it and that "we feel really good about" her husband, according to Cookie.

Liza was eleven at the time. A year before, she'd been a smiley girl with oversized glasses who won a national poetry contest, one of fourteen elementary schoolers in the country.[14] She loved snuggling with our cat, Doris, and watching *Mister Rogers' Neighborhood* with my mom, who found the show soothing.

THE NEXT DAY, Cookie texted me a plea not to include the story of what happened to my niece—and, by extension, to all of us: "It doesn't benefit anyone. Brings up trash that may have happened. I see no value in it at all."

"I'm sorry, I know you're hurting," I wrote back. But her husband "and the church people who told you to blindly believe him—and to ignore a suffering child—are the perpetrators here, not me." For the second time in as many days, I urged her to apologize to Liza, explaining that an apology might lead to healing and that Liza, now forty-nine, still thought of what her stepdad had done to her "almost every day." Without accountability, I explained, it's harder for victims to find closure. Shame always becomes the cloak that shuts healing down.

A week later, Cookie was ready to apologize, but Liza refused to take her call. "She's had forty years to make amends," she told me. An apology this late in the game could not possibly be genuine, she believed.

EARLIER THAT YEAR, the literary icon and Nobel Prize winner Alice Munro was revealed to have denied her daughter's allegations of childhood sexual abuse against her stepdad, Munro's husband, even after he pleaded guilty in court to indecent assault. The bombshell, delivered after Munro's death, contained the fact that Munro had for decades lashed out at her daughter and blamed a misogynistic society, not her husband, for the abuse. "If this were true, the life [Munro] knew was over," the novelist Roxana Robinson explained. "If she could make it not true, her life could continue."[15]

"PEDOPHILIA" WAS NOT A word I imagined using when I began this home-going project. Children living with stepdads or live-in partners are ten times more likely to experience abuse than those living with married biological parents.[16] One in four American girls are sexually abused before the age of eighteen—more than a third by family members—and only 12 percent of child sexual abuse cases get reported. Very few perpetrators, as in Liza's cases, are ever arrested, prosecuted, or in any way held to account.[17] Of those who are, they're rarely covered in the press except when prominent people are featured, such as in the case of the Penn State coach Jerry Sandusky or revelations about abuse in the Catholic Church.[18] Even then, solutions and prevention are rarely addressed, while the ripples of this underreported epidemic fan out across generations.[19]

THOSE STATS KEPT SLAPPING me in the face: in intimate conversations with friends who'd been raped by their uncles and dads and never reported it; in interviews with QAnon classmates whose wackadoodle theories about Sandy Hook and Tom Hanks (*Mister Rogers*, for fuck's sake!) were being whipped up by the rants of Alex Jones and other grifters who make money off freaking out vulnerable people. In interviews with Silas and Maddie and damn near every youth center kid I met. In Liza's recollection of watching her beloved grandma, my mom, walk down a shiny elementary school hallway to pick her up the day she told a school counselor and everything changed.

What did all the non-reckoning with such toxic secrets have to do with the supersizing of our polarization and outrage? Was it that the secrets we bury are the same things we are most apt to fear? As Diana Zuckerman, the research psychologist, put it, "If you know it from your personal experience, then it doesn't seem so outrageous to accuse other people of it, right?"[20]

THE WEEK AFTER the Urbana-Graham football game, a teenage girl and youth center member came to the Urbana Youth Center to report that she'd been sexually assaulted by a classmate at the game. She'd already described the incident to the principal and the school resource officer, and was immediately asked, "What were you wearing?" Because an investigation didn't seem to be forthcoming, she'd come to ask Weller if he could help. Two weeks after the assault, the girl was still forced to sit in two classes with her alleged perpetrator, who'd been caught on camera assaulting her the year before.

Matt Lingrell, the police chief I'd gone to high school with, told me an investigation had taken place but, without backup evidence beyond the teen's account, no charges were filed.[21] He had yet to receive funding for a second school resource officer.

FOR SILAS, THE DRAMATICS continued apace. His mother relapsed after more than a year of sobriety. When CPS workers found out, they immediately removed his youngest half-siblings, now four and five, and placed them with family members on their dad's side. His older teenage siblings were put in emergency custody with Silas, who was now all of nineteen.

He had managed to secure his own two-bedroom apartment with Max in a complex with a swimming pool; it was next to a park. He still loved his job, he told me, noting how ironic it was that he oversees the selling of car parts, considering how badly he once needed them. When the school called Silas about problems with his teenage charges, his store manager was flexible. A co-worker at the store had recently told him, "I don't like your lifestyle, but I don't care what you do. You're a hard worker."

I said I was sorry that his plan for full independence from his family had been thwarted.

"It's all right," Silas said. "I planned on it [raising the kids] for most of my life; I knew it was going to happen. It's just shitty that it happened when I thought it wouldn't."

He and Max had recently made the last payment on their Honda, posting a photo of the title and his car keys on Instagram. It was too early to say grace over any of it. But for now, Silas at least felt physically removed from the hamster wheel of his parents' dysfunction. "I'm going to make sure these two kids coming up behind me break the cycle, too."

Mrs. Flowers offered to buy whatever he needed for his new place. Mr. Sapp, worried about the pressure it would put on his relationship with Max, went by to visit. I stopped in, too, on one of my last visits. Silas's siblings were due to arrive in two weeks, and Max and Silas had already moved most of their belongings into the two bedrooms. Max and Silas were sleeping on a foldout couch in the living room, which was covered in boho tapestries, a Pride flag, and SpongeBob art. When I commented on how neat looking everything was, Silas nodded toward Max and said, "That is his happy place—cleaning."

In high school, Max told me, his schoolteacher parents attended a rural church that actively preached against homosexuality. But after watching Max struggle with depression and multiple suicide attempts, his dad, a science teacher, undertook his own research, after which he finally came around to "I don't think it's a choice," and they joined a more open-minded congregation in town. On move-in day, Max's parents helped the couple move and bought them kitchen supplies, including an air fryer, microwave, pots and pans, and dishes. "They see that as, like, what you're supposed to do for your child," Max explained.

Silas told me he was "absolutely done with" his mom, but they still spoke about the children on the phone. Max added, "It's a lot. Not a lot of teenagers are raising teenagers, but I love those kids. I would not feel comfortable if we were here living our lives and they were still in foster care." As imperfect and flimsy as it all seemed, the best word to describe what I saw in their novel family arrangement was "grace."

On Christmas Eve of 2024, Silas got down on one knee in front of the foldout couch and asked Max to marry him.

*Fifteen*

# THE PRICE OF IGNORANCE

*Lightning strikes above a Champaign County farm in the
summer of 2024 as polarization blanketed the nation.*

A popular Government, without popular information, or the
means of acquiring it, is but a Prologue to a Farce or a Tragedy;
or perhaps both. Knowledge will forever govern ignorance:
And a people who mean to be their own Governors must arm
themselves with the power which knowledge gives.[1]

—JAMES MADISON, 1822

Late last fall on my last trip home, my cop buddy Chad Seeberg
drove us deep into the western Ohio countryside. He'd re-
newed his lapsed gun club membership so he could teach me
how to defend myself if it came to it. Into the back of his extended-
cab truck, he had thoughtfully packed a bulletproof vest, ear protection, a bread-box-sized container of ammo, and five different guns,
ranging from a .22 to a double-barreled 20-gauge shotgun.

As he drove, we talked about candidate Trump's plans to deport immigrants, even legal ones, and to do away with gender-affirming care, something twenty-six states had already restricted.[2] We discussed how shocked some of our mutual friends would be by my unvarnished descriptions of our hometown.

"If you don't live it, you don't know it," he said. "I understand the darker piece of it; I've had friends [from Urbana] I've had to talk through a mental health crisis or substance abuse." He'd arrested people addicted to OxyContin and heroin and fentanyl, one of whom was positive for hepatitis C and had hidden a used needle in his pocket that stuck Seeberg as he patted the man down. (Seeberg had to endure an excruciating year of hepatitis testing before doctors concluded that he didn't have the disease.)

Deaths of despair are disproportionately concentrated in places where misinformation spreads rampantly—in high-poverty communities with low college education attainment, scarce access to local doctors, and scant local news. Small Ohio cities like the Springfields, Urbanas, and Marysvilles are places that tend to be the most overlooked by the Democratic Party and urban elites. "Emerging neurological research has shown clear links between despair and vulnerability to misinformation, right-wing radicalization, and violence," noted a Brookings Institution study Chad shared with me.[3]


I THOUGHT OF DR. RACHEL TOWNSLEY CHURCH, the sole physician working out of Urbana's recently opened federally qualified health center, where most patients are low income. Roughly half her patients turn down her recommendations for COVID vaccines. (Champaign County's vaccination rate is 46.9 percent, far lower than the state's average of 59.2.)

Though Church is three decades younger than me, we share parallel Hillclimber stories, down to our Most Improved softball trophies and fond memories of playing trumpet in the UHS Marching Band. "I *love* David M. Sapp!" Church enthused, when I mentioned his name. When Church returned to Urbana after her medical residency two years ago, a local cardiologist sent her a fruit basket with the note "We're so proud you came back." Talk about exceptional: Few UHS kids go on to become doctors, and almost none of those return home to practice.

*When a med-school professor expressed shock that Dr. Rachel Townsley Church would return to Urbana to practice, she said, "Why? This is where I've always wanted to live."*

When Church, thirty-one, got married in 2023, her bridesmaids were three of her favorite cows, on loan from the shrinking dairy farm where she was raised. "At this point, I call 'em cow therapy because it just makes me feel good to hang out with 'em," her dad, Mark Townsley, told me, describing the winnowing effect of big-ag consolidation on his 160-acre family farm.[4] Whereas there were once more than forty-five dairy farms in the county, now there were fewer than ten.[5]

The couple's only child, Church had grown up showing cows and participating in Future Farmers of America. Profit margins were so thin that both her parents worked other full-time jobs, and the family vacationed once every five years.

"I used to dream about going to vet school, but I couldn't handle people spending thousands of dollars to keep a cat alive when people can't get that," Church said. Her medical education at Ohio State was

*Dr. Rachel Townsley's dad, Mark Townsley, teaches career
education and tends his 160-acre dairy farm before and after
school. "I'm prouder of who she is—kind-hearted—than what she's
accomplished," Rachel's mother, Lorraine Townsley, told me.
"The work ethic of farming's what made her."*

mostly paid for by a program that incentivizes students to become primary care providers.

When I asked Church how she stays upbeat, she said, "By celebrating the small wins, like patients just showing up, or getting their blood pressure and diabetes under control. Sometimes I feel like I'm the one person in their week who sits and listens to them. The loneliness, it's huge."[6]

She and her husband had recently joined a progressive church in Springfield that offers English Language Learners classes for Haitians and heartily supports the LGBTQ members of its congregation. During her medical residency, Church did a U-turn on her long-held conservative beliefs about gay people, after befriending several fellow residents who were queer.

Asked if she delivered gender-affirming hormone care at the clinic, she whispered, "Yes."

"Suicide rates among trans people are out of control, and we know that gender-affirming care helps prevent that."

When I told her my favorite quotation about medicine, delivered in 1926—"For the secret of the care of the patient is in caring for the patient"[7]—she said she wanted to frame it and hang it on her wall.

SEEBERG REMINDED ME THAT Americans had discriminated harshly against Irish immigrants in the nineteenth century. Landlords subdivided tiny flats housing upward of thirty people and charged sky-high rents by the week *because they could*. Among the demands of the nativist Know-Nothing Party were a twenty-one-year naturalization period for immigrants, mandatory Bible reading in schools, and immediate deportation of all Irish foreigners. Instead of claims about eating people's pets, the Know-Nothings called the Irish "vile imposters, liars, villains, and cowardly cutthroats." Virulent conspiracies were taken as gospel: Irish-Catholic priests were accused of raping nuns and strangling the babies that resulted, and it didn't matter that none of it was true.

And the Jews in Weimar Germany weren't "foreigners" or "political enemies" or "vermin" . . . until Hitler, named chancellor in 1933, eventually convinced enough people that he could deem them so. The tipping point came when he exacted pledges of loyalty from every branch of government, including the police and the military, then systematically went about outlawing their existence. America's slide into fascism was already playing out as the philosopher Richard Rorty envisioned it in 1998: "The gains made in the past forty years by black and brown Americans, and by homosexuals, will be wiped out."

When I showed Seeberg the photo of my angry ex looking like a Civil War reenactor, he said, "He's regressing." His friend in Urbana had recently spotted a van full of commuting Haitians, en route to the

Urbana factory where they work, on his property. Trying to avoid being seen in public, the Haitians had turned up his gravel road, mistaking it for a public back road.

"He believes everything out of the tangerine toddler's mouth, and he was so amped up about it," Seeberg said. "I told him, 'Think about how they see it,' and he said, 'I don't know, man, I don't know.'"

If Trump, Vance, and company could make enough people afraid—of change, of differentness, of smug bureaucrats and Antifa and those of us besmirched by rageaholics who once loved us as YOU PEOPLE and YOUR FUCKING TEAM—then all bets on democracy were off.

In her masterful 2017 book, *One Long Night: A Global History of Concentration Camps*, the journalist and my dear friend Andrea Pitzer detailed how, over several continents and across 130 years, unchecked immigrant baiters had gathered enough political support to deport foreign-born people or put them in camps by concentrating power and dividing the populace. Trump was now promising, for starters, to carry out the largest mass deportation in American history, imprison his opponents, do away with future elections, and roll back Title IX protections for transgender students.

On a glorious day in the fall of 2024, just fifteen minutes from the nation's capital, I met Pitzer for a walk at the Great Falls Park to get her take. As she saw it, MAGA adherents were trying to spark "mini-fires" closer to home, far away from the Mexican border—in places like Springfield and Aurora, Colorado, where Venezuelans were "overrunning" that city, according to Trump and Stephen Miller, who called a vote for Kamala Harris a vote to live "in occupied territory."[8]

If a wider swath of undecided voters in America's heartland could be made fearful—the "mushy middle," Pitzer called these more apolitical citizens—then destabilization and violence were more likely to occur. "It only takes a little extreme horror for everybody to get scared," she said. "And scared people will trade a lot for a sense of stability."[9]

Racist tropes used to instigate violence were the primer for getting Americans to accept four more years of Trump-led institutional atrocities. That summer, a friend and former war photographer now living in France urged my husband and me to move abroad. "The collapse always happens quicker than people think," he told us. His friend in Bosnia had lost both his house in the city and his rural cabin during that region's civil war and ended up living out the war's final months on a neighbor's floor.

Soon, Trump would light another mini-fire in Charleroi, Pennsylvania, describing the Haitians who had legally settled there as "lawless gangs."[10] At another rally the same week, harking back to the Springfield migrants, he told a group of supporters, "You have to get them the hell out." The crowd chanted, "Send them back!"

My ex was now on the verge of becoming a YouTube celebrity, telling a host on BlazeTV, falsely, that Haitian migrants in Springfield here on Temporary Protected Status had EBT cards with five-figure balances and were automatically getting $600 to $1,600 in monthly Social Security benefits—a claim that absolutely lit up the fury of more than fifteen hundred commenters.[11] While TPS recipients are eligible for Medicaid, food stamps, and cash assistance in limited cases, it's not automatic. The vast majority were working at places like McGregor and *paying into* Social Security through their payroll taxes, not drawing from it. But such misinformation shows why it's near impossible to have real democracy in decision-making when people have such limited information about what's going on. "THEY WILL BE

IN EVERY SMALL TOWN," one commenter wrote. "NO PLACE
TO RUN."

As Pitzer and I hiked the falls, the election was deadlocked. She
gave democracy roughly a 55 percent chance of holding out after the
election. But it all depended upon what everyday Americans decided
to do in the aftermath.

I wasn't quite as optimistic. If Trump won, it would partially be
because many conservatives could not see, let alone denounce, that
the worst of America had taken shape in their corners of the country,
much of it puppet mastered by faraway rich people. It would also be
because liberals failed to actually talk to non-college-educated conservative Americans, not all of whom are racist and sexist.

As the election of 2024 approached, a group in Urbana organized
their second Trump Train, a seventy-two-mile tour of the county featuring scores of trucks, semis, motorcycles, and other vehicles, all
sporting Trump flags and signs. A vintage VW truck displayed a
photo of Trump with his ear bloodied and his fist raised. The parade
began and ended at what used to be the Corn Nuts factory and made
its way through the public square, past the forlorn Man on the Monument. More than 180 vehicles beeped and waved and raged about an
election they were already convinced would be stolen.

"I love how we had patriots stopping traffic for us at intersections,
without anyone asking!" one participant enthused. Food trucks were
brought in for the speech portion, candy thrown from the trucks to
onlookers. It reminded me of the homecoming parade I'd participated in with Betty the year before, only louder, more robust, and
oddly more joyful.

For a variety of reasons, the computer chip plant in New Albany, one of Biden's signature deals, was nowhere close to fruition. Neither of the presidential candidates substantially addressed the opioid crisis or the more than half a million kids who'd been abandoned by it, including Maddie and Silas. Not only had Democrats, traditionally the ones who care about public-health measures, failed to provide a clear path out of the crisis; they were also failing to show they cared about people struggling with the high costs of living.

The changes wrought on Urbana were a microcosm of the country's larger failures to address the collapsing economic order brought on by global trade, the transfer of control from public to private, and the growing impotence of what was once a free, fair, and fact-checked local press. When I asked an investigative journalist friend, recently retired from a national news organization, whether she wished she was still covering politics and the economy, she said no. "It doesn't seem to matter anymore what the legacy media does. Half the country doesn't believe what we report anyway."

SCHOOL ATTENDANCE was still in a downward spiral. In JD Vance's hometown of Middletown, an hour south of Urbana, the chronic absenteeism rate was 44.5 percent—not that Vance mentioned it.[12] His educational platform was all about beefing up private school vouchers and religious education and doing away with the Department of Education. If you want to quantify the price of ignorance, here's one number: The State of Ohio was now spending nearly $1 billion annually on private school vouchers that mainly benefited kids who are already attending private schools.[13]

In the first two weeks of the new school year, the truancy officer Brooke Perry visited a record 153 homes. A month into the year, 120 students were already homeschooling, up from 115 at the end of the previous year. Superintendent Thiel expected the number to grow during the school year as truancy charges threatened to accrue and parents defensively pulled out their kids. Almost two-thirds of third graders weren't proficient in language arts or math, but they'd been passed onto the fourth grade anyway.[14]

The sovereign-citizen wife whose farm we'd visited the year before had been pulled over for speeding and, finally, spent a night in jail for her outstanding truancy warrants. Her husband threatened to file kidnapping charges against police. They were threatening, too, to sue Brooke.

Lindsey, the teenager who attacked Brooke that spring, had since assaulted three others. She'd been court ordered to a behavioral health rehab on a therapeutic horse farm, where she stayed for eighteen days before being released to her grandmother. Shirley, her grandmother, "looks awful," Brooke said. "She is so worn down and out."

On our last visit, Brooke and I crisscrossed the county, delivering a polite high school senior who'd overslept to an alternative-ed school in Springfield. We drove a seven-year-old who was presently homeless and staying with relatives to Graham Elementary. An uncle who answered the door said the boy's grandma had been "too sick" to send him to the bus stop, which was only fifty yards from her front stoop. The boy's hair was slumped up on one side, but he was happy to go to school because his teacher was nice, he told us in the car. His favorite subject was coloring.

"I like coloring, too," Brooke said. "It's fun." The seventh anniversary of her bus accident was almost upon her; her PTSD was in overdrive.

A block away from my old Walnut Street house, a mother of two was running a pit bull rescue when city officials condemned her home, Brooke told me, referring to another ongoing case. The family was presently living in a camper and roaming the county for spaces to park at night, after police kicked them out of the Walmart parking lot. The teens were supposedly doing school online, but Brooke had her doubts.

When I told her that Urbana had just been named by *Ohio Magazine* as one of Ohio's Best Hometowns, a bit of publicity that Mayor Bean and company were already touting as an economic development tool, Brooke said, "I'd like to know who they interviewed for that!"

"You should rename your book *Hot Mess Express*," she said.

IN LATE 2024, Justin Weller and Dave Uhl made inquiries about buying *The Urbana Daily Citizen*, the paper I delivered and later wrote for. Their best-case scenario: "I want to just buy it and unhinge [the remaining two writers] from all the bullshit," Uhl said.

"They need to be on the front lines," Weller said.

"Or drag their happy asses into the real world where they don't seem to want to go!" Uhl said.

Weller had learned the hard way that spotlighting problems in a small town can easily backfire. People in Urbana—the country-club set, anyway—have a heightened sense of civic ownership in contrast to people who live in, say, Columbus, who don't pretend to understand half of what's going on in their communities. "People here think they know where they live. But when you share things they have no idea about, things that unmoor them from what they think they know, they'll attack whoever's sharing it." I was being warned, again, about irate villagers.

"It's that grief thing," Uhl added. "You've got to give them time to breathe, to understand the dreamy vision you had doesn't have to be dissolved."

"Yeah," Weller added, "but it has to be modified by reality . . . instead of just sitting on your hands and wanting to paint only with the nice colors."

Do-gooders like Lance Jackson, the youth center volunteer who'd predicted Americans would end up in districts à la *The Hunger Games*, had changed his mind about moving to Oberlin. Blue dots turned out to be a lot more expensive than his northern Champaign County red hamlet, where the Jacksons lived in a comfortable paid-off house, surrounded by neighbors who mostly still revered him as the teacher-coach who'd helped their kid graduate and/or get into college; the guy who once defied his own principal by babysitting for a student's infant while teaching his class, every day, for three months.

But he was torn now because he still could not share with his neighbors the happiest and most basic of family news: that his daughter was soon to wed a woman.

Jackson was pessimistic about the postelection landscape. "I think it's going to get violent. January 6 will look like a walk in the park no matter who wins. If Kamala wins, people around here will not take a Black female as their leader."[15]

In Georgia, election officials were planning to wear lanyards equipped with panic buttons.[16] Associated Press reporters across the country were being trained to work in combat zones, learning how to assess which walls were thick enough to hide behind during battles, with orders to wear goggles to guard against tear-gas attacks. In Arizona's Maricopa County, election officials erected two layers of fencing around its vote-tabulation center, with SWAT teams stationed on the roof and officers patrolling the perimeter on horseback. In Wilkes-Barre, Pennsylvania, a fortress of landscaping boulders aimed for a more aesthetically pleasing polling-place vibe.

AT THE SHOOTING RANGE with Chad, my aim was so bad that most of my shots landed in the bullet-trap backstop many yards from the target. When a guy in the firing line next to us wanted to know why I was there, Chad said, "To learn about protection," and the man cheered.

I wondered if he was following the edicts of the Ohio Gun Owners, who were still urging followers to train daily and ammo up for the end-time. "If local law enforcement is not going to do anything about [the Springfield situation], let's us local militia remedy the situation," one member enthused. A third of Republicans and 23 percent of Americans now believed that "true American patriots may have to resort to violence in order to save our country," a 5 percent increase among Republicans and 8 percent increase among the American public since 2021.[17] Almost three-quarters of Americans worried about politically motivated violence in the election's aftermath.[18]

"When the men with guns who have always claimed to be against the system start wearing uniforms and marching with torches and pictures of a leader, the end is nigh," warned the historian Timothy Snyder in his *On Tyranny: Twenty Lessons from the Twentieth Century*. "When the pro-leader paramilitary and the official police and military intermingle, the end has come."[19]

Who would join them? I wondered. And who would join the path of the Underground Railroad conductor Udney Hyde, who pledged to break the laws of man but keep the laws of God?

BY THE TIME CHAD brought out his third gun for me to shoot—a Glock—I knew in my gut that I would never own one. But it took spending two hours at a shooting range to understand what my husband and our city friends had been telling me all along: that having a gun in the house was more likely to put myself and my family at risk.

I had recently read "If I Owned a Gun," an essay by Andre Dubus III. Of the afternoon his father came within inches of accidentally killing him with a .22, the writer recalled, "My father may have apologized or maybe I did for standing where I had been, but what comes more clearly is my father's deeply reddened face, the way he lowered the rifle and looked down at the locked and unlocked guns around him as if they were scorpions he had once considered pets."[20]

The shooting was loud even with ear protection, and Chad and I were both sweating through the bulletproof vests. Each gun had a different safety apparatus, and when I pointed out that the smallest one eerily resembled a plastic toy gun, Chad nodded and said "exactly." While the exercise didn't exactly terrify me, it made me queasy. When I declined to fire the remaining weapons, the double-barreled shotgun and a semiautomatic folding rifle, Chad said, "No worries," and carefully, as if handing a newborn over to her mother, put them back in their cases.

It was a sweltering, hotter-than-normal October day. Across the globe, the escalation of climate change was upping the risk of violent conflict, which, in turn, was undermining "societies' ability to cooperate," leading to yet more climate change, according to a recent report.[21] That month, my kid's band held fundraisers for mutual-aid groups assisting the Appalachian victims of Hurricane Helene and started giving away Narcan, the overdose antidote, at their merch table.

Ten months earlier, in late winter—well ahead of Ohio's peak thunderstorm season—repeat clusters of tornadoes touched down across my western Ohio home region. At nearby Indian Lake, one killed three people and injured twenty more. That February, my newly widowed sister, Terry, found herself huddled inside a closet on her electric scooter in the middle of the night. It reminded me of her late husband's dying request—that Terry and Liza move into a duplex built into the side of a hill. As we teetered toward the election, I found myself wondering, was the bunker John envisioned on his deathbed delirium, or was it prescience?

YEARS AGO, an addiction scholar I interviewed told me something I thought of nearly every time I set foot in my hometown: "Rigid thinking is a trauma response."[22]

Rigid thinking propelled by decades of job losses alongside pill mills to pacify the wounds, creating more billionaires and a growing underclass of people grappling with sky-high ACE scores. Rigid thinking culminating in the widespread normalization of obfuscated greed: If that little girl in the lilacs poring over the library's copy of *Harriet the Spy* can go to college and have nice things, won't that just make it harder for my own kids to get ahead?

It won't. The answer to poorly performing public schools isn't to pull out all the high achievers and segregate them from the stragglers; it's to strengthen the most fundamental unit of a democratic society— our public schools. The answer to our epidemic of loneliness isn't to seek solace in conspiracy theories; it's to participate in real life with other human beings, including those we don't know.

With a nod to the Ohio Gun Owners, may I suggest that we instead:

> Touch grass.
>
> Take a walk with a friend.
>
> Buy diapers for a nonprofit dedicated to serving low-wage moms.

*Help mutual-aid groups led by people in struggle.*

*Where it is safe to do so, try to mend frayed connections by practicing grace (in the words of Barbara Kingsolver: "Love stays alive if you tend it like a flame").[23]*

*Support local news.*

*Run for local office and/or support candidates who are trying to change things for the better for the most people.*

*Repeat.*

Like many of my friends who are scared about living under a fascist regime, I love the idea of moving to Portugal. I also dream about living in my ancestral Irish homeland, where my hip pain went away just as Liza's eczema did. But there is a world of resistance to hatred and the systemic betrayal of democracy that demands us to stay and fight. We must scramble for hope fiercely, the way a farm girl wrestles a muddy sow.

WHEN OUR KIDS WERE in elementary school, my husband and I signed up to help our local Refugee and Immigration Services organization, hoping to model service. We were assigned to be English tutors for a family of eight Liberians, newly arrived from the Ivory Coast refugee camp where they'd been living since the start of Liberia's civil war.

But the Dolue-Glay family needed so much more than language lessons. They needed jobs and winter coats and someone to teach them how to drive. Their kids needed in-depth tutoring, rides to their first teeth cleanings, instructions on how to operate a Coke machine. ("There is a person inside that machine!") They needed every damn thing.

It was incredibly moving, like the first time they witnessed snow: The children were so excited they called us, then immediately dropped the phone on the floor to go wallow in it. It was also overwhelming, like when the principal repeatedly called us out of work because the oldest son, who had PTSD, could not stop throwing tantrums. After two years of near-daily contact, after we helped the Dolues apply to build their own Habitat for Humanity house, we stepped back in utter exhaustion. Unless there's a family emergency, we see them now mainly just in April, to help with taxes.

But first, demonstrating a reservoir of patience I cannot begin to conjure, my husband taught the dad, Tailey, a taciturn man I never quite warmed to, how to drive. The one time I rode with Tailey, he turned left at a stoplight without yielding to oncoming cars. I seized the wheel and jerked us onto the median, narrowly preventing a head-on crash. "You cannot keep driving with Tailey, or you're going to die!" I told my husband. (He didn't listen, and Tailey eventually passed his driving test after several tries.)

I was closer to his wife, Zeor (pronounced ZEE-or), who laughed easily and seemed less burdened than her husband, though they were both exhausted from working manual-labor jobs while caring for five school-age kids and Zeor's nonagenarian mother. I'd helped Zeor land her first American job at a deli, a Roanoke institution where she made $9 an hour shredding cabbage for slaw and where the owner refused to learn her name, instead calling her Zero.

The night before their first American Thanksgiving, Zeor joined me in our kitchen, and I taught her how to make some of my standard dishes, including my mother-in-law's favorite Junior League recipe for Holiday Mashed Potatoes (the secret being copious amounts of sour cream, butter, and cream cheese) and my mom's green bean casserole (the secret being to open lots of cans). While we were cooking, Zeor mentioned in broken English that her eldest daughter, still in a refugee camp in Ghana, had just delivered a baby girl. I hadn't even known she was pregnant.

Just as casually, Zeor then explained that by tradition her daughter had asked her to name the baby.

"And?" I asked.

"The baby is called Beth Macy Glay."


As MY HOUSE PERCOLATED with simmering starches—my happy place—that night, I lent Zeor a bathing suit, and we sank into our backyard hot tub. It had been a huge splurge on our teacher-reporter salaries to buy it; it took more than a year to pay it off. As Zeor settled into the water, she made a guttural noise in her native tongue. I was familiar with the exclamation, a cross between a gasp and a cluck, which roughly translated to "holy shit."

Then a huge smile spread across her face.

"Oh . . . you . . . *white people!*" she said.

That was twenty years ago. The last time I saw Zeor, her mother had died at the age of 104. To pay for the funeral, we chipped in with another couple, friends of ours who'd mentored one of their sons and paid for most of his college, the portion financial aid no longer covered. He's now married, an accountant living in a D.C. suburb, and expecting his own child.

Zeor now works as a custodian for a Veterans Administration hospital. She and Tailey still send money back to relatives in Africa, but now they also send funds for the construction of a house in Liberia. They plan to move back home when they retire.

Unless you are born into money, unless you are one of the luckiest *white people*, as they now view life in America, it is just too hard to thrive.

Across the United States, bullies have upended our peace and prosperity by turning too many of us against our most vulnerable people: women and girls, the poor, queer people, immigrants, people of color. They have turned the people of our hometowns—and members of our own families—into people we still love but often struggle to like.

At a Trump rally near my house three days before the election, I asked a vendor what his most popular T-shirt was. It was a toss-up between SAY NO TO THE HOE and ROSES ARE RED, KAMALA'S NOT BLACK, JOE HAS DEMENTIA, AND HUNTER'S ON CRACK. Two young men waiting to get inside the arena said they couldn't wait for Trump to become the "forty-seventh president—and the forty-eighth, forty-ninth, and fiftieth."

I rolled my eyes, but the joke was on me. In my home county, three out of every four people voted for Trump and Vance. Chief among the fire hose of disruptions at the start of Trump's second presidency was his blanket pardoning of the January 6 insurrectionists, including Jessica Watkins, the bartender from my home county and a former member of the far-right Oath Keepers militia.[24] Trump won with one of the smallest popular-vote margins in American history, but he won 91 percent of the counties lacking a professional source of local news, trouncing Harris by an average of 54 percentage points.[25]

The bullies are no longer just on the playground; they're on our school boards, in our mayor's offices, behind the Resolute desk. They're casting stones on social media platforms owned by bigger bullies who profit not by sharing fact-checked reports but by connecting lonely people who crave the addictive, rapid-fire punch of belonging and fear, fight or flight, us versus them—because it helps them sell more shit.

The bullies are in the YouTube comments of my kid's band, including one motherfucker who hopes my child—the one who happily jitterbugged with his demented grandma—will join the 41 percent of trans women who attempt suicide before they turn forty.

The day after the election, I called Amy—my fellow Urbana expat—to commiserate. She blamed Trump's win on "that same micro-dick energy that wants to keep us in the kitchen because we've already surpassed all the dudes living in their parents' basements addicted to porn and video games.

"I feel so naive," she said, sighing. "These [Trump supporters] we grew up with, they're still playing these diabolical comic book characters while we've just been . . ." She trailed off.

"Singing Kumbaya," I said.

In mid-February, my ex-boyfriend Bill, a hard-core smoker who carried a canister of loose nicotine and rolling papers with him wherever he went, came down with a serious case of pneumonia. He had told me in the summer of 2023, "At this point I'm thinking if something gets me, it gets me." He called the Affordable Care Act nothing but a fraud on "regular-ass people" and added, "If I just keel over at seventy-six, it'll be good."

Lacking health insurance, he went to the hospital later than he probably should have for his pneumonia and died a few days later of heart failure.

His obituary noted that Bill "loved to immerse himself in the world of fantasy" and that he "dedicated his waking hours working towards bettering the city and helping the homeless." In an interview with NewsNation, Bill had blamed the city's rise in homelessness squarely

*Bill Monaghan (second from left) was the most liberal person I knew
in the mid-1980s. I interviewed him about his rightward
turn several times over the course of my home-going project.
A former newspaper reporter, Bill is shown here at
a Springfield town hall in September 2024.*

on Springfield's Haitians, whose presence, he believed, was the main cause of rising housing costs.[26]

On X, he promoted racist and antisemitic screeds, including a "documentary" claiming that immigrants were invited into the country at the behest of Jewish moguls eager to erase white America as payback for the Jewish suffering in World War II. In his mind, the Haitian influx was unscrupulously designed to provide cheap labor for corporations to make up for the "unreliable worthless drug addicts who refuse to go to work."[27]

Bill had spent his final months fully ensconced in the debunked white-nationalist Great Replacement Theory, supporting such notions that the Jewish Sackler family developed OxyContin with the intent of killing off whites and that the Biden administration's Jewish members led the way on getting Temporary Protected Status for Haitians for similar reasons.

The day of Bill's funeral, the Trump administration announced it was halting TPS for Haitians, including most of the roughly fifteen thousand living in Springfield. Bill died at sixty-three.

THIRTY MILLION POOR and low-wage people didn't bother to vote in the 2024 election, in part because nobody talked to them.[28] The non-voters, alas, included Silas, who explained the day after, "I just feel like all politicians say extremes when they're running, but it's much harder and complicated to get what they want done."

That was before Trump 2.0 banned trans people in the military, signed an order recognizing only male and female genders, and tried to ban trans care for minors—all in his first week. It was before Ohio Governor Mike DeWine signed a bill into law requiring schools to mandate religious instruction release time and to force teachers to out a student's gender identity to their parents.[29] Between work and his teenage charges, Silas said, he hadn't had time to devote to politics.

"The system hasn't worked very well for towns like Urbana, Ohio," the Democratic strategist David Axelrod told me after the election. If conservatives seem uninterested in preserving democracy, "it's because the status quo has not worked for the large numbers of Americans who feel alienated."[30] The minimum wage has been $7.25 since 2009.

"The question is, How do we reestablish a dialogue with people about what's going on in their lives that is respectful and from which policymakers can learn but also that we as Americans learn about each other not as menacing people but as our neighbors?"[31] Axelrod said.

IT MAY BE MAGA's world now, but if we want to hold onto our freedoms and our democracy, there is work to be done, voters to register, resistance to sow. It will take more than an oversized hoodie, even a bulletproof one, to keep our children safe. It will take people willing to understand that facts matter, and that real leaders model how to be human, not belittle.

When more Americans prosper, as they did during the aftermath of World War II, when people weren't constantly fretting about food and rent and whether their beater with a heater would get them to work, they have the bandwidth to see beyond their foxholes to address bigger questions about basic decency and human rights.

I believe Donald Trump cared more about staying out of prison than he cared about the people of my hometown. But harnessing a 20 percent inflation rate that too many comfortable Democrats shrugged off and a pattern of division so worn that people no longer feel its grooves, the consummate showman conned most voters into thinking he cared.[32] I blame Trump and his billionaire enablers, not them.

## ACKNOWLEDGMENTS

When I find myself slamming on my car brakes to avoid a collision, my right arm instinctively juts out as if to shield my niece Liza, even when no one is there. As a kid, she loved sitting next to me in my old VW Bug and shifting gears. It's been decades since I drove beater cars with bad brakes, but that deep muscle memory still reminds me of our entwined DNA. Liza, your participation in this project means everything to me. I wish I could have shielded you more.

Thanks to my sisters Terry and Cookie and our brother, Tim, all of whom lovingly opened their hearts, memories, and homes to me through laughter, disagreements, and occasional tears. I learned so much from long discussions with my hometown classmates Betty Sherman, Joy Ware Miller, Amy Puglia Hunter, Dave Curnutte, Terri Thompson, and Mark Evans. Betty and Phil Sherman were especially generous hosts, as were Tonya and Ed Evans. Former *Urbana Daily Citizen* editor Gary Schenkel, my first professional boss, pitched in with reporting advice, data gathering, and on-the-ground research, as did his librarian wife, Kay Schenkel.

I'm grateful for feedback from friends, scholars, and writers who sustained me and helped shape my thinking, especially my bestie, Martha Bebinger, who talked me through every quandary with unfettered love and near-daily strategy sessions (plus yoga). Thanks also to

Bill Bishop, Mary Bishop, Sarah Jones, Kelsang "Nami" Namgyal, Carole Tarrant, Andrea Pitzer, Jen Brothers, Rich Martin, Margaret Newkirk, Jeff Sharlet, Carl Erik Fisher, Nick Jacobs, Steven Conn, Amy Azano, Jane Hundley, Sharon Rapoport, Lon Wagner, Anthony Flaccavento, Sarah Wildman, and Mim Young.

Photographer Josh Meltzer, my dear friend and longtime collaborator, joined me on several trips home, bucking me up when I was sad before I knew it myself, never judging, and helping me see my hometown anew.

Agent Dorian Karchmar shaped my initial idea into a research-driven quest. But no one contributed more sideline cheering, emotional backstopping, and elevated thinking than my editor, Scott Moyers, who took the time to read and discuss long summaries of my interview notes, read so very many drafts, and even traveled to Urbana to meet some of the people in the book, asking eye-opening questions of them and me as well as contributing some of my favorite lines. This next-level editing is so rare, his name should be on the cover, too.

Elsewhere at Penguin Press, Helen Rouner, Ann Godoff, Gail Brussel, Danielle Plafsky, Elijah Rey-David Matos, Sarah Hutson, Matt Boyd, Ingrid Sterner, and Michael Brown shepherded the publication of this project with creativity and aplomb. Special thanks to the John Simon Guggenheim Memorial Foundation whose fellowship supported my travel and research.

No one protects my personal windshield from errant stones more than my husband, Tom Landon, a former paper boy whose secret sauce is a blend of steadiness, great humor, and unfaltering good judgment. To our kids Sasha and Max: Thanks for your love and technical support (and remember: When paddling through rapids, always follow Dad).

Finally, I bow down to the educators celebrated in this book, all of whom exhibited traits of my own life-mending teachers and mentors: public school heroes Pamela Bullard Mack, Margaret Tabor, Ray Laakaniemi, Vicki Hesterman, and the late Robert K. Martin; and the late Bob Giles, the Nieman fellowship curator who changed my life; the late Frosty Landon, my editor turned uncle-in-law; and most of all my late mom, Sarah Macy Slack, my first reader, pluck-seeder, and maker of ways. She was in her eighties when she paid cash for her first new car, then astonished us all by showing up in my Virginia driveway in a cherry red Monte Carlo with dual exhaust and a spoiler on the back. Liza drove.

# NOTES

## EPIGRAPHS

1. Annie Woodford, "Those Factories Had Heart-Pine Floors," in *Where You Come from Is Gone* (Macon, Ga.: Mercer University Press, 2022), 5.
2. Flannery O'Connor, *Wise Blood* (New York: Farrar, Straus and Giroux, 1952), 165.
3. Frederick Douglass, from a series of dialogues with white enslavers, 1855.

## CHAPTER ONE: PRECIPICE

1. Allana Akhtar, "This Is Where to Go If You Want Higher Education for Free," World Economic Forum, Sept. 26, 2019.
2. Jon Marcus, "10 Years Later, Goal of Getting More Americans Through College Is Way Behind Schedule," Hechinger Report, Jan. 14, 2019.
3. Liz Weston, "The US Has Fallen Behind Other Countries in College Completion," Reuters, Sept. 9, 2014.
4. 2021 census data, www.biggestuscities.com/city/urbana-ohio, and compared with 6.7 percent of children living in poverty in 1990. U.S. Census.
5. Stacy Cox (Champaign County director of Job and Family Services), interview by author, April 11, 2023.
6. Heather Cox Richardson, "Letters from an American," Substack, Sept. 13, 2023.
7. David H. Feldman and Donald E. Heller, "The Wall Street Journal Is Wrong About Pell Grants," *Politico*, May 9, 2022.
8. "Percentage of U.S. Students' Expenses for Tuition, Fees, Room and Board Covered by Pell Grants from 2003/2004 to 2023/2024," Statista, 2024, www .statista.com/statistics/222444/share-of-us-students-expenses-covered-by-pell -grant/.
9. David Reich and Brandon Debot, "House Budget Committee Plan Cuts Pell Grants Deeply, Reducing Access to Higher Education," Center on Budget and Policy Priorities, Oct. 21, 2015.

10. Sarah Flanagan, interview by author, Jan. 17, 2023.
11. Felix Richter, "Americans Owe $1.75 Trillion in Student Debt," World Economic Forum, Aug. 30, 2022.
12. Matthew Desmond, *Poverty by America* (New York: Random House, 2023), 52.
13. David Deming, "The College Backlash Has Gone Too Far," *Atlantic*, Oct. 3, 2023.
14. "In 2023, We Tracked 1,430 Hate and Antigovernment Groups Across the U.S.," Southern Poverty Law Center, June 4, 2024, www.splcenter.org/hate-map.
15. Flowers, interview by author, March 23, 2023.

### CHAPTER TWO: TRUST

1. Jane Hundley, from notes I took during our therapy sessions; this one was from the spring of 1999.
2. Rich Ebert (Champaign County Economic Partnership director), interview by author, Sept. 25, 2023.
3. Evan P. Middleton, *History of Champaign County, Ohio* (Indianapolis: B. F. Bowen, 1917), 335.
4. Workers of the Writers' Program of the Work Projects Administration, *Urbana and Champaign County* (Urbana, Ohio: Gaumer, 1942), 49.
5. "Freed Slave Counted Among Early Settlers," newspaper clipping, date and publication unknown, Champaign County Historical Society. Stanhope was initially called Stanup, the story went, because he'd learned to "stand up" whenever a Washington family member entered the room; he lived to be 114. Tom Stafford, "Valet to History," *Springfield News-Sun*, date unknown. Stories for this section were also drawn from "Taking a Stand for Freedom," a project of the Ohio History Service AmeriCorps program, 2011, and from multiple documents compiled by the Champaign County Historical Society.
6. Ralph M. Watts, *History of the Underground Railroad in Mechanicsburg* (Columbus, Ohio: F. J. Heer, 1934).
7. Edward O'Conner Purtee, "The Underground Railroad from Southwestern Ohio to Lake Erie" (PhD diss., Ohio State University, 1932), 27.
8. Kathy Schulz, *The Underground Railroad in Ohio* (Charleston, S.C.: History Press, 2023), 21.
9. Workers of the Writers' Program of the Work Projects Administration, *Urbana and Champaign County*, 49.
10. Evans, interview by author, Feb. 24, 2023, and follow-up messages, Jan. 23, 2024.
11. Ted Macy to Sarah Macy, postmarked Nov. 22, 1974.
12. Betty Sherman, email to author, Aug. 10, 2022.
13. Terry's letters to Mom recounted the financial help, 1982–83.
14. President Johnson gave the speech in 1964, a year before he signed into law the Higher Education Act.
15. Beth Macy, "The Door That Claiborne Pell Opened," *Chronicle of Higher Education*, Jan. 16, 2009.

# NOTES

### CHAPTER THREE: BUBBLES

1. Anne Case and Angus Deaton, "Accounting for the Widening Mortality Gap Between American Adults with and Without a BA," *Brookings Papers on Economic Activity*, Sept. 28–29, 2023.
2. Deaton and Case, as noted in Michael T. Nietzel, "Americans Without College Degrees Live Shorter Lives, Brookings Study Finds," *Forbes*, Oct. 3, 2023.
3. David Wheeler, "What Counts as a Rural College," *Chronicle of Higher Education*, April 18, 2024.
4. Anne Case and Angus Deaton, *Deaths of Despair and the Future of Capitalism* (Princeton, N.J.: Princeton University Press, 2020), 50.
5. Matt Lingrell (Urbana police chief), email to author, Oct. 10, 2023. The number of mental health emergency calls went from roughly 40 per year in 1984 to 270 in 2022. By 2023, it had increased to 370.
6. Dean Ortlieb (fire chief), interview by author, March 26, 2024.
7. Monica Potts, "Is College Worth It? Voters Are Split," *FiveThirtyEight*, Oct. 24, 2022.
8. Donald J. Trump, Twitter, July 10, 2020.
9. Juliana Kaplan, "Angus Deaton Won a Nobel Prize in Economics. Now He Says He Got It Wrong on Globalization," *Business Insider*, April 7, 2024. Other economists who changed their minds include Janet Yellen, Mario Draghi, and Paul Romer.
10. Angus Deaton, "Rethinking My Economics," International Monetary Fund, March 2024.
11. Michael Collins, "The Abandonment of Small Cities in the Rust Belt," *Industry Week*, Oct. 10, 2019.
12. Michael Collins, "American Workers: Caught in the Jaws of Change," *Industry Week*, Aug. 4, 2022. See also David Autor et al., "On the Persistence of the China Shock," Brookings Institution, Sept. 9, 2021.
13. Ebert, interview by author, Sept. 25, 2023.
14. Axelrod, interview by author, Nov. 26, 2024.
15. Flaccavento, interview by author, April 23, 2024, and several email follow-ups.
16. Josh Bivens, "Globalization and American Wages," Economic Policy Institute, Oct. 10, 2007.
17. Beth Macy, "Who's Speaking Up for the American Worker?," *New York Times*, June 25, 2015.
18. Jeff Faux, "U.S. Trade Policy—Time to Start Over," Economic Policy Institute, Nov. 30, 2016.
19. Dan Kaufman, "On the Line," *New Yorker*, Nov. 6, 2023.
20. Donald E. Heller, "Pell Grants Are Getting Their Due in the 2020 Campaign," *Conversation*, Oct. 17, 2019.
21. Cookie, interview by author, Aug. 9, 2023.
22. The Grimes family sold the company to Midland-Ross in 1977, which sold it in

1997 to Allied Signal before the enterprise merged with Honeywell in 1999. *Urbana Daily Citizen* clippings from those years.

23. Nathan P. Kalmoe and Lilliana Mason, *Radical American Partisanship: Mapping Violent Hostility, Its Causes, and the Consequences for Democracy* (Chicago: University of Chicago Press, 2022), 34.

24. Brian Kelley, email to author, Nov. 11, 2024.

25. Burns, interview by author, Feb. 27, 2023.

26. Burns, email to author, Nov. 7, 2024.

27. Khanna, interview by author, June 6, 2023.

28. Gibbs, interview by author, Oct. 11, 2023.

29. Ashley Perham, "Vending Machine Distributes 600 Free Naloxone Doses in 1st Year," *Charleston Gazette-Mail*, April 16, 2024.

30. Emily Ekins, "63 Percent of Republicans Say Journalists Are an 'Enemy of the American People,'" Cato Institute, Nov. 1, 2017.

31. Helen Coster, "More People Are Avoiding the News and Trusting It Less," Reuters, June 14, 2022.

32. Kalmoe and Mason, *Radical American Partisanship*, 46–47. See also "Threats to American Democracy Ahead of an Unprecedented Presidential Election," PRRI, Oct. 25, 2023.

33. "This Conservative Thinks America's Institutions 'Earned' the G.O.P.'s Distrust," *The Ezra Klein Show, New York Times* podcast, Aug. 5, 2023, citing a Pew Center Survey showing that trust in federal government has dwindled from 73 percent in 1964 to 9 percent today, and 61 percent of Republicans think public schools are having a negative impact on the country. See also "Public Trust in Government: 1958-2024," Pew Research Center, June 24, 2024, where trust is shown to have improved modestly from 16 percent to 21 percent of Americans saying they trust the government to do what is right most of the time.

### CHAPTER FOUR: DESCENT

1. Stout, interview by author, March 23, 2023.

2. Ohio Board of Elections, Nov. 17, 2020, www.boe.ohio.gov/champaign/c/elecres/20201103results.pdf.

3. Burns, interview by author, March 23, 2023.

4. Spencer S. Hsu, "More Oath Keepers Convicted with Rhodes for Jan. 6 Attack Are Sentenced," *Washington Post*, May 26, 2023.

5. Charles Homans and Alyce McFadden, "Today's Politics Divide Parties, and Friends and Families, Too," *New York Times*, Oct. 18, 2022.

6. Maya Wiley, "Leadership Conference Poll: 54 Percent Fear America Is on the Path to Another Civil War," Leadership Conference on Civil and Human Rights, Oct. 13, 2022.

7. Research from city directories at the Champaign County Library, 1914–59.

8. Abby James, quoted in William E. Smith and Ophia D. Smith, *A Buckeye Titan*

# NOTES

(Cincinnati: Historical and Philosophical Society of Ohio, 1953), 150. "If she had to go on living in Urbana, life was not worth a pin," the authors wrote.

9. Workers of the Writers' Program of the Work Projects Administration, *Urbana and Champaign County*, 46.
10. Phil Angelo, "Swedenborgian Church Is Small but Strong," *Urbana Daily Citizen*, Feb. 17, 1979.
11. Middleton, *History of Champaign County, Ohio*, 550.
12. Selvaggio, interviews by author, Aug. 10, 2023, and April 17, 2024.
13. Reisinger, interview by author, Feb. 27, 2024.
14. Bishop, email to author, Feb. 7, 2022.
15. Staff report, "Woman's Body Found in Home," *Urbana Daily Citizen*, Feb. 1, 1990.
16. Kathleen Fox, "Employees Claim Chi-Vit Has Cut 14 Jobs, Reduced Salaries," *Urbana Daily Citizen*, Sept. 23, 1993.
17. Kathleen Fox, "Nabisco Closing Corn Nuts Plant; 75 Face Layoff," *Urbana Daily Citizen*, Jan. 27, 1999.
18. Sarah Macy Slack, letter to author, Feb. 2, 1993.
19. Poetry by Gene Slack, typed over in a letter to the author, Sarah Macy Slack, 1989 postmark.
20. Stead Sellers, "Explaining America with Raj Chetty," *Washington Post Live*, Aug. 16, 2023.
21. Seeberg, interview by author, July 30, 2024.
22. Andrew Welsh-Huggins, "7,000 Construction Workers Are Needed for Ohio's Largest Economic Development Project," PBS, Aug. 22, 2022.
23. Morgan Trau, "Ohio Union Leader Frustrated as Intel Delays $20 Billion Project," Ohio Capital Journal, Feb. 5, 2024.
24. Allen, interview by author, Aug. 9, 2023.

## CHAPTER FIVE: MIGRATIONS

1. Flowers, interview by author, Oct. 10, 2023.
2. Gary K. Clabaugh, "The Educational Legacy of Ronald Reagan," U.S. Department of Education, 2004, files.eric.ed.gov/fulltext/EJ684842.pdf.
3. Ethan W. Ris and Eddie R. Cole, "Promises Made: The Truman Commission Report at 75," *Peabody Journal of Education* 98, no. 3 (2023).
4. Will Bunch, *After the Ivory Tower Falls: How College Broke the American Dream and Blew Up Our Politics—and How to Fix It* (New York: William Morrow, 2022), 52–57.
5. Branch, interview by author, May 4, 2023.
6. Levitsky, interview by author, Feb. 23, 2023.
7. Hunter, interview by author, Feb. 8, 2024.
8. Don Heller, interview by author, Sept. 18, 2023.
9. Goldrick-Rab, interview by author, Oct. 3, 2023.
10. Ingram, email to author, Feb. 19, 2024.

# NOTES

11. Beth Macy, "The Scarlet P: Why Pell Grant Holders Aren't Slackers," *Chronicle of Higher Education*, Jan. 15, 1999.
12. Beth Macy, "Pell's Poster Child," *Christian Science Monitor*, March 18, 1999.
13. Beth Macy, "From Rusty Fences to Wrought-Iron Gates," College Board, Jan. 2000.
14. Beth Macy, "Working-Class Zero," *Salon*, Feb. 16, 2000.
15. Heller, interview by author, Sept. 18, 2023.
16. Alana Semuels, "America's Great Divergence," *Atlantic*, Jan. 2017.
17. Bean, interview by author, Aug. 8, 2023.
18. Ohio School Report Cards, Sept. 2023.
19. Urbana City Schools, annual report, 1985.
20. Cecilia Yelton (prevention director at TCN Behavioral Health Services), interview by author, Nov. 26, 2024.
21. Dr. Rachel Townsley Church, interview by author, Sept. 26, 2023.
22. Lingrell, interview by author, Sept. 28, 2023.
23. Data from fire chief Dean Ortlieb, March 25, 2023.
24. Nathan Sever (UHS principal), interview by author, Sept. 29, 2023.
25. Cassie Cress, interview by author, May 10, 2023.
26. April Jackson (now retired teacher), interview by author, Jan. 23, 2024.
27. Rick Ridgeway (Orbis), interview by author, Sept. 26, 2023.
28. Nino Vitale (Johnson Welded Products), interview by author, Jan. 22, 2024.
29. Johnson, interview by author, Feb. 28, 2024.
30. Interim dean Adam Parrillo, "Metallica Rocks Clark State with Scholarships," Clark State College, Aug. 26, 2022.
31. Avery Kreemer, "Ohio House OKs Ban on Gender-Affirming Care for Minors," *Dayton Daily News*, June 21, 2023.

### CHAPTER SIX: HOMECOMING

1. Sapp, interview by author, June 23, 2023.
2. Elizabeth Mann Levesque, "Improving Community College Completion Rates by Addressing Structural and Motivational Barriers," Brookings Institution, Oct. 8, 2018, www.brookings.edu/articles/community-college-completion-rates-structural-and-motivational-barriers/.
3. Cress, interview by author, May 10, 2023.
4. Rhitu Chatterjee, "CDC: Childhood Trauma Is a Public Health Issue and We Can Do More to Prevent It," NPR, Nov. 5, 2019. Researchers concluded that preventing childhood abuse could have kept up to 1.5 million students from dropping out of school.
5. Rader, interview by author, Jan. 19, 2024.
6. Brooke Perry, interview by author, Sept. 27, 2023; Police Chief Matt Lingrell, interview by author, Sept. 28, 2023. (The ages of the deceased were twenty-four and seventy-four.)
7. Karla Markley Hall, interview by author, Sept. 20, 2023.

# NOTES

8. Keith Orejel, "Why Trump Won Rural America," *Dissent*, Oct. 16, 2017.
9. Jacobs, interview by author, April 29, 2024.
10. Nicholas F. Jacobs and Daniel M. Shea, *The Rural Voter: The Politics of Place and the Disuniting of America* (New York: Columbia University Press, 2024), 10.
11. Jacobs, interview by author, July 9, 2024.
12. Clare E. Anthony et al., "On the Frontlines of Today's Cities: Trauma, Challenges, and Solutions," National League of Cities, 2021.
13. Senator Tim Kaine, interview by author, April 21, 2024.
14. Heather Tiefenthaler, interview by author, April 20, 2024; Heather Tiefenthaler, text to author, June 21, 2024.
15. Mason, interview by author, April 5, 2023.
16. Cramer, interview by author, April 4, 2023.
17. Israel, interview by author, Jan. 25, 2024.
18. Bell, interview by author, Jan. 25, 2023.
19. Richard Rorty, *Achieving Our Country: Leftist Thought in Twentieth-Century America* (Cambridge, Mass.: Harvard University Press, 1998), 89–90.
20. Rorty, *Achieving Our Country*, 86.
21. Sarah Macy to Terry Macy Vigus, Nov. 2, 1983, five days before Dad's death.
22. Rev. Douglas M. Watts advertisement, *Urbana Daily Citizen*, Sept. 11, 1982.
23. Heather Cox Richardson, *Democracy Awakening: Notes on the State of America* (New York: Viking, 2023), 54–57.

### CHAPTER SEVEN: STRANGERS

1. Sarah Macy Slack to Terry Macy Vigus, Sept. 6, 1992.
2. Desmond, *Poverty by America*, 151.
3. Advancing New Standards in Reproductive Health, "Introduction to the Turnaway Study," University of California, San Francisco, Dec. 2022, 4, intranet.bixbycenter .ucsf.edu/training/training/ansirh.html.
4. Justice Ruth Bader Ginsburg, dissent, Gonzales v. Carhart, 550 U.S. 124 (2007).
5. Author to Urbana city and law enforcement officials, March 16, 1988, from a copy Mom kept. Urbana's police chief, Matt Lingrell, said police records from that period were destroyed in a 2008 flood; email to author, Nov. 30, 2023.
6. Joel E. Mast, "Prosecutor Imploring Valore to Set Obscenity War Standards," *Urbana Daily Citizen*, Jan. 30, 1987.
7. Evans, interview by author, March 1988.
8. Mast, "Prosecutor Imploring Valore to Set Obscenity War Standards."
9. Chris Landon, letter to author and husband, Jan. 3, 1992.
10. Zuckerman, interview by author, Oct. 28, 2024.
11. Cookie, interview by author, Aug. 9, 2023.
12. Bessel van der Kolk and Ezra Klein, "Transcript: Ezra Klein Interviews Bessel van der Kolk," *The Ezra Klein Show*, *New York Times* podcast, Aug. 24, 2021.
13. Angie Reed Finnerty, interview by author, Aug. 9, 2023.

# NOTES

14. James, interview by author, Nov. 7, 2023.
15. Justin Gest, "What Happens When White People Become a Minority in America?," *Foreign Policy*, March 22, 2022. Also see Isabel Wilkerson, *Caste: The Origins of Our Discontent* (New York: Random House, 2020), 322–23.

## CHAPTER EIGHT: TRIBALISM

1. The American Community Survey estimated Urbana's population to be 11,156, but the economic development director, Doug Crabill, puts the number higher, between 11,000 and 12,000, with 4,766 people commuting from outside the city to Urbana for work, mainly in manufacturing.
2. Gary Schenkel (freelance researcher and former *Urbana Daily Citizen* editor), email to author, Nov. 13, 2024.
3. Marcia Bailey (former economic development director), interview by author, Nov. 9, 2023.
4. Chad L. Aldis, "Remember Whom Open Enrollment Serves," Thomas B. Fordham Institute, Oct. 30, 2013.
5. Lingrell, interview by author, Sept. 28, 2023.
6. Muirhead, interview by author, Aug. 10, 2023.
7. Bry, interview by author, Aug. 18, 2023.
8. Julie Henson, interview by author, Aug. 6, 2024.
9. Natalie Yoder, interview by author, Feb. 27, 2024.
10. Zach Everson, "Thiel Was Good for $10 Million, but J. D. Vance's Other Billionaire Backers Were Good for Nothing," *Forbes*, May 6, 2022.
11. Pamela Bullard Mack, interview by author, Feb. 22, 2023.
12. Dunn, interview by author, Aug. 9, 2023.
13. James Baldwin, "To Be in a Rage, Almost All the Time," *1A*, NPR, June 1, 2020, www.npr.org/2020/06/01/867153918/-to-be-in-a-rage-almost-all-the-time. Baldwin was asked by a radio host about being Black in America in 1961.
14. April Jackson, interview by author, Jan. 23, 2024.
15. Lance Jackson and Weller, interviews by author, May 9, 2023.
16. Lance and April Jackson, interview by author, June 28, 2023.
17. Conn, interview by author, Nov. 6, 2023.
18. "No, American Schools Are Not Encouraging Pupils to Identify as Cats," *Economist*, Oct. 20, 2022.

## CHAPTER NINE: RED-PILLED

1. Curnutte, interview by author, March 16, 2023.
2. Sam Gardner, "In the Hunter Family, Mother Knows Best . . . Every Day," Fox Sports, May 10, 2015.
3. Charles Curtis, "The Legend of Georgia State Coach Ron Hunter's March Madness Stool," *USA Today*, March 16, 2018. Hunter was limited to coaching from a

stool because he had a torn Achilles tendon but couldn't contain himself when his son made the game-winning shot.

4. Hunter, interview by author, Feb. 8, 2024.
5. "New PRRI Report Reveals Nearly One in Five Americans and One in Four Republicans Still Believe in QAnon Conspiracy Theories," Public Religion Research Institute, Feb. 24, 2022, www.prri.org/press-release/new-prri-report-reveals-nearly-one-in-five-americans-and-one-in-four-republicans-still-believe-in-qanon-conspiracy-theories/.
6. Thompson, interview by author, June 28, 2023.
7. McCain, interview by author, March 16, 2023.
8. Derek Thompson, "The True Cost of the Churchgoing Bust," *Atlantic*, April 3, 2024.
9. Workers of the Writers' Program of the Work Projects Administration, *Urbana and Champaign County*, 53.
10. Colby Itkowitz, "Ohio Supreme Court Rejects GOP-Drawn Congressional Map as Unfairly Partisan," *Washington Post*, Jan. 14, 2022.
11. U.S. Attorney's Office, Southern District of Ohio, "Former House Speaker Sentenced to 20 Years in Prison for Leading Racketeering Conspiracy Involving $60 Million in Bribes," press release, June 29, 2023. Former FirstEnergy executives and a former public utility commissioner were also indicted.
12. Politics desk, "This Analysis Shows Which Voters Rejected Ohio's Issue 1 Measure," *PBS News Hour*, Aug. 9, 2023.
13. Shanto Iyengar et al., "The Origins and Consequences of Affective Polarization in the United States," *Annual Review of Political Science* 22, no. 1 (2019): 129–46. Sixty-seven percent of Americans identify as the so-called "exhausted majority," according to Stephen Hawkins et al., "Hidden Tribes: A Study of America's Polarized Landscape," More in Common, 2018.
14. DeWitt, interview by author, Feb. 26, 2024.
15. "Upward of 85 percent do not cling to conspiracy theories like Democrats running child sex rings." Jacobs and Shea, *Rural Voter*, 353, 349.
16. Bruce K. Alexander, "My Final Academic Article on Addiction," Simon Fraser University, April 19, 2022. Alexander discusses this at length with Carl Erik Fisher, "Why We Can't Therapize Our Way Out of Addiction, with Dr. Bruce Alexander," *Flourishing After Addiction* (podcast), March 5, 2024.
17. Kingsolver, interview by author, Nov. 2, 2022, www.youtube.com/watch?v=uS-glbhS1-WU.
18. Matthew Rosenberg and Julian E. Barnes, "A Bible Burning, a Russian News Agency, and a Story Too Good to Check Out," *New York Times*, Aug. 12, 2020.
19. Bill Monaghan, email to author, May 18, 2023.
20. Corbett Daly, "Clinton on Qaddafi: 'We Came, We Saw, He Died,'" CBS News, Oct. 20, 2011.
21. "Ohio Job Loss During the NAFTA-WTO Period," Public Citizen, quoting

Bureau of Labor Statistics, 2018, www.citizen.org/article/ohio-job-loss-during-the -nafta-wto-period/.

22. Shay Frank, "New Position Created to Reduce Violent Crimes in Springfield," WYSO, Nov. 13, 2023.

23. Nat Malkus, "Return2Learn Tracker," American Enterprise Institute, www.return tolearntracker.net.

24. "The City of Springfield, OH: Collaborative Efforts Among MHRB and McKinley Hall to Increase Access to Opportunity for Justice-Involved Individuals," Bureau of Justice Assistance, Sept. 30, 2022, bja.ojp.gov/funding/awards/15pbja-22-gg -04453-coap.

25. David Dayen, "Obama's Foreclosure Relief Program Was Designed to Help Bankers, Not Homeowners," Billmoyers.com, Feb. 14, 2015; Matt Stoller, "How Democrats Killed Their Populist Soul," *Atlantic*, Oct. 24, 2016.

26. "Busted Trust," *Economist*, April 20, 2024; Jeffrey M. Jones, "Americans Trust Local Government Most, Congress Least," Gallup News, Oct. 13, 2023.

27. Julia Belluz, "Nobel Winner Angus Deaton Talks About the Surprising Study on White Mortality He Just Co-authored," *Vox*, Nov. 7, 2015.

28. Jacobs and Shea, *Rural Voter*, 237.

29. Israel, interview by author, Jan. 5, 2024. Israel credited research summarized by Shankar Vedantam and Bill Mesler in *Useful Delusions: The Power & Paradox of the Self-Deceiving Brain* (New York: W. W. Norton, 2021), introduction and 66–67.

30. Arlie Russell Hochschild, *Stolen Pride: Loss, Shame, and the Rise of the Right* (New York: New Press, 2024), 9, 34, 45.

31. Jeff Helman, interview by author, Aug. 7, 2024.

32. Jacobs and Shea, *Rural Voter*, 253–54.

33. Matthew Desmond, "Dollars on the Margins," *New York Times Magazine*, Feb. 21, 2019. See also Sendhil Mullainathan and Eldar Shafir, *Scarcity: Why Having Too Little Means So Much* (New York: Henry Holt), 2013.

### CHAPTER TEN: INTERVENTIONS

1. Perry, interview by author, Sept. 27, 2023.

2. "Sovereign Citizens Movement," Southern Poverty Law Center, 2023, www .splcenter.org/fighting-hate/extremist-files/ideology/sovereign-citizens-movement.

3. Rachel Goldwasser, "Sovereign Citizenship Takes Hold Among Younger, Affluent, Female Communities," Southern Poverty Law Center, June 4, 2024.

4. Dan Abrams, "Court Cam: Deputies Do Battle with Man Who Barged into Courtroom," A&E, July 22, 2022.

5. Thiel, email to author, April 23, 2024. Thiel also sent the LifeWise data.

6. Dana Goldstein and Troy Closson, "'A Wave That's on the Decline?': Trump to Talk to Parents Leading the Culture Wars," *New York Times*, Aug. 30, 2024.

7. Mike Hixenbaugh, "Prayer, Bible Lessons, and a Big Red Bus: How an Ohio Group Is Bringing God to Public School," NBC News, March 25, 2024.

# NOTES

8. Katherine Stewart, *The Power Worshippers: Inside the Dangerous Rise of Religious Nationalism* (New York: Bloomsbury Publishing, 2022), 2.
9. Champaign County Schools, Search Institute Survey, Community Health Assessment, May 2022. Thirteen percent more of Urbana's eighth graders report having depression in the past month, compared with those in 2005, and 4 percent more report having attempted suicide.
10. Tiefenthaler, interview by author, April 19, 2024.
11. Megan Henry, "Ohio Bill Would Require School Districts to Create Released Time for Religious Instruction," Ohio Capital Journal, May 17, 2024.
12. Nuria Martinez-Keel, "Oklahoma Schools Ordered to Use Bible in History Teaching," *Oklahoma Voice*, June 27, 2024.
13. Larry McClemons, "'Every Teacher' in Oklahoma Must Teach the Bible? That'll Keep Them from Leaving," *Washington Post*, July 26, 2024.
14. Bill Moyers, "The United States of ALEC," Moyers & Co., Sept. 28, 2012. See also John Oliver's 2014 segment on ALEC, www.youtube.com/watch?v=aIMgfBZrrZ8, and Editorial, "The Big Money Behind State Laws," *New York Times*, Feb. 12, 2012. See also Jane Mayer, "The Big Money Behind the Big Lie," *New Yorker*, Aug. 9, 2021. See also Jane Mayer, *Dark Money: The Hidden History of the Billionaires Behind the Rise of the Radical Right* (New York: Anchor Books, 2016), 426–27.
15. Hannah Natanson, "America Has Legislated Itself into Competing Red, Blue Versions of Education," *Washington Post*, April 4, 2024.
16. Denis Smith, "Public Schools, Vouchers, Privatization, and Educational Choice: Be Careful What You Wish For," Ohio Capital Journal, Sept. 16, 2021. Original text appeared in Kenneth R. Conklin, "Education Transmits a Culture," 2004, www.angelfire.com/hi2/hawaiiansovereignty/edtransmitsculture.html.
17. Thiel, interview by author, April 18, 2024.
18. Webb, interview by author, July 31, 2024.
19. Webb, email to author, Aug. 2, 2024.
20. 2022–23 Report Card for Urbana High School, reportcard.education.ohio.gov /school/print/037994.
21. Blondin, interview by author, May 18, 2024.
22. Emily Hemphill, "Tim Kaine Solicits Feedback on Workforce Training Bill," *Daily Progress*, March 27, 2024.
23. Kaine, email to author, July 7, 2024: "It currently has more than 50 sponsors . . . will likely be voted out of committee in an overwhelmingly bipartisan vote. Then we'll be looking to pass it on the floor before year end. A similar proposal is moving through the House."
24. Author interviews, Robert Lerman, May 14 and 15, 2024. See also Oren Cass, *The Once and Future Worker: A Vision for the Renewal of Work in America* (New York: Encounter Books, 2018), 110–13.
25. Helman, interview by author, Aug. 7, 2024.

# NOTES

### CHAPTER ELEVEN: MEDIATION

1. David Gilbert, "Inside a US Neo-Nazi Homeschool Network with Thousands of Members," *Vice News*, Jan. 29, 2023.
2. Zach Tuggle, "'I Felt Disgusted.' Ohio Home-Schooling Leader Stunned by Parents Using Nazi Teachings," *Bucyrus Telegraph-Forum*, Feb. 1, 2023.
3. Brad McElhinny, "Senator: Homeschooling Not to Blame for 14-Year-Old Girl's Death," *MetroNews*, June 10, 2024.
4. Calvin Lee, "Sovereign Citizens: Sitting on the Docket All Day, Wasting Time," *Minnesota Law Review*, March 2, 2022.
5. Perry, interview by author, Aug. 10, 2023. I did ride-alongs with Perry on most of my trips to Urbana in 2023 and 2024.
6. Gratz, interview by author, Aug. 1, 2024.
7. Robert Halpern, *The Means to Grow Up* (New York: Routledge, 2009), 203.
8. Lerman, interviews by author, May 14 and 15, 2024.
9. Rachel Cahill and Sofia Charlot, "SNAP Employment and Training Program: Best Practices for Ohio," Center for Community Solutions, May 6, 2024.
10. Flowers, interview by author, Jan. 24, 2024.
11. Biddle, interview by author, Dec. 7, 2023.
12. Sarah Mervosh and Francesca Paris, "Why School Absences Have 'Exploded' Almost Everywhere," *New York Times*, March 29, 2024.
13. Allensworth, interview by author, Nov. 3, 2023.
14. Nat Malkus, senior fellow at the American Enterprise Institute, whose research was reported by Mervosh and Paris, in "Why School Absences Have 'Exploded' Almost Everywhere."
15. Bill Bean, interview by author, Aug. 8, 2024.
16. Reisinger, interview by author, Feb. 27, 2024.
17. Madison Allen, interview by author, June 12, 2024.
18. Amy Hunter, Cassie Cress, Lance and April Jackson, Hayla Parker, and Margaret Tabor, interviews by author, March 28, 2024.
19. Nellie Bowles, "A Dark Consensus About Screens and Kids Begins to Emerge in Silicon Valley," *New York Times*, Oct. 26, 2018.
20. Editorial Board, "The Startling Evidence on Learning Loss Is In," *New York Times*, Nov. 18, 2023. The study on the efficacy of outstanding teachers' influence on students came from the Center for Research on Education Outcomes at Stanford University.
21. Reeves, interview by author, March 11, 2024.
22. "The Lynching at Urbana," *New York Times*, June 5, 1897.
23. Special to The Dispatch, "The Exciting Scenes Following the Brutal Outrage of Mrs. Gaumer," *Columbus Evening Dispatch*, June 4, 1897.

### CHAPTER TWELVE: ASCENSION

1. Dunn, interview by author, Aug. 10, 2023.
2. Terry Vigus to Sarah Macy, Sept. 30, 1982.

3. George Goehl, "How We Got Trump Voters to Change Their Mind," *Atlantic*, Oct. 26, 2020.
4. According to the Brain Injury Association of America, people with a severe head injury are at higher risk of developing epilepsy for up to fifteen years. Tim Macy, interview by author, Sept. 30, 2023.
5. Bean, interview by author, Aug. 8, 2023.

### CHAPTER THIRTEEN: GENIALITY

1. Timothy H. H. Thoresen, *River, Reaper, Rail: Agriculture and Identity in Ohio's Mad River Valley, 1795–1885* (Akron, Ohio: University of Akron Press, 2018), 79–85, 102–3.
2. Champaign County Sheriff's Office, "St. Paris Police Chief Arrested at Champaign County Fair," press release, *Urbana Daily Citizen*, Aug. 6, 2024.
3. Jeff Diamant, "About Four-in-Ten U.S. Adults Believe Humanity Is 'Living in the End Times,'" Pew Research Center, Sept. 8, 2022. Forty-seven percent of Christians believe it, including majorities in the historically Black (76 percent) and evangelical (63 percent) communities.
4. Andrew J. Tobias, "Mitch McConnell Allies Plan Massive $83M Ad Campaign to Take Down Sherrod Brown," Cleveland.com, Feb. 7, 2024.
5. Thomas B. Edsall, "The MAGA Formula Is Getting Darker and Darker," *New York Times*, May 18, 2022, quoting Buckley.
6. Marty Schladen, "Politicians Are Parroting Racist Lie with 'Great Replacement' Rhetoric, Anti-hate Groups Say," Ohio Capital Journal, Aug. 26, 2024.
7. Mason, interview by author, Aug. 28, 2024.
8. Rob Reiner and Dan Partland, *God & Country: The Rise of Christian Nationalism*, Oscilloscope Laboratories, 2024, inspired by the book *The Power Worshippers*, by Katherine Stewart.
9. Alex Isenstadt, "Ralph Reed's Army Plans $62 Million Spending Spree to Boost Evangelical Turnout," *Politico*, March 11, 2024.
10. Jeff Sharlet on Marc Maron's podcast, episode No. 1466, Aug. 31, 2023.
11. David Bauder, "Decline in Local News Outlets Is Accelerating Despite Efforts to Help," Associated Press, Nov. 16, 2023.
12. Sharlet, interviews by author, Sept. 12 and 26, 2024.
13. Mann, email to author, Aug. 23, 2024.

### CHAPTER FOURTEEN: GRACE

1. Slagle, interview by author, March 26, 2024.
2. Weller, email to author, Sept. 19, 2024.
3. Uhl, interview by author, Oct. 4, 2024.
4. Sorensen, interview by author, June 8, 2023.
5. Bean, interview by author, Aug. 8, 2023.
6. Weller, interview by author, Aug. 9, 2024.

7. William Brangham, "Ohio City with Haitian Migrant Influx Thrust into Political Spotlight," *PBS News Hour*, Sept. 10, 2024, www.pbs.org/newshour/show/ohio -city-with-haitian-migrant-influx-thrust-into-political-spotlight.

8. Email to author, name withheld at reporter's request, Sept. 15, 2024.

9. Miriam Jordan, "An Ohio Businessman Faces Death Threats for Praising His Haitian Workers," *New York Times*, Sept. 30, 2024.

10. Michael Rubinkam, "Ohio Sheriff Condemned for Social Media Post," Associated Press, Sept. 21, 2024.

11. Payne, interview by author, Jan. 31, 2024.

12. Sydney Dawes, "Hate Groups Converge on Springfield After False Claims About Haitian Immigrants," *Dayton Daily News*, Oct. 1, 2024.

13. Jose Soto, "Remembering Pauly Likens, 14-Year-Old Transgender Girl Killed in Pennsylvania," Human Rights Campaign, July 11, 2024.

14. Staff, "Students Writing Published," *Urbana Daily Citizen*, date omitted from the clipping but sometime in 1985.

15. Roxana Robinson, "Reckoning with Alice Munro's Darkest Secret," *Time*, July 18, 2024.

16. Diana Zuckerman and Sarah Pedersen, "Child Abuse and Father Figures: Which Kind of Families Are Safest to Grow Up In?," National Center for Health Research, 2024.

17. "Statistics About Sexual Violence," National Sexual Violence Resource Center, www.nsvrc.org/sites/default/files/publications_nsvrc_factsheet_media-packet _statistics-about-sexual-violence_0.pdf.

18. Lori Dorfman, "Issue 19: Case by Case: News Coverage of Child Sexual Abuse," Berkeley Media Studies Group, May 2011.

19. John Gramlich, "What the Data Says About Crime in the U.S.," Pew Research Center, April 24, 2024. According to 2023 FBI statistics, 44.7 percent of rapes and sexual assaults are reported to police.

20. Zuckerman, interview by author, Oct. 28, 2024.

21. Lingrell, email to author, Oct. 21, 2024.

### CHAPTER FIFTEEN: THE PRICE OF IGNORANCE

1. James Madison to William T. Barry, Aug. 4, 1822, Founders Online, founders .archives.gov/documents/Madison/04-02-02-0480.

2. "Map: Attacks on Gender-Affirming Care by State," Human Rights Campaign, Aug. 2024, www.hrc.org/resources/attacks-on-gender-affirming-care-by-state-map.

3. Carol Graham and Emily Dobson, "Despair and Vulnerability to Misinformation: An Interactive Tool," Brookings Institution, July 13, 2023.

4. Mark and Lorraine Townsley, interviews by author, Sept. 27, 2023.

5. Grant Davis (Ohio State University Extension educator), email to author, Nov. 6, 2024. Dairy farm data also confirmed by the retired local veterinarian Don Sanders.

6. Church, interview by author, Feb. 27, 2024.
7. Dr. Francis Peabody, lecture delivered Oct. 21, 1926, as discussed by J. Willis Hurst, "Dr. Francis W. Peabody, We Need You," *Texas Heart Institute Journal* 38, no. 4 (2011).
8. Stephen Miller, posted on X, Aug. 31, 2024.
9. Pitzer, interview by author, Sept. 19, 2024.
10. Neil Vigdor and Simon J. Levien, "Trump Stokes Fears About Haitian Migrants in a Pennsylvania Community," *New York Times*, Sept. 24, 2024.
11. Julio Rosas, "Local Man EXPOSES City Officials on Migrant Crisis," BlazeTV, Sept. 25, 2024, www.youtube.com/watch?v=8ji2gx2LxjM.
12. Eileen McClory, "Chronic Absenteeism Still High Across the State," *Springfield News-Sun*, Sept. 24, 2024.
13. Megan Henry, "Ohio Spent Nearly a Billion Dollars on Private School Voucher Scholarships in 2024," Ohio Capital Journal, Oct. 25, 2024.
14. Ohio School Report Cards, Urbana City Schools, 2023–24 school year data, report-card.education.ohio.gov/district/044941.
15. Jackson, interview by author, Aug. 9, 2024.
16. "A Foregone Confusion," *Economist*, Sept. 14, 2024.
17. Staff, "After Three Years and Many Indictments, the 'Big Lie' That Led to the January 6th Insurrection Is Still Believed by Most Republicans," Public Religion Research Institute, Jan. 5, 2024.
18. Tania Israel, "How Worried Should You Be About Post-election Violence?," *Psychology Today*, Oct. 23, 2024.
19. Timothy Snyder, *On Tyranny: Twenty Lessons from the Twentieth Century* (New York: Crown, 2017), 42.
20. Andre Dubus III, "If I Owned a Gun," in *Ghost Dogs: On Killers and Kin* (New York: W. W. Norton, 2024), 117.
21. Elizabeth Kolbert, "Letter from Greenland: When the Ice Melts," *New Yorker*, Oct. 14, 2024, 26. The study she cites is "Global Tipping Points," published by the University of Exeter in 2023.
22. Nikki King, interview by author, quoted in Beth Macy, *Raising Lazarus: Hope, Justice, and the Future of America's Overdose Crisis* (New York: Little, Brown, 2022), 89.
23. Barbara Kingsolver, Instagram post, Nov. 6, 2024.
24. White House, "Granting Pardons and Commutation of Sentences for Certain Offenses Relating to the Events at or near the United States Capitol on January 6, 2021," Jan. 20, 2025. See also: Christopher Wiggins, "Donald Trump Commutes Sentence of Trans Woman Convicted for Role in January 6 Insurrection," *Advocate*, Jan. 21, 2025.
25. Paul Farhi and John Volk, "In News Deserts, Trump Won in a Landslide," The Medill Local News Initiative, Northwestern University, Dec. 5, 2024.
26. Rich McHugh and Marty Hobe, "Springfield Residents Talk to NewsNation," NewsNation, Sept. 13, 2024.

# NOTES

27. "The Haitian Invasion of Springfield, Ohio, and the Replacement of America, Part 1 of 2," Banned History, YouTube, https://www.youtube.com/watch?v=uPwK_DLgX7Y.
28. "Waking the Sleeping Giant," Poor People's Campaign, Oct. 2021, www.poorpeoplescampaign.org/waking-the-sleeping-giant-poor-and-low-income-voters-in-the-2020-elections/; John Blake, "This Fiery Evangelical Pastor Offers a Blueprint for Democrats' Revival in Trump's Second Term," CNN, Nov. 25, 2024.
29. Megan Henry, "Ohio Gov. Mike DeWine Signs Forced-Outing, Mandated Religious Release Time Policy Bill into Law," *Ohio Capital Journal*, Jan. 8, 2025, https://ohiocapitaljournal.com/briefs/ohio-gov-mike-dewine-signs-forced-outing-mandated-religious-release-time-policy-bill-into-law/.
30. "Minimum Wage," Wage and Hour Division, United States Department of Labor, https://www.dol.gov/agencies/whd/minimum-wage/history/chart.
31. David Axelrod, interview by author, Nov. 26, 2024.
32. Alfredo Ortiz, "Inflation Hits 20 Percent Under Biden, Pushing Small Businesses to the Brink," *The Hill*, May 15, 2024.

# IMAGE CREDITS

# INDEX

Page numbers in italics indicate photographs.

# INDEX

# INDEX

# INDEX

# INDEX

# INDEX

# INDEX

# INDEX

# INDEX

# INDEX